The Cambridge Introduction to
Mikhail Bakhtin

In this introduction to Mikhail Bakhtin, Ken Hirschkop presents a compact, readable, detailed, and sophisticated exposition of all of Bakhtin's important works. Using the most up-to-date sources and the new, scholarly editions of Bakhtin's texts, Hirschkop explains Bakhtin's influential ideas, demonstrates their relevance and usefulness for literary and cultural analysis, and sets them in their historical context. In clear and concise language, Hirschkop shows how Bakhtin's ideas have changed the way we understand language and literary texts. Authoritative and accessible, this Cambridge Introduction is the most comprehensive and reliable account of Bakhtin and his work yet available.

Ken Hirschkop is Professor of English Language and Literature at the University of Waterloo. A recognised international authority on Bakhtin's work, he has co-edited *Bakhtin and Cultural Theory* (1989, 2005) with David Shepherd, written *Mikhail Bakhtin: An Aesthetic for Democracy* (1999), and contributed articles on Bakhtin to many leading journals.

The Cambridge Introduction to
Mikhail Bakhtin

KEN HIRSCHKOP

CAMBRIDGE
UNIVERSITY PRESS

University Printing House, Cambridge CB2 8BS, United Kingdom

One Liberty Plaza, 20th Floor, New York, NY 10006, USA

477 Williamstown Road, Port Melbourne, VIC 3207, Australia

314–321, 3rd Floor, Plot 3, Splendor Forum, Jasola District Centre, New Delhi – 110025, India

103 Penang Road, #05–06/07, Visioncrest Commercial, Singapore 238467

Cambridge University Press is part of the University of Cambridge.

It furthers the University's mission by disseminating knowledge in the pursuit of education, learning, and research at the highest international levels of excellence.

www.cambridge.org
Information on this title: www.cambridge.org/9781107109049
DOI: 10.1017/9781316266236

© Ken Hirschkop 2021

This publication is in copyright. Subject to statutory exception and to the provisions of relevant collective licensing agreements, no reproduction of any part may take place without the written permission of Cambridge University Press.

First published 2021

Printed in the United Kingdom by TJ Books Limited, Padstow Cornwall

A catalogue record for this publication is available from the British Library.

Library of Congress Cataloging-in-Publication Data
Names: Hirschkop, Ken, author.
Title: The Cambridge introduction to Mikhail Bakhtin / Ken Hirschkop.
Description: Cambridge, United Kingdom ; New York, NY : Cambridge University Press, 2021. | Series: Cambridge introductions to literature | Includes bibliographical references and index.
Identifiers: LCCN 2020055433 (print) | LCCN 2020055434 (ebook) | ISBN 9781107109049 (hardback) | ISBN 9781107521094 (paperback) | ISBN 9781316266236 (epub)
Subjects: LCSH: Bakhtin, M. M. (Mikhail Mikhaĭlovich), 1895-1975–Criticism and interpretation.
Classification: LCC PG2947.B3 H56 2021 (print) | LCC PG2947.B3 (ebook) | DDC 801/.95092–dc23
LC record available at https://lccn.loc.gov/2020055433
LC ebook record available at https://lccn.loc.gov/2020055434

ISBN 978-1-107-10904-9 Hardback
ISBN 978-1-107-52109-4 Paperback

Cambridge University Press has no responsibility for the persistence or accuracy of URLs for external or third-party internet websites referred to in this publication and does not guarantee that any content on such websites is, or will remain, accurate or appropriate.

Contents

Acknowledgements	*page* vii
A Note on the Translations	x
Chronology	xi
List of Abbreviations	xvi

1 Introduction 1

2 Life 5

Youth: 1895–1917	8
Friendships: 1918–1929	11
Exile, Escape, and the War: 1930–1946	21
Saransk: 1946–1961	27
Rediscovery, Rehabilitation: 1961–1975	28

3 Context 30

Philosophy: Influences and Options for the Young Bakhtin	32
Language: Soviet Struggles over Literary Criticism in the 1920s, and Bakhtin's Linguistic Turn	39
Excursus: Voloshinov's Linguistic Turn	48
Literature: Socialist Realism and Arguments about the Novel in the 1930s	53
The 1950s and 1960s: Consolidation and a Quiet Life	56

4 Works 59

Some Preliminary Observations	59
List of Bakhtin's Published Works	60

The Concepts and Arguments 68
Author, Hero, Art, Responsibility 69
Dialogism as Polyphony 75
Dialogism as Heteroglossia 88
The *Bildungsroman* and the Chronotope
   (with a Brief Glance at the Future) 105
The Novel, Contemporaneity, and the Future 118
Popular-Festive Culture and the Novel 128
Speech Genres, Utterances,
   and Metalinguistics 142

5 Reception 146

6 A Brief Conclusion 159

Notes 161
Further Reading 185
Index 187

Acknowledgements

This may be the last book I write on Bakhtin; part of me certainly hopes so. That being the case, it's worth looking back on the circumstances and people that led me to this point. Two of those people could not possibly have known the seeds they were sowing. There was the popular high school teacher of Russian, whose possible sacking led me to sign up for instruction in a language I had no interest in at the time (I was persuaded to do so by my friends, who *were* interested in Russian, and, being me, I never got round to switching out). There was my high school friend, Klemens Meyer, who lent me his copy of *Problems of Dostoevsky's Poetics* when I was taking an evening course on the Novel and the City and needed some help with *Crime and Punishment*. That such small gestures could shape a career is evidence of the role that serendipity may play in our lives.

Once I got going, however, the help was explicit and generous. There was a master's thesis on Bakhtin in London under Jane Grayson's selfless and careful supervision and a doctoral one supervised by the tireless, and always interested Terry Eagleton. There was, importantly, a world of Bakhtin scholars, who met periodically to talk and share, and who created a scholarly community that was varied, open, stimulating, and quite a lot of fun to belong to. Among those who should get credit for this community – because communities, even enjoyable ones, take work – are Clive Thomson, who organised the first International Bakhtin Colloquium and edited the six still invaluable issues of the *Bakhtin Newsletter*, and David Shepherd, who – once the dam broke in the Soviet Union – organised numerous visits of Russian Bakhtin scholars to the UK and established the Bakhtin Centre at the University of Sheffield.

The generosity and open-mindedness that distinguish the community of Bakhtin scholarship have been a joy to behold. Readers of this book may know that literary studies in North America and Europe are often the scene of passionate and somewhat acrimonious dispute, despite the relatively low stakes: the rise of politically orientated and motivated criticism and theory has led to some strikingly heated arguments in the detailed work of literary scholarship. In Russia and the Soviet Union, the stakes were, in the immediate sense, much, much higher: after all, in the past people had been murdered by the Soviet state for having the 'wrong' view on literary matters (Bakhtin's friend Pavel Medvedev was one such victim). Bakhtin scholars, in Russia and elsewhere, are a heterogeneous group, straddling the various divides that structure twentieth- and twenty-first-century literary scholarship. They not only follow different methods and have divergent literary interests, but they are devoted, in their larger intellectual lives, to very different causes, some political, some religious, some philosophical. They have, however, not let these differences get in the way of their scholarly endeavours: I have shared ideas with, been supported by, and had important conversations with Bakhtin scholars whose general worldview could not have been more different from my own, at home and in Russia. While I have my own strong political views and a deep sense of the intersection between political life and literary scholarship, this is complemented by an abiding conviction in the importance of open, critical, and independent scholarship, led by the facts and the most compelling arguments. I've been privileged to be part of a scholarly community organised around the same convictions. This book, which stands on the foundation of the work of many scholars, of all different sorts, is a testament to that community.

Within that community, there are a few people whose work on and on behalf of Bakhtin has proved fundamental and on which I have relied heavily. The late Michael Holquist was warm and encouraging throughout our acquaintance, and his advocacy for Bakhtin, tireless work as an editor and translator, and infectious enthusiasm got Bakhtin scholarship moving in the English-speaking world. Caryl Emerson has generated a stream of insightful, thoughtful commentary and has given us what is, in my view, the best existing English-language translation of any Bakhtin work (her readable, but precise *Problems of Dostoevsky's Poetics*). The late Sergei Bocharov was one of the men who rediscovered Bakhtin and who lovingly aided and guided him in his last fifteen years, but after Bakhtin's death he may have done him an even greater service. His editorship of the Academy of Science's *Collected Works* was an extraordinary achievement, establishing the foundation for all work on Bakhtin in the future. The late Iurii Medvedev and his wife, Daria, were tireless, sophisticated, and persuasive advocates for the work of Iurii's father, Pavel Medvedev, and their hard work debunked much of the mythology surrounding Bakhtin and made available Medvedev's fascinating *oeuvre*. The late Nikolai Pan'kov edited a Bakhtin journal, *Dialog Karnaval Khronotop*, that revolutionised the field and produced detailed philological and biographical studies that have no equal in Bakhtin scholarship. Craig

Brandist has done more to elucidate the intellectual history of Bakhtin's work than any other writer, and his detailed, sophisticated studies have illuminated the entire landscape of Bakhtin's work. Galin Tihanov has produced a series of brilliant and original analyses of Bakhtin, which have changed the way we understand and appreciate his work.

While these people made the scholarship possible, others made the book possible. I'm indebted to Ray Ryan for persuading me to write it and for showing exceptional patience while I did so. Edgar Mendez has been a superb and helpful desk editor. Galin Tihanov, mentioned above, was a careful and insightful reader of the first version of the manuscript, and his comments and suggestions improved it considerably. Dylan Woods, one of my graduate students at Waterloo, cast a sympathetic but relentlessly critical eye over the whole manuscript, and if the book is at all readable and useful, the credit belongs to him. Beth Morel was a wonderful, scrupulous copyeditor.

Through all this, the love and support of my family – who cannot understand why I spend so much time on one guy – have been indispensable. Thanks to my partner, Joanne, my daughter, Roisin, and my son, Jacob.

Parts of Chapter 5 were commissioned for and will be published in Michał Mrugalski, Schamma Shahadat, Danuta Ulicka, and Irina Wutsdorff (eds.), *Literary Theory between East and West: Transcultural and Transdisciplinary Movements from Russian Formalism to Cultural Studies* (Berlin: de Gruyter). Permission to use them in this volume is gratefully acknowledged.

A Note on the Translations

In references to Bakhtin's works, the first page reference will be to the English translation of the text and the second reference to the Russian original, in almost every case drawn from the version published in Bakhtin's *Collected Works* rather than the version first published in Russian (the exceptions are the books on Dostoevsky and Rabelais, where I refer to the original published editions). Where no English translation is available, the single page reference is to the Russian text. I have often modified the English translation, sometimes substantially. More disturbing for the reader, I have sometimes had to modify the title of the work as well, in cases where the *Collected Works* have given a familiar text a new title (which is, in almost every case, actually the text's old, original title). Where that is the case, I indicate it below and give the reader a heads-up when I first mention the particular work. Full bibliographical details are found in the list at the beginning of the Works chapter.

Transliteration is according to the Library of Congress system, but without diacritical marks. I have made exceptions for names with well-known transliterations. Unless otherwise indicated, all emphases are from the original text (even where they have not been reproduced in the existing English translation).

Chronology

Date	Event	Texts
16 November 1895	Mikhail Mikhailovich Bakhtin is born in Orel, Russia.	
1905	The Bakhtin family moves to Vilnius (Lithuania) and Bakhtin enters gymnasium there.	
1911	The Bakhtin family (except Nikolai) moves to Odessa (Ukraine).	
1913	Bakhtin may have begun attending classes at Novorossisk University in Odessa, without having registered.	
1916	Bakhtin moves to Petrograd, where he may have attended classes at the University, again without having registered.	
1918	Bakhtin moves to Nevel', where he meets M. I. Kagan, M. V. Iudina, L. V. Pumpianskii, and V. N. Voloshinov, among others.	
1919		'Art and Answerability' published
1920	Bakhtin moves to Vitebsk, where Voloshinov and Pumpianskii have moved and where he meets P. N. Medvedev.	
February 1921	Bakhtin contracts osteomyelitis, from which he will suffer his whole life.	

xi

Chronology

Date	Event	Texts
16 July 1921	Bakhtin marries Elena Alexandrovna Bersh-Okolovich.	
1920–24		Work on early philosophical essays
May 1924	The Bakhtins move to Leningrad.	
1924		'The Problem of Form, Content and Material'
1924–25	Bakhtin delivers cycles of lectures on Neo-Kantian philosophy and 'Hero and Author in Aesthetic Activity' in Leningrad. Continues meeting with Pumpianskii, Iudina, Voloshinov, and Medvedev.	
24 December 1928	Bakhtin is arrested.	
June 1929		*Problems of Dostoevsky's Art* is published
22 July 1929	Bakhtin is sentenced to five years in Solovki labour camp. Bakhtin spends July to December in hospital (for recurring osteomyelitis).	
23 February 1930	In response to lobbying by Bakhtin's friends and contacts, his sentence is changed to five years' exile in Kustanai (Kazakhstan).	
29 March 1930	The Bakhtins move to Kustanai.	'Problems in the Stylistics of the Novel' (outline)
April 1931	Bakhtin is hired as an accountant for the local Consumers Union	
1930–36		'Discourse in the Novel' composed
July 1934	Bakhtin's sentence is complete, although he will remain in Kustanai for another two years.	
Summer 1936	The Bakhtins travel to Leningrad and Moscow; Mikhail sees Kagan, Iudina, Medvedev, and Zalesskii.	Bakhtin seeks to publish 'Discourse in the Novel' as a book; agreed by publisher but MS never submitted.

Chronology xiii

Date	Event	Texts
26 September 1936	The Bakhtins move to Saransk, so that Mikhail can take up a post teaching literature at the Mordovian State Pedagogical Institute.	
March 1937	Bakhtin is denounced by the Institute's Party Committee.	
July 1937	The Bakhtins move (without a permit) to Moscow, stay with Zalesskis. Bakhtin meets several times with Kagan in August.	
September 1937		Bakhtin proposes to publisher that he substitute a manuscript on the *Bildungsroman* for 'Discourse in the Novel' (it is agreed).
Winter 1937–38	After failed attempts to settle in Moscow, the Bakhtins relocate to Savelevo, where they will stay until the end of the war in 1945. Bakhtin will teach at local schools, but he will visit Moscow for his research.	
1937–39		Work on *Bildungsroman* project, 'Forms of Time', Rabelais research
17 February 1938	Bakhtin's right leg is amputated to the knee.	
Fall 1940	Bakhtin dictates Rabelais dissertation at his sister's flat in Moscow.	Initial typescript of Rabelais dissertation is completed
14 October 1940	Bakhtin delivers lecture 'Discourse in the Novel' at the Gorky Institute. The work is published under the title 'Towards the Prehistory of Novelistic Discourse'.	
24 March 1941	Bakhtin delivers lecture 'The Novel as a Literary Genre' at the Gorky Institute. The work is published under the title 'Epic and Novel'.	

Chronology

Date	Event	Texts
1940–46		Various texts on the novel, continuing revision of Rabelais typescript
September 1945	The Bakhtins move to Saransk, so that Bakhtin can take up post as head of Department of General Literature at the Mordovian State Pedagogical Institute.	
15 November 1946	Oral defence of Bakhtin's dissertation on Rabelais at the Gorky Institute.	
19 April 1950	Revised version of dissertation submitted to the Higher Attestation Commission.	
9 June 1951	Authorities refuse to award Bakhtin the degree of Doctor of Philological Sciences. In June 1952 he will receive the degree of Candidate of Philological Sciences.	
March 1958	Bakhtin is made head of Department of Russian and Foreign Literature at what is now the Mordovian State University.	
November 1960	Bakhtin receives first letter from Bocharov, Kozhinov, Gachev, et al.	
February 1961	Bakhtin receives invitation from publisher Einaudi to revise *Problems of Dostoevsky's Art* for publication in Italy.	
June 1961	Visit of Bocharov, Kozhinov and Gachev to Bakhtin.	
August 1961	Bakhtin retires from post at Saransk.	
September 1963		*Problems of Dostoevsky's Poetics* published
1965		*The Work of François Rabelais [...]* published
30 May 1967	Bakhtin is formally rehabilitated.	

Date	Event	Texts
October 1969	The Bakhtins move to the Kremlin hospital near Moscow, where they will stay through the winter.	
May 1970	The Bakhtins move to home for the elderly in Klimovsk.	
14 December 1971	Elena Alexandrovna Bakhtina dies in Podolsk hospital.	
30 December 1971	Mikhail Bakhtin is moved to the home for writers in Peredelkino.	
September 1972	Bakhtin moves to flat in Moscow.	
February–March 1973	Interviews with Duvakin are recorded.	
7 March 1975	Bakhtin dies at home.	

Abbreviations

61N.	'1961. Notes'. The first half of these notes constitutes the second half of 'The Problem of the Text in Linguistics, Philology, and the Human Sciences', in *Speech Genres and Other Late Essays*, 118–31; the second half of the notes has been translated as 'Towards a Reworking of the Dostoevsky Book', Appendix II to *Problems of Dostoevsky's Poetics*, 283–302; Russian, *Collected Works, Vol. 5*, 329–60.
AARab.	'Additions and Amendments to "Rabelais"'. Translated as 'Bakhtin on Shakespeare: Excerpt from "Additions and Changes to *Rabelais*"', *PMLA* 129, 3 (2014), 524–37; Russian, *Collected Works, Vol. 4 (1)*, 681–731.
AH.	'Author and Hero in Aesthetic Activity'. *Art and Answerability*, 4–256; Russian, *Collected Works, Vol. 1*, 69–263.
Conv.	Conversations with V. D. Duvakin. 1973. *Mikhail Bakhtin: The Duvakin Interviews, 1973*; Russian, *Besedy c V. D. Duvakinym*.
DN.	'Discourse in the Novel: On Issues in the Stylistics of the Novel'. *The Dialogic Imagination*, 259–422; Russian, *Collected Works, Vol. 3*, 9–179.
FTC.	'Forms of Time and of the Chronotope in the Novel'. *The Dialogic Imagination*, 84–258; Russian, *Collected Works, Vol. 3*, 341–511.
Lect.	'Lectures and Comments of 1924–25 by M. M. Bakhtin'. Translated in Susan M. Felch and Paul J. Contino (eds.), *Bakhtin and Religion: A Feeling for Faith*, 205–37; Russian, *Collected Works, Vol. 1*, 326–42.
NLG.	'The Novel as a Literary Genre'. Translated as 'Epic and Novel'. *The Dialogic Imagination*, 3–40; Russian, *Collected Works, Vol. 3*, 608–43.
NRab.	'Notebooks for "Rabelais"'. No English translation; Russian, *Collected Works, Vol. 4 (1)*, 605–75.

OBild.	'On the *Bildungsroman*'. Parts of it appeared in English translation as the final two sections of 'The *Bildungsroman* and its Significance in the History of Realism', in *Speech Genres and Other Late Essays*, 19–59; Russian, *Collected Works, Vol. 3*, 218–335.
OQThN.	'On Questions in the Theory of the Novel'. No English translation; Russian, *Collected Works, Vol. 3*, 557–607.
PDA.	*Problems of Dostoevsky's Art*. There is no complete English translation, but much of it can be found in the translation of the later, substantially revised *Problems of Dostoevsky's Poetics*; Russian, *Problemy tvorchestva Dostoevskogo*.
PDP.	*Problems of Dostoevsky's Poetics*. Same title in English translation; Russian, *Problemy poetiki Dostoevskogo*.
PFCM.	'On Issues in the Methodology of the Aesthetics of the Verbal Artwork. I. The Problem of Form, Content, and Material in Verbal Art'. Note the essay is generally known by its subtitle alone, which is the title (slightly altered) of the English translation in *Art and Answerability*, 257–325; Russian, *Collected Works, Vol. 1*, 265–325.
PSG.	'The Problem of Speech Genres'. *Speech Genres and Other Late Essays*, 60–102; Russian, *Collected Works, Vol. 5*, 159–206.
Rab.	*The Work of François Rabelais and the Popular Culture of the Middle Ages and Renaissance*. In English the book is titled *Rabelais and His World*; Russian, *Tvorchestvo Fransua Rable i narodnaia kul′tura srednevekov′ia i renesansa*
Sat.	'Satire'. Translated in Ilya Kliger and Boris Maslov (eds.), *Persistent Forms: Explorations in Historical Poetics* (New York: Fordham University Press, 2016), 369–91; Russian, *Collected Works, Vol. 5*, 11–38.
TPA.	'Towards a Philosophy of the Act'. *Towards a Philosophy of the Act*; Russian, *Collected Works, Vol. 1*, 7–68.
TPhFHS.	'Towards Philosophical Foundations for the Human Sciences'. No English translation; Russian, *Collected Works, Vol. 5*, 7–10.
WN.	'Working Notes from the 1960s and Early 1970s'. Parts translated in 'From Notes Made in 1970–71' and 'Towards a Methodology for the Human Sciences' in *Speech Genres and Other Late Essays*, 132–72; Russian, *Collected Works, Vol. 6*, 371–439.

Chapter 1

Introduction

In late 1965 a young Bulgarian critic came to Paris on a scholarship, in order to study literature there. She was introduced by another Bulgarian – Tzvetan Todorov, who had arrived a few years earlier – to Roland Barthes, then a leading literary critic and theorist, who in turn invited her to join his weekly seminar. Her first presentation was about the work of a Russian critic that few in Paris had ever heard of: Mikhail Bakhtin. She described his brilliant work on Dostoevsky, summed up in a book he'd published a few years earlier. A few years later that Dostoevsky book appeared in French translation, and Julia Kristeva, who had given the seminar talk, provided a preface, titled 'Une poétique ruinée' ('A ruined poetics').[1]

Why the odd title? Kristeva claimed that Bakhtin had attempted to think about language in a new way: not as a formal system that speakers learned and used to transmit bits of information (as the reigning structuralist model suggested), but as something that the speaker could twist and slant, expressing an attitude to the words used and to the person one was addressing. Language was something always 'depending on the concrete relationship which the user maintains here and now with his utterances'; it could be held at a distance, be spoken ironically or parodically, even stylised (if the speaker wanted to sound 'like' a certain sort of speaker).[2] Bakhtin had tried to describe this as a 'poetics', using the concepts he inherited from the Russian Formalists and structural linguistics, but the result was a patchwork of new ideas, fragmented by their reliance on an older terminology.

It's a provocative, thoughtful image: Bakhtin's new conception taking shape as the ruins of an old one, but Kristeva didn't know the half of it. For there's a sense in which Bakhtin's entire *oeuvre*, his whole intellectual project, ended up as so many ruins. He had, over the course of his eighty years, tried over and over again to articulate his ideas in public and get them a fair hearing, but was constantly frustrated. He started with an ambitious project in moral philosophy, which he then put aside in the 1920s. He managed to publish a book on Dostoevsky in 1929, but was arrested before it saw the light of day and it lay, like buried treasure, undiscussed for thirty years. He wrote books that didn't get published, an entry for an encyclopaedia that was cancelled, an article for a journal that was closed down, and a doctoral dissertation that took six years to be examined and another five (with constant rewriting) to be accepted for a degree. He wrote in many, many notebooks, filling them with short and long paragraphs that hazarded exciting ideas, which then lay undeveloped and unseen for decades. In short, what Bakhtin left to the world, after a lifetime of thinking and writing, was not a shelf full of polished books and essays, but a grab bag of fragments, uncompleted projects, and works that had, in one or another way, been distorted. Scholars, however isolated, eccentric, and unsociable they may be, depend on a public sphere of criticism and argument: the latter tests their ideas, helps them find definitive form, opens them up to wider concerns. Bakhtin had big ideas and no audience: as a result, we have the ruins of a project. Our job is to go through the ruins and extract what we can, to repair what we can repair, to extend and reconstruct where that is possible, and, finally, to admit that we can't make the ruins into a finished building, can't undo the history that produced them.

Why are we even aware of the ruins? Because in the early 1960s a trio of determined and passionate young scholars discovered Bakhtin's 1929 book in a library, found out – to their surprise – that the author was still alive, paid him a visit, and decided to devote a remarkable amount of their academic life and resources to a campaign for his rehabilitation. In a way, one could say that Bakhtin's reception – which I'll discuss at the end of this *Cambridge Introduction*, in keeping with the standard format for this series – preceded his biography and context. Bakhtin had not been a public figure. There was no biography to speak of and the context of his work was, to a great extent, a history of repression: he'd been arrested in 1929, served five years in internal exile, had spent the late 1930s and the war years hiding, and had finally managed a degree of normalcy by getting a post at a fairly remote provincial university (remote enough so that people who had known him earlier assumed he was dead). It was only after two of the young scholars, S. G. (Sergei Georgievich) Bocharov and V. V. (Vadim Valerianovich) Kozhinov, succeeded in getting some of the unpublished material into print in the 1960s and 1970s, that the moment of reception finally arrived and the scholarly community tried to figure out who this man was and what he had, precisely, accomplished.

Even when that moment arrived, interpretation wasn't a straightforward process. Bakhtin was himself reticent to talk about his past, and records at the time were still difficult to access. As a result, there was a struggle of sorts over Bakhtin's legacy, a struggle among different groups in the Soviet Union, each seeking to identify this emerging luminary with their cause. Structuralists and semioticians, Marxist critics of structuralism and semiotics, and Russian

'Slavophile' nationalists all claimed him as their spokesperson. When the archive is in ruins and the life barely documented, it's easy to fill in the gaps according to your preferences: there were, accordingly, multiple biographies and multiple descriptions of context, each designed to support a different interpretation of the man and his work. There were arguments about why he became a literary critic: was it a matter of intellectual evolution, or was he forced onto this path because the Soviet government wouldn't publish his early writing in philosophy? There were arguments about the early philosophy: was it inspired by Russian religious philosophy or German Neo-Kantianism? There were disputes about his friends: were his closest ones the Marxists Voloshinov and Medvedev, the Jewish philosopher Kagan, or two Jews who converted to Russian Orthodoxy, Pumpianskii and Iudina? (We will be introduced properly to all these people in the following chapter.)

You may have picked up this volume thinking that Bakhtin had smoked one of his manuscripts during the Second World War. You may believe that he wrote works published under the names of his friends Voloshinov and Medvedev. You may have been thrilled by his essay 'Discourse in the Novel', but wondered why it included so few references to the work of other scholars working on stylistics. 'Towards a Methodology of the Human Sciences' may be, despite (or perhaps because of) its fragmentary nature, one of your favourite Bakhtin texts. Now that the dust has settled, we can say with some confidence (but not absolutely, because there just isn't conclusive evidence) that there was no manuscript to be smoked, that Bakhtin may have helped with but didn't write the books by Voloshinov and Medvedev, that there were plenty of footnotes in 'Discourse in the Novel' (they were not included in the versions that were translated), and that Bakhtin never put together 'Towards a Methodology of the Human Sciences' (it was pieced together from various notebooks by an editor, without any authorisation from Bakhtin).

The ruin of a poetics and then what we might call a struggle over what to do with this archaeological site, which, as we shall see, ended up having far more visitors, in the Soviet Union and beyond, than anyone could have expected. There were competing ideas about how to interpret and curate the ruins and a sense of urgency about sorting them out. As I write this in 2019, the ruins have become a kind of theoretical Stonehenge: adored, surrounded by various myths and conjectures, a must-see for any tourist of literary theory, and – at this point – only to be viewed at a distance. The reader of this *Cambridge Introduction* probably knows Bakhtin from the various translations that arrived like so many wonderful gifts from the 1980s onwards, from the monographs that tried to make sense of his life, and from critical texts that were probably based on those same translations. We should think of all those now as the first go at reconstruction, produced with some haste though with the best of intentions, at a time when doing the job the way it should be done seemed impossible. But today things are much different. The reform of the Soviet Union in the 1980s and its eventual collapse in 1991 removed many of the constraints on Bakhtin scholarship: archives were opened, scholars from Russia were able to communicate freely with scholars from abroad, and scholarly work could be published without censorship. Between 1996 and 2012 a team of specialists at the Russian Academy of Sciences produced a six-volume *Collected Works*, a scholarly edition that far surpassed, in detail and editorial care, any Bakhtin publication that preceded it. Are there still differences of opinion about the man and his work? Without doubt. But now we have the old texts in proper form and plenty of new texts as well.

We've come, you could say, to a turning point in the reception of Bakhtin, the moment at which we can finally put together something like a reasonable biography, a thorough account of his context, and a reliable description and analysis of the works themselves. That is exciting, but it makes the writing of this *Cambridge Introduction* a little more complicated than it should be. On the one hand, this book should be like a toolbox with an instruction manual: within its pages, the reader should find concepts and arguments – theoretical tools – which will be useful for their work in literary and cultural analysis, together with sensible advice on how these can be used. While many who read this book will have picked up a few of those tools already (dialogism, or the chronotope, say) and tried to use them, this introduction ought to show them how to apply them in ways they might not have thought of or to tasks they didn't realise were appropriate.

On the other hand, this book has to set the record straight. There are myths that need to be dispelled – about Bakhtin, about his friends and his colleagues, and about some of his works. There is a complicated context to be accounted for. And there are works that need to be reinterpreted in the light of new editions or even introduced to the English-language reader. In the pages that follow I do my best to balance and coordinate the two tasks: to present a usable and interesting Bakhtin for students and researchers; and to present what is in some respects a new Bakhtin. Where a re-edited text differs substantially or importantly from the one we're familiar with, I'll make sure to note the differences. Where there are texts that remain untranslated but that offer something new and interesting, I'll make sure to alert the reader to their existence. It will require a bit of juggling, but I will try to ensure the patient reader is rewarded.

Chapter 2

Life

Mikhail Bakhtin led an extraordinary life, extraordinary in its difficulty and extraordinary in its achievements. 'To live a life is not as simple as to cross a field', goes an old Russian proverb, and the crossing was particularly brutal and complicated for a Russian born in 1895, who would have to experience, in turn, the First World War (1914–18), the Russian Revolutions and the ensuing Civil War (1917–21), the onset of Stalin's repression in the late 1920s, the nightmare of collectivisation in the 1930s, the purges and murders that climaxed in 1937, and the Second World War (1939–45). Many of these events touched Bakhtin's life directly – he was in Leningrad during the revolution, and during the Civil War he moved to the town of Nevel´ simply to obtain food. He was arrested in 1929 and sent in exile to a town in Kazakhstan for five years, where he witnessed people starving to death in the streets during the famine and collectivisation. When he attempted to start a normal life after his sentence of exile, his first academic appointment came to a sudden end, as the purges of 1937 threatened his position, forcing him to run away. While he survived the war years working as a high school teacher, his mother and sisters died. His doctoral dissertation, submitted in 1940, became a subject of ideological struggle – it was even referred to in the Soviet press. He finally obtained a steady academic appointment when he was fifty. A difficult life and a hard to pin down life, as a quick glance at the 1984 English-language biography, written by Katerina Clark and Michael Holquist, reveals: there is sketchy (and, we now know, partly incorrect) information about his family, a good deal of detail on Bakhtin's activity and friendships from 1917 till 1929, very little about his life from 1930 till 1960 (except for a brief account of his thesis defence), and more detail about his life from 1960 until his death in 1975.[1] It is hardly surprising, for while Bakhtin survived – itself an achievement, for most of his close friends were dead by 1940 – he lived on the fringes of the Soviet system, recognised as an extraordinary and inventive mind, but, despite his best efforts, unable to gain official status.

After Stalin's death in 1953 there was a struggle for the leadership of the Communist Party, won eventually by Khrushchev, under whose watch there was considerable liberalisation of Soviet cultural life. It was this liberalisation that made possible the publication of a revised version of Bakhtin's book on Dostoevsky in 1963 and the publication of a revised version of his doctoral thesis on Rabelais in 1965. Bakhtin's life, however, remained complicated, because his rehabilitation depended on a shifting set of alliances and compromises. There were critics who liked his work because it looked like a sophisticated rebuttal of Russian Formalism, which they opposed from a fairly orthodox Communist position. There were Formalists – Viktor Shklovsky, for example – who supported Bakhtin because they thought of him as a subtle thinker who was distant from the Communist Party line.[2] There were critics who thought Bakhtin represented opposition to the entire culture of the Soviet Union, in the name of either a repressed Russian Orthodox or repressed Russian nationalist tradition.

These unstable alliances complicated Bakhtin's life in the 1960s and 1970s, but they also complicated his *previous* life. Bakhtin was not forthcoming about the details of his earlier years and he had himself obscured matters by occasionally – for understandable reasons – playing fast and loose with the truth on official documents. Now that people eager to claim him for their cause were trying to discover who he was and had been, there was a rush to fill the biographical void. As is so often the case when documents are not available or accessible, rumour and surmise filled the void instead. The rumours were not aimless – they had a point. If you said Bakhtin had aristocratic origins, that gave him a certain air of nobility (and hostility to Soviet Communism).[3] If you claimed he had smoked one of his manuscripts, it illustrated his indifference to worldly success.[4] If you said he wrote some books and articles published under the names of his friends, this could imply that he couldn't write under his own name and that he was able and willing to disguise his thoughts with an alien terminology.

Bakhtin did not intervene to scupper the rumours or settle the disputes (although it turned out he had engaged in thirteen hours of interviews in 1973 with the literary scholar V. D. Duvakin, which came to light two decades later). When he died in 1975, the world was aware of his study of Dostoevsky – republished in 1963 as *Problems of Dostoevsky's Poetics* (the 1929 version had been titled *Problems of Dostoevsky's Art*) – his book on Rabelais, a few fragments on the novel, and, notoriously, books and articles authored by his friends V. N. (Valentin Nikolaevich) Voloshinov and P. N. (Pavel Nikolaevich) Medvedev, which, it was claimed, had actually been written by Bakhtin. *That* claim had first been made publicly by the semiotician V. V. Ivanov, at a meeting to celebrate Bakhtin's seventy-fifth birthday in 1970, although afterwards various Russian scholars said it had been a common belief amongst the local intelligentsia.[5] In 1975 a collection of essays with four works on the novel and one long philosophical critique of Russian Formalism came out in Russia. In 1979 a Russian collection was published that included a long, early philosophical fragment, excerpts from a book on the *Bildungsroman* (the novel of 'formation' or 'education'), some essays on linguistics, and two collections of aphorisms and comments – some philosophical, some linguistic, some religious, some literary – called, enigmatically, 'Towards a Methodology of the Human Sciences' and 'From Notes Made in 1970–71'. Now there was some explaining to do, for the Bakhtin *oeuvre* looked like a heterogeneous grab bag of work: some fairly technical philosophy that was like phenomenology, a philosophical critique of Formalism, works on the novel written in a militant tone and aiming at a sociological stylistics, a scholarly but enthusiastic recovery of popular carnival culture, and philosophical musings from later life.

Explanations were forthcoming. Some commentators suggested that Bakhtin had always intended to write philosophy and to be a philosopher, but the restrictions imposed on philosophy by the Soviet government forced him to change course, to shift to literary criticism and the philosophy of language, all the while disguising his intentions with the kind of sociological language that would appeal to Marxists. Others thought the early philosophical works were just, well, early works, which Bakhtin abandoned when his intellectual path took him in a different direction. Some thought the occasional use of religious language revealed the true Bakhtin, while discussions couched in the language of linguistics and social theory were mere window dressing for the Soviet censors. Others saw the religious language as occasional and relatively uninteresting compared to the richly elaborated studies of novelistic style and imagery. All were struck, however, by the sheer productivity and originality of a man who seemed to have worked in more or less complete intellectual isolation.

The evidence for each explanation was fairly thin, often relying on unsourced oral testimony. But to be fair, unsourced oral testimony was often all that was available, given the power of Soviet censorship. The result is one of the great ironies of Bakhtin scholarship: the fullest and most detailed elaboration of the explanation favoured by a substantial number of Bakhtin's Russian supporters – Bakhtin was a religious philosopher forced by circumstances to work on literature and linguistics – appeared not in Russia itself, but in Clark and Holquist's 1984 biography. There the case was made for the importance of Bakhtin's early philosophical writings and for Bakhtin's authorship of texts by his friends Voloshinov and Medvedev, supported in many instances by the testimony of unnamed Russian sources.

8   Life

The biography would become the standard reference for Bakhtin readers both abroad and in the Soviet Union.

But history had another card to play and Bakhtin's life was to be upended, rewritten, yet again. In the 1980s, the emergence of a reform leadership in the Soviet Communist Party, headed by Mikhail Gorbachev, led to the policies of *glasnost´* (openness) and *perestroika* (reconstruction), which in turn led to further publication of work on and by Bakhtin. Gorbachev's liberalisation unleashed forces he could not control and in 1991 the Soviet Union itself disintegrated and with it many of the limitations that had hobbled Bakhtin scholarship. In 1992 a Russian journal devoted purely to Bakhtin was launched and it began to publish memoirs, studies of archival work, interviews, and critical studies. In 1993 the transcripts of the interviews from 1973 began to be published. In 1996 the Russian Academy of Sciences began to publish the Bakhtin *Collected Works*, a proper scholarly edition of everything by Bakhtin that had been already published – the two books, the essays, the notes – and much that was new, including the contents of many of Bakhtin's notebooks. The end result was a sea change in Bakhtin scholarship. Arguments began to be made on the basis of archival evidence and documentary sources. Texts that had been censored appeared in uncensored form. The grey areas in Bakhtin's life, like that period between 1930 and 1960, began to acquire some colour and detail. But some of the biographical facts people had accepted up till that point were contradicted by new evidence, so the biography itself also changed.

What follows is a summary of Bakhtin's life according to the current state of scholarship. (And who knows? History may have another card up its sleeve.)[6] There are still uncertainties and aspects of Bakhtin's life we know little about. In some respects what follows is different from the common understanding of Bakhtin's life in the English-speaking world, and sometimes the story is different from the one told by Bakhtin himself in his lengthy interviews with Duvakin – because it is contradicted by documentary evidence. Where there are facts in dispute, I've indicated it in the notes. It's still a complicated life. But the complications are now mostly complications in the life itself, rather than in the tortured process of telling it.

Youth: 1895–1917

The story begins in Orel, a Russian town roughly 350 kilometres south-west of Moscow, where Bakhtin's father, Mikhail Nikolaevich, worked for the Orel Commercial Bank. Mikhail Mikhailovich Bakhtin was born on 4/16

November in 1895, second child to Varvara Zakharovna Bakhtina, in what would become a family with six children (the first date is according to the Julian calendar then in effect in Russia; the second is the date according to the modern, Gregorian calendar). The family was middle class, not – as was claimed by Bakhtin's elder brother Nikolai and by Mikhail himself – descended from Russian aristocrats, but they were clearly well off, with a very large, comfortable house and servants. Nikolai was one year older than Mikhail; their sisters Mariia, Ekaterina, and Natalia were born between 1899 and 1909 and there was also an adopted sister, Nina. There would be, over the next several decades, a good deal of moving about, as a family and individually, and a great deal of tragedy: the Bakhtins were not destined to be as close as they might have hoped. They would not see Nikolai after 1918, when he went to fight in the Russian Civil War (he emigrated afterwards), and although Mikhail Bakhtin would remain in contact with his mother and sisters, it would be sporadic from 1929 onwards. And, to be frank, we will lose contact with them as well, for there is very little information available about their lives, their interests, and their fates.

According to Mikhail's and Nikolai's (not invariably accurate) recollections, the Bakhtin household was, in traditional terms, extremely 'cultured'. Both Nikolai and Mikhail were reportedly educated by a governess in their youth, who taught them German, and Bakhtin also learned French at an early age. We do know that the bank required his father and the family to move to Vilnius, in Lithuania, in 1905. There, Nikolai and Mikhail, a year later, would enter a gymnasium – that is, an academically orientated secondary school – where they received a fairly standard classical education, which would include Latin and ancient Greek. There, also, they met Mikhail Lopatto and Leib Meerovich Pumpian, both of whom have further roles to play in this history.[7]

In 1911 another change in post compelled the Bakhtins to move to Odessa, a Black Sea port notable for its large Jewish population and ethnic diversity, although Nikolai stayed on in Vilnius to complete gymnasium. In 1912 Nikolai moved to Odessa and entered the local university, Novorossiskii University, and Bakhtin scholarship enters something of a black hole. For Mikhail claimed, in one of the 1973 interviews, that he, too, entered Novorossiskii University in Odessa and enjoyed being taught by a number of its notable professors, before transferring to Petrograd University. But this is only one possible account of Bakhtin's postsecondary education: at various points he claimed to have spent two years at university in Odessa and two in Petrograd (as Saint Petersburg was known from 1914 to 1924), four years at Petrograd, just two years at Petrograd, and two years at Marburg University in Germany. There is, however, no official record of Bakhtin being enrolled in any university at the time, although there are records for his brother Nikolai. Did Bakhtin simply borrow Nikolai's academic history later in life, for purposes of employment? Both Bakhtin's erudition and his fairly detailed recollections of his university days in Odessa and Petrograd (in the interviews with Duvakin) imply he tagged along with his older brother and attended classes either as an auditor or unofficially.[8] But the absence of records means we don't know what happened for sure.

In any case, Mikhail moved to Petrograd at some point in 1916, attending classes until 1918. He, Nikolai, Lopatto, and the man now named Lev Vasil'evich Pumpianskii (Pumpian, born Jewish, had converted to Russian Orthodoxy in 1911 and changed his name) took up where they left off: they now met regularly as a group, which seems to have been dedicated to creating parodies of the serious works they studied by day, mimicking notable intellectual figures, and playing charades.[9] But by the end of 1916 both Pumpianskii and Nikolai Bakhtin were in the Russian Army. Bakhtin was not – he had osteomyelitis in one of his legs.

This left Bakhtin in what was fast becoming revolutionary Petrograd. Speaking in retrospect, he claimed that although the Petrograd University student body was full of warring political factions, who sometimes fought in the corridors, he stayed well away, devoting himself to his presumably unofficial studies. Was Bakhtin uninterested in politics? He has described himself as 'completely apolitical' (Conv 65/78), but he clearly had views. When the February 1917 revolution overthrew the monarchy, Bakhtin had no faith in the leadership of Alexander Kerensky, who had been installed as leader of the Provisional Government. The lack of faith was based on ordinary political calculation – he thought 'these intellectuals were completely unable to rule the government, unable to defend the February revolution' (Conv 106/132) – as well as some personal experience.[10] Kerensky, had been, in fact, the lover of the wife of his friend Boris Zalesskii, and he impressed neither Zalesskii nor Bakhtin. 'And therefore it was inevitable', Bakhtin later told Duvakin, 'that the most extreme elements would prevail' (Conv 107/133–4), meaning that either the monarchy would be restored or the Bolsheviks would triumph.[11]

He did not view the latter prospect with joy. The proletariat, in his view, was 'not a historical class, it has no values – actually it has nothing. Their whole lives they struggle only for narrow material things' (Conv 108/134). Having no belief in the prospect of socialist revolution and no faith in the political will or ability of the liberal movement (represented by Kerensky), Bakhtin stayed out of the way. In his own words, 'I sat at home, I read; when there was heating, I sat in the library' (Conv 108/134).

His brother Nikolai joined the White Guard (i.e., the counter-revolutionary army) in 1918, and became, in turn, a sailor, a member of the French Foreign Legion, a wounded member of the French Foreign Legion, a Russian émigré in Paris, and finally a classicist in England (he would gain a doctorate at Cambridge, where he became close friends with Ludwig Wittgenstein, and then taught at the universities of Southampton and Birmingham). Mikhail would never see him again, and Nikolai, careful not to endanger his brother, would communicate with their mother only thereafter.[12]

Friendships: 1918–1929

The rest of the Bakhtins were in Petrograd. Pumpianskii, who had been stationed in the provincial city of Nevel' during the war, visited and persuaded Mikhail to come to Nevel', where food was plentiful (it was hard to come by in Petrograd). It was a move with remarkable consequences. For there Bakhtin met most of the people who would be his intellectual companions for the next twenty years. Pumpianskii had met a young pianist named M. V. (Mariia Veniaminovna) Iudina in Nevel'; he persuaded her to convert to Russian Orthodoxy, as he himself had done earlier. A young philosopher named M. I. (Matvei Isaevich) Kagan had just returned from eight years in Germany, where he had studied with the Neo-Kantians Hermann Cohen, Ernst Cassirer, and Paul Natorp (the stay had been longer than anticipated, as he was interned when the First World War started). B. M. (Boris Mikhailovich) Zubakin – poet, mystic philosopher, leader of the Rosicrucian order – was, like Pumpianskii, stationed in Nevel' as part of his military service. Zubakin's friend Valentin Voloshinov, the future author of *Marxism and the Philosophy of Language*, but then a music scholar, had come to Nevel' at Zubakin's urging.

The friendship was not merely a matter of enjoying each other's company: all had serious intellectual and cultural commitments, which were, in the old-fashioned sense, 'vocational', not professional or recreational, but something akin to a mission. Their socialising was therefore always mixed with, if not dominated by, intellectual exchange and debate. Bakhtin has recounted daily walks with Iudina, accompanied sometimes by Pumpianskii as well, during which he would talk about his new ideas for an ethical philosophy; the lake around which some of the walks were taken was accordingly honoured with the title 'the lake of ethical reality'.[13] These three, together with some combination of Kagan, Zubakin, Voloshinov, and perhaps others, would also meet at regular intervals at someone's home to discuss important philosophical

12   *Life*

books and important philosophical issues, in what was sometimes called their 'Kantian seminar'. But debate was by no means limited to private occasions and venues, because at this immediately post-revolutionary moment there was a lot to debate and both public interest and support for popular education and discussion. Bakhtin, Pumpianskii, and Kagan – together with some other local intellectuals, Ia. Gutman and I. N. (Iosif Naumovich) Gurvich – formed the Nevel´ Scholarly Association, which organised a series of debates and lectures in the town, hosted at what we can assume was the newly christened Karl Marx People's Club. At a time of revolution, everything is up for grabs, and the topics were suitably ambitious: 'God and Socialism', 'Christianity and Critique', 'The Meaning of Life', 'The Meaning of Love'.[14] Nor was popular education and culture just a matter of lectures: there were plays and concerts with introductory talks and at least plans for a production of the Sophocles tragedy *Oedipus at Colonus*, 'directed by the connoisseurs of Hellas and Greece, Citizens Bakhtin and Pumpianskii'.[15]

Bakhtin scholars, however, only occasionally refer to the Nevel´ Scholarly Association: they prefer to focus on what they call the 'Bakhtin Circle' or the 'Nevel´ school of philosophy'.[16] The Russian circle (*kruzhok*) was an informal, but in its way rigorous, form of intellectual research and debate. Because Russia had been dominated by the Tsarist autocracy, which kept close control on all official centres of intellectual life, 'circles' of intellectuals, meeting informally to discuss particular texts or issues of common interest, had been a distinctive feature of Russian culture since the 1840s. If informality is the measure, then the label might be appropriate, insofar as Bakhtin, Iudina, Pumpianskii, and Kagan often met at homes or on rural walks. In other respects, however, it makes no sense. For one thing, the label is purely retrospective: unlike, say, the Moscow Linguistic Circle, instituted explicitly in 1915, the Vienna Circle formally instituted in 1929, with an explicit programme, or even the Petrashevsky circle of the 1840s (which generated the Russian term), no one spoke of a Bakhtin Circle in the 1910s or 1920s, and for good reason. Bakhtin, Kagan, and Pumpianskii did not share a programme or a philosophy, though they had overlapping interests; indeed, Bakhtin himself did not have enough of a worked-out system at that point to be the focus of a circle. It is probably, therefore, time to retire the notion of a 'Bakhtin Circle'. If one ever existed, it was in the late 1920s, when Voloshinov, Bakhtin, and Medvedev seemed to work in concert towards a new philosophy of language and literature and, at that point, it would be misleading to name it after Bakhtin alone.

Instead, what we have are serious intellectuals who become friends, who are faced with an extreme social and political crisis in Europe, and who work from a shared set of intellectual resources, in large part because they share them with one another. They did not, for the most part, think about the crisis in political terms. Kagan, it's worth pointing out, had been a Social Democratic (i.e., Communist) activist from 1904 to 1908 and had been jailed in 1905 for his trouble (he claimed in later life he had once hidden the young Josef Stalin).[17] His return to Russia after the end of the war in 1918 seems to have occasioned ambiguous feelings. His wife and daughter recalled a moment soon after his return when, looking out the window, he exclaimed, 'This is the first time in the world this has been done' and he was excited by this social experiment.[18] In a brief memoir of his own, however, he claims that in 1918, he was initially 'horrified by all that had taken place', but that by the summer of 1924 had had a change of heart – he had 'fully accepted the completed revolution'.[19] Pumpianskii, by contrast, described himself as 'on the sidelines' – although in 1927 he would commit himself wholeheartedly to the revolution.[20] So far as we can tell from his reminiscences with Duvakin, Bakhtin had been sceptical of the Bolshevik revolution at the outset and remained so later. In any case, their writing from this period discusses the current crisis as a cultural rather than explicitly political one, and in terms of the long durée: as the outcome of a long historical process, dating back as far as the Renaissance, rather than immediate political circumstances.

In 1920, Pumpianskii had to move to the larger town of Vitebsk, in order to act as a translator for the Red Army; Bakhtin followed him in the autumn. As Iudina had moved to Petrograd, to continue her musical studies, and Kagan to Orel, in order to teach, it looks like Bakhtin could have been intellectually stranded. But while Nevel′ had had a surprising amount of cultural activity, Vitebsk, a provincial capital, had far more. It was home to the Vitebsk School of Art, which had been founded by Marc Chagall and which, from 1920 onwards, was directed by Kasimir Malevich, founder of the avant-garde movement Suprematism, with whom Bakhtin would spend a good deal of time.[21] In Vitebsk Bakhtin would meet the young I. I. Sollertinskii, then a student of Hispanic languages but soon to become a scholar of music and later the director of the Leningrad Philharmonic, a leading critic of modern music, and a close friend of Shostakovich.[22] Bakhtin would teach aesthetics and philosophy of music at the Vitebsk Conservatory and classes at the Institute of People's Education. Most important, he would meet the literary critic, Pavel Medvedev, already a lecturer at the local pedagogical institute and soon to be the rector of a newly established Proletarian University in Vitebsk. Medvedev had been the last mayor of Vitebsk and briefly (from 1917 until 1918) a member of the left wing of the Socialist-Revolutionary Party – in other words, he was politically active in a way that Bakhtin's other friends were not. He seems to have been one of those rare people who combined serious intellectual ability with a talent and liking for administration. Such a man would not only accomplish a good deal, but also be an invaluable friend to Bakhtin, who possessed the first set of qualities, but not the second.[23]

Bakhtin met more than new friends, for it was in Vitebsk that he met Elena Alexandrovna Bersh-Okolovich, who worked at the local library, whom he would marry in July 1921, and to whom he would remain married until her death in 1971. In keeping with the sexism of the society in which Bakhtin lived, we know remarkably little about the woman who was Mikhail Mikhailovich's companion throughout the course of his life. The fullest picture we have was painted by a colleague of Bakhtin's in the 1940s and 1950s, when he had moved to Saransk to teach at the local pedagogical institute. Having noted that Elena Alexandrovna was someone 'made wise by life experience, an extremely intelligent woman', E. V. Estifeeva describes her as quite different in temperament from her reserved and reticent husband. The people who lived in the Bakhtins' building sensed in Mikhail Mikhailovich a 'distance [...] that generated a feeling of respectful relations'. Elena Alexandrovna was different: 'Immediately threads of kind and friendly relations bound her to many inhabitants of the building. They sought her advice, shared their impressions about what was going on at the institute, confided their secrets.'[24] This seemed to have been combined with a remarkable toughness and determination, centred on supporting an ailing husband: the rest of the picture shows us a woman hauling firewood and fetching water, all the while enforcing severe economies, motivated by the 'desire to provide some kind of support for Mikhail Mikhailovich, in case she died before him'.[25]

But that must have seemed a remote possibility throughout the marriage: Mikhail had suffered throughout his life from chronic osteomyelitis, a condition that required surgery in February of 1921, and later in 1938. If his newfound love was a support, she was not the only one, for we also know that Voloshinov moved to Vitebsk to look after Bakhtin, renting rooms with him from a woman whose daughter he would marry shortly thereafter. Voloshinov, whose expertise at that point was in music, found work arranged by the indefatigable Medvedev.

M. I. Kagan had moved to Moscow, and Bakhtin – happily for us – corresponded with him. The letters speak of grand projects: 'Lately I have been working almost exclusively on the aesthetics of verbal creation' (February 1921); 'I began a work on which I now intend to continue: "The Subject of Ethics and the Subject of Law"' (October–November 1921); 'Now I am writing a work on Dostoevsky, which I hope to finish very soon' (January 1922).[26] The archive, however, consists of unfinished works.

There are fragments of a work of moral and ethical philosophy, which Bakhtin's editors call 'Towards a Philosophy of the Act'. There is also another, longer fragment, which editors named 'Author and Hero in Aesthetic Activity', which might well be a chapter from the planned ethical philosophy or might be the work on 'the aesthetics of verbal creation' Bakhtin mentions to Kagan – both fragments are undated, and they overlap enough to say they are related, but not enough to say exactly how.

In any case, Bakhtin returned to Petrograd in May of 1924, by which point the city had been rechristened Leningrad. The accumulated friends from Nevel' and Vitebsk continued to meet, although they were now a small part of a much larger civic public sphere, consisting of a wide range of salons, unofficial circles, cultural societies, and new Soviet institutions. It was a time of fierce argument in the Soviet Union – within the Communist Party and the government itself and among an extraordinarily varied group of intellectuals: some actively currying favour with the Soviet leadership, some struggling for a version of cultural revolution that they thought would complement the political one, some hostile to the political regime but still convinced some kind of cultural renewal was required.

What was Bakhtin doing in this tumultuous period? We know about some of his activity, but not nearly as much as one would think, because he did not earn his keep by means of an established, salaried post with an institution that would keep official records. There are notes taken by Pumpianskii for two sets of lectures by Bakhtin – one titled 'Hero and Author in Aesthetic Creation' (apparently from July 1924) and a set of lectures on Kantian critical philosophy, from later that year. From letters and notes we know that the group of friends from Nevel' and Vitebsk – Iudina, Pumpianskii, Bakhtin, Voloshinov, Medvedev, and a few others – looked at work in psychoanalysis in 1924–25 and works in theology in 1925–26.[27] From Bakhtin's own reminiscences and recollections, we've learned that he was a regular attendant at cultural evenings hosted by Medvedev, by Iudina, and by A. S. Rugevich (another Vitebsk persona, originally a friend of Voloshinov's), that he had been attending meetings of the Religious-Philosophical Society in Petrograd since the mid-1910s, and that he went to a wide range of readings and talks across the city.[28] He seems to have survived on fees from private lessons and occasional teaching posts, although the main breadwinner in this period may have been Elena Alexandrovna.[29]

The obvious comparison, frequently made in the critical literature, is with Voloshinov and Medvedev. The former, having returned to university in 1922 and having completed a degree in linguistics by 1924, became a postgraduate and then researcher at the Institute for the Comparative History of

Eastern and Western Languages and Literatures (ILIaZV was its Russian acronym), where he worked from 1925 to 1930. ILIaZV was a hothouse for some of the Soviet Union's most interesting and independent intellectuals: Russian Formalists and Formalist fellow-travellers, like Boris Eikhenbaum, Boris Tomashevskii and Viktor Zhirmunskii; the leading followers of the proto-structuralist linguist Baudouin de Courtenay, Lev Shcherba and Lev Iakubinskii; the eventual creators of 'semantic paleontology', Olga Freidenberg and Izrail' Frank-Kamenetskii; and finally the linguist Nikolai. Ia. Marr, whose Japhetology would overwhelm and stifle Soviet linguistics from the late 1920s onwards (although he left the Institute in 1927). Craig Brandist has described the institute's remarkable spread of work, which stretched from the description of manuscript collections and the publication of dictionaries to work in experimental phonetics and linguistic and literary theory.[30] As Brandist has pointed out, the reorganisation of the institute in 1927 divided it into a language and a literary section, but the decision to focus research on certain themes meant that many scholars at the institute freely mixed literary and linguistic study. One of those themes was the study of languages in the contemporary city and village, which would lead directly to Zhirmunskii's study *National Language and Social Dialects* in 1936 and indirectly to the clearly urban accounts of language we will encounter in Bakhtin's 'Discourse in the Novel'.[31]

Medvedev, too, would end up at ILIaZV, acquiring a research post there in 1928. He had returned to Petrograd with his family in 1922 and had been almost immediately appointed editor of a journal associated with a theatrical company (although the journal would be closed by the government in 1924).[32] As a consequence, for a couple of years at least he had a platform for writing and editing. In 1925 he would be appointed to a research post at the Institute for Russian Literature (Pushkin House), and at around the same time he was elected to the board of the Leningrad section of the All-Russian Union of Writers (then a non-governmental organisation). It's clear he was exceptionally active as a speaker and writer in the 1920s, who was not afraid to get involved in the polemics of the time. In 1928 he became an editor at Gosizdat, the State Publishing House. But, like most intellectuals in the period, he found earning a living difficult, even though he was an established literary scholar and a talented administrator of cultural institutions.

We know not only more about what Voloshinov and Medvedev were doing, but also more about what they were thinking, because they not only belonged to public institutions but also published articles and books in the lively but conflictual world of Soviet literary and cultural scholarship.[33] What was Bakhtin writing between 1924, when he arrived in Leningrad, and the end of 1928, when he was arrested? There are two texts we can be confident about: a critique of Russian Formalist literary criticism, titled 'The Problem of Form, Content and Material in Verbal Artistic Work', which has been dated to 1924, and the book *Problems of Dostoevsky's Art*, which was published in Leningrad in early 1929 (although submitted several months earlier). The former is a philosophical critique of Russian Formalism, which, according to current Bakhtin scholarship, was to have been published in the journal *Russkii sovremennik* (*The Russian Contemporary*), but wasn't, because the journal was shut down by the Soviet government in 1924. There is, however, no evidence of the planned publication in the journal – no advance notice and nothing in the recollections of its editor, K. Chukovskii.[34] The book on Dostoevsky, while it has its philosophical moments, is very different: it's focused on Dostoevsky's 'revolutionary innovation in the field of the novel as an artistic form', which Bakhtin called 'dialogism' (PDA, 276/4). From this point forward, Bakhtin's writing would be almost wholly devoted to literary theory and analysis. The question that leaves us with is how Bakhtin got from A – ethical philosophy with a focus on aesthetics – to B, literary theory dominated by a new philosophy of language and the idea of dialogism.

How one answers that question seems to determine how one interprets Bakhtin's work as a whole (or it might be the other way round: how one thinks about Bakhtin's life in general predisposes one to a certain interpretation of this period). In Bakhtin scholarship the result has been a classic and characteristic stand-off, in which our understanding of Bakhtin's trajectory is intertwined with disputes over the dating of certain works and the authorship of several others (and questions, as well, about whom Bakhtin felt closest to intellectually). 'Author and Hero in Aesthetic Activity' has, as I mentioned, no date (and neither, for that matter, does the critique of Russian Formalism). The scholars providing editorial commentary for its Russian publication (among them Sergei Bocharov) have argued that it must have been written before 1924 because they believe it must have been written before 'The Problem of Form, Content, and Material', which they date to 1924.[35] Brian Poole, on the other hand, has argued that it was probably written much later, because its argument depends on familiarity with philosophical work that was not published until 1926.[36] Why does it matter?: because in each case the dating is part of a larger narrative.[37] Bocharov and others have argued that Bakhtin always thought of himself as a philosopher, that the work represented in 'Towards a Philosophy of the Act' and 'Author and Hero in Aesthetic Activity' – 'written in the treasured and pure language of his philosophy' – was what he intended to devote his life to.[38] He had, the argument runs, initially dedicated himself to this philosophical work and had tried, in the form of 'The Problem of Form, Content, and Material', to publish it, but found himself rebuffed by the Soviet government when they closed the journal. As Bocharov has put it, 'Bakhtin could draw his own conclusions from the failure of the journal and of his own article': he accepted the fact that he would never be able to publish his philosophical work and had to take a different tack.[39] He therefore turned, the argument concludes, from philosophy to linguistics and literary theory for purely tactical reasons, publishing his own work under the names of his friends Voloshinov and Medvedev, beginning with articles on linguistics and literary theory in 1925 and 1926 and culminating in their well-known books from the late 1920s: *Freudianism: A Critical Sketch* (Voloshinov, 1928), *Marxism and the Philosophy of Language* (Voloshinov, 1929), and *The Formal Method in Literary Scholarship* (Medvedev, 1928) (all together known, in Bakhtin scholarship, as 'the disputed texts').[40] By the time of the Dostoevsky book, Bakhtin had accepted his fate and become a literary scholar. But all these texts are written 'in a mask', including the book on Dostoevsky, which, though it has Bakhtin's name on the cover, deploys a theoretical language that is in effect an intellectual disguise.[41]

But if Bakhtin was writing 'Author and Hero' in the mid-1920s, that narrative is much less plausible. Bakhtin would have been still beavering away on his philosophy after the supposed 1924 rebuff and would therefore not be motivated to switch fields, to write books for his friends, and so on. Instead, Bakhtin would be continuing to do his thing, while Voloshinov and Medvedev, more interested in Marxism, though sharing a lot of Bakhtin's philosophical inclinations, did theirs. Bakhtin's shift to what he does in the Dostoevsky book then looks like a consequence of the *influence* of Voloshinov and Medvedev on his work. We know Voloshinov stayed with Bakhtin in his dacha (summer cottage) in the summer of 1928, and it's reasonable to think Bakhtin decided to look in Dostoevsky for the 'dialogical' style Voloshinov was looking at more broadly.

Two alternative interpretations of a five-year stretch of Bakhtin's life, a stretch which, perhaps ironically, was probably the least difficult of those first fifty years. For what it's worth, I believe the second interpretation is much more convincing. First, because the one dated philosophical text we have – Pumpianskii's summaries of Bakhtin's 1924 lectures (Lect 209–18/236–44) – sounds like work that precedes 'Author and Hero' rather than work that follows it, like an attempt to explore a new area rather than a précis of work already done. Second, because of the ambiguity of Bakhtin's own testimony. As one scholar has wittily put it, the evidence for Bakhtin's authorship consists of 'reminiscences about reminiscences', that is, people recounting conversations with Bakhtin in which he recounts what supposedly happened fifty or sixty years ago (the strongest piece of such evidence is a conversation from 1970, recounted in detail by Bocharov twenty-three years later).[42] By contrast, when Kozhinov asked Bakhtin about the matter in a letter at the end of 1960, Bakhtin replied in the following, now infamous, terms:

> The books *The Formal Method* and *Marxism and the Philosophy of Language* I know very well. V. N. Voloshinov and P. N. Medvedev were my close friends; in the period when these books were written we worked in very close creative contact. In fact, at the foundation of these books and my book on Dostoevsky lies a shared conception of language and speech production. In this respect V. V. Vinogradov is entirely right. One has to point out that the presence of a shared conception and contact in work does not lessen the self-sufficiency and originality of any of these books. Regarding the other works of P. N. Medvedev and V. N. Voloshinov, they lie on a different plane, they do not reflect a shared conception and I took no part in their composition.[43]

In the Duvakin interviews he referred to Voloshinov as 'the author of *Marxism and the Philosophy of Language*, a book that is, so to speak, attributed to me' (Conv 72/88). Third, the argument for Bakhtin's authorship revolves around a dubious contrast of character: Bakhtin, the unworldly philosopher, who wants to pursue the higher truth and avoid the dirty muck of politics and professional advancement; Voloshinov and Medvedev, the talentless Communist hacks, lacking both the intellectual resources to produce such philosophically sophisticated books and the moral fibre to resist Communism. When Sergei Bocharov claimed that Bakhtin belonged, in his own view, to a 'hidden, secret layer of culture', he provided a revealingly selective list of its members: 'Iudina, Pumpianskii, M. I. Kagan, A. A. Meier, Vaginov – all these, who made up Bakhtin's close and tight circle in the 1920s, were unofficial people', he insisted, pointedly excluding the two people with whom Bakhtin was working most closely at the time, presumably on the basis that they were too 'official'.[44] The contrast, and the accompanying characterisations, are false on both ends. As we will demonstrate below, Bakhtin, far from becoming a voluntary recluse, with a preference for unofficial activity, was constantly trying to integrate himself into Soviet scholarly life, even long after the supposed 1924 rebuff. Nor is there is any good reason for thinking Medvedev and Voloshinov lacked the intellectual wherewithal to produce their texts: both had a clear record of substantial writing and research that leads to the books in question.[45] The conclusion seems inevitable: Bakhtin spends those years in Leningrad turning his ethical philosophy into a philosophy of literature, in which 'author and hero' take the role of *I* and *other*, cashing out this bold substitution in a remarkable study of the works of Dostoevsky.

20 Life

It may be indicative of the balance of evidence that the claims for Bakhtin's authorship have, over time, become steadily more modest and muted. Even at the beginning, Ivanov had said that 'the basic text belonged to Bakhtin', while Voloshinov and Medvedev 'made only small insertions and changes of individual parts'.[46] Kozhinov had claimed that '[h]e simply dictated it'.[47] As evidence for the opposing view mounted, Bocharov conceded that 'one can probably not exclude all forms of participation by the signatory authors in working over or adjusting the texts'.[48] S. Averinstev suggested people just agree to disagree, labelling the texts in question 'deutero-canonical', as if their status was akin to the Christian dispute over the canonical contents of the Hebrew Scriptures.[49] Finally, in the *Collected Works*, which were initially to have included the disputed texts, the editors cut their losses by saying that 'the authorial participation of M.M.B. in these works is beyond doubt and was affirmed by the author in conversations with different interlocutors, but it remains an open question what form the authorship and co-working with the signed authors took'.[50] In the end, the *Collected Works* excluded the disputed texts.

The authorship question, though, isn't just a question about authorship. The issue is whether from the supposed 1924 rebuff till the end of his days Bakhtin is writing 'in a mask', that is, in a language and about topics that are distant from his true intellectual leanings. For if Bakhtin turned to stylistics, to literary criticism, and to linguistics tactically, then everything he writes in this vein afterwards is a case of writing in a mask, in the inauthentic language of linguistics and sociology. Thus Bocharov – a brilliant and sympathetic critic – took to describing even Bakhtin's Rabelais study as an instance of 'his own authorship in half-mask'.[51] Once the mask is on, it allows one to pretend the entire Bakhtin corpus has a secret meaning. And, indeed, in one of his later commentaries Bocharov suggested that 'the kernel of his [Bakhtin's] thought remains untouched and sufficiently secret – *unusable*'.[52]

To be fair, no one knows what actually happened between 1924 and 1929. It's characteristic, and tragic, that we only really know what happens to Bakhtin when he is arrested by the OGPU (the Soviet internal security force, later named the KGB) on the evening of 24 December 1928, that is, when the Soviet government becomes directly involved in his life. Almost immediately after his arrest, Bakhtin was interrogated by A. R. Stromin-Stroev and Ivan Petrov; in his conversations with Duvakin, he went out of his way to commend the civility with which the interrogations were conducted, and he noted, with apparently genuine sympathy, that both of his interrogators were themselves executed by the government in the 1930s (Conv 132–3/164 and

347n32). The charge against Bakhtin was membership in an organisation deemed 'anti-Soviet' and 'counter-revolutionary', in this case a discussion group headed by A. A. Meier called 'Resurrection'. In fact, roughly 200 people were arrested in connection with 'Resurrection', including Pumpianskii (who was released shortly after) and Meier himself.[53] Bakhtin denied being a member of the group and, in the course of the interrogation, described his informal participation in various meetings between 1924 and 1927. His interrogators concluded that he had 'delivered lectures with an anti-Soviet spirit in various circles'.[54]

Bakhtin's arrest was part of a concerted campaign, launched in the spring of 1928, to repress and terrorise intellectuals in the Soviet Union. The repression was aimed not only at independent intellectuals like Bakhtin, but also at intellectuals friendly to the regime who were advocating a line different from the one recently adopted by the Communist Party. On 22 July 1929 Bakhtin was sentenced: five years in the Solovki labour camp. Bakhtin had friends and defenders willing to stand up for him, even within the ranks of the Bolsheviks. The book on Dostoevsky had won warm praise from Anatolii Lunacharskii, the head of the Commissariat of Enlightenment.[55] His wife and Iudina knew Maksim Gorky's wife, Eketarina Pavlovna Peshkova, and persuaded her to ask Gorky to intervene – in response he sent two telegrams to the OGPU asking for Bakhtin's sentence to be reduced. Bakhtin's poor health – his chronic osteomyelitis, earlier bouts of tuberculosis, and meningitis – was invoked as a reason for changing the sentence, as labour camp was tantamount to a death sentence for him. The pressure paid off, and on 22 February 1930, the sentence was changed to internal exile, in the town of Kustanai, in the Soviet Republic of Kazakhstan. Bakhtin would have to live there for the remainder of his five-year sentence.

Exile, Escape, and the War: 1930–1946

On 29 March 1930, Mikhail Mikhailovich Bakhtin and Elena Alexandrovna Bakhtina moved to Kustanai, in Kazakhstan, so that he could serve his sentence of internal exile. The next sixteen years would be brutally difficult for them: they would endure a terrible situation in Kustanai, manoeuvre quickly to escape being caught up in the purges of 1937–38, and then survive the Second World War. They were, in many respects, lucky to survive: most of their friends and family did not. But Bakhtin did not merely survive – he was also extraordinarily productive. Not merely in terms of volume, though he did write two complete books, rough materials and drafts for two more, two finished essays, and drafts of several more. In this sixteen-year period Bakhtin worked out a theory of the novel that is also a 'dialogical' philosophy of language, a provocative account of the working of ideology, a theory of novelistic plot, and a comprehensive theory of popular and official culture. The Bakhtin we know as the innovative theorist of the novel and inventor of a dialogical view of language belongs to this undoubtedly stressful period. It's an astonishing achievement.

Kustanai was a small provincial city, in the north-western corner of Kazakhstan, one of the constituent socialist republics of the Soviet Union. Kazakh society had been largely a society of nomadic herders, although areas like Kustanai, close to the northern border, had arable enough land for settled agriculture. In 1931, Bakhtin got a job as an accountant for the Regional Consumer Union, which he held until 1936: his responsibilities were largely bookkeeping, although he also lectured occasionally on economic topics. In 1934 he would even publish an article on the experience of collectivisation.[56] But collectivisation was not simply an economic policy, and its effects on Kustanai, and the lives of the Bakhtins, were serious.

The aim of collectivisation, launched by the Soviet government in 1929, was to make Soviet agriculture more productive and easier to control by replacing individually owned peasant landholdings with larger collective enterprises. Most Kazakhs were not peasant landholders or tenants to begin with: they were nomadic herdsmen and herdswomen, so collectivisation for the most part meant changing not the property structure of Kazakh agriculture but reorganising Kazakh productive life entirely. No matter what the intentions, collectivisation was one of the signal disasters of the Soviet era, politically and economically. In economic terms, it did not result in the anticipated rise in agricultural production. Politically, it entailed compelling millions of peasants to join collectives they did not want to join, waging a murderous and brutal war against all who opposed it (in the name of dispossessing the kulaks), and, when famine struck in the early 1930s, ignoring the fact that millions of people were dying of starvation. In Kazakhstan, 1.5 million people died in the famine of 1931–33, roughly one out of every three Kazakhs living in the republic. In Kustanai this meant the Bakhtins were surrounded by, as Bakhtin described it much later, 'people half-dead from hunger on the streets [...] children blue in the face [...] the dying'.[57] Ironically, Bakhtin the exile, having a skilled job, survived on a higher salary than the local inhabitants.

It's in this context that Bakhtin worked out his first theory of the novel. In the town itself, surrounded by unimaginable misery, he effectively reorientated his life's work, which now broadened its focus to the novel, to questions of genre, and to a new linguistic idea, 'heteroglossia'. The essay 'Discourse in the Novel' was researched and drafted in the period 1930–34. We know very little about his day-to-day life in this period, although we know that in 1934, after his term of exile officially ended (the clock had started when he was sentenced in July 1929), he visited Leningrad and Moscow, before returning to Kustanai for another two years, unsure of what to do. As he put it to Duvakin years later, knowing he was forbidden from settling in Leningrad or Moscow, he thought 'why trade one Kustanai for another Kustanai'? (Conv 192/237) In fact, Kustanai had been enriched, if one can put it that way, by a wave of new political exiles in 1934, including the former leading Party member Grigorii Zinoviev, and G. J. Flakserman, a Bolshevik activist (the decision to storm the Winter Palace was made in her flat) and wife of the Menshevik N. N. Sukhanov. Flakserman would end up typing up the draft of 'Discourse in the Novel' some time in 1934 or 1935.

In the summer of 1936 the Bakhtins visited Moscow, and Mikhail was reunited with Kagan. He gave him a copy of 'Discourse in the Novel' to read and he wrote a letter to a Soviet publisher proposing it as a book (the essay refers to itself as a 'book' not an essay). He also saw Medvedev, among others, and, as in the past, Medvedev was willing and able to help Bakhtin: in this case by means of his former student, G. S. (Georgii Sergeevich) Petrov, who was now Dean of the Faculty of Language and Literature at the Mordovian State Pedagogical Institute in Saransk. The latter arranged for Bakhtin to be appointed to the post of docent (roughly, a Lectureship in the UK or Associate Professorship in the States) in 1936. In September the Bakhtins moved there and Mikhail Mikhailovich began teaching. It was to be a short-lived appointment. As the Stalinist purges gained steam in 1937, it became clear that Bakhtin, as a recent exile, would be in danger.[58] In February a Party committee meeting noted that a recent exile was working in their midst; in March they demanded his sacking – Bakhtin left a few days after. Knowing he was in serious danger, he moved unofficially, in fact illegally – he did not have the required residence permit – to Moscow.[59] While in Moscow he and his wife moved residence frequently, relying on the hospitality of friends and in particular that of Bakhtin's sister Natalia and her husband. By all accounts, they hoped to stay in Moscow, but this proved impossible, and they ended up moving to the town of Savelevo, about 130 kilometres from Moscow, where Bakhtin would work as a schoolteacher until the end of the war.

In the face of these extreme stresses and pressures, Bakhtin produced, in effect, a second theory of the novel, focusing on questions of plot and narrative rather than style. This theory was to have culminated in the book

Bakhtin supposedly smoked. The actual written results are a little different: an outline for a projected book on the European *Bildungsroman* and an extraordinarily long (716 manuscript pages) set of notes and drafts, a 'laboratory text', as his editors call it, in which Bakhtin explores and rehearses many of his arguments.[60] It's characterised in the following manner by his editors:

> [...] it is apparently chronologically the first example of what we know as classical and typical laboratory texts by Bakhtin, in which the leading ideas of the author alter each other, as if emerging out of the theoretical mist, intertwining and intersecting with one another[61]

The text does indeed wander, and it covers some very interesting territory (it is, in fact, much more interesting, and much more wide-ranging, than the outline of the book for which it is supposedly the preparation). The latter half of this long text would be reworked by Bakhtin in the 1970s as 'Forms of Time and of the Chronotope in the Novel'; the first half was published in 2012 as 'On the *Bildungsroman*'. That both of these are, in effect, part of the same long text shows us that Bakhtin was looking for a way to think about the novel as something distinct in terms of plot and narrative, and that the idea of the chronotope – which, in fact, appears in the first few pages – came up in the course of his research.

The *Bildungsroman* study had celebrated the ever finer and more comprehensive integration of the individual life story into the history around it. It's impossible not to wonder at the irony of this, for Bakhtin probably wanted to put as much distance as possible between himself and the history surrounding him. He had managed to avoid being rearrested in the Stalinist purges of 1937–38, but his friends were far less fortunate. Kagan had refused, under orders, to massage the figures for energy production and he was sure arrest would follow – he died of a heart attack in December 1937 while he awaited his fate at home. Medvedev's constant activity, his articulation of sophisticated but independent Marxist positions in literary theory and criticism, made him a target once the purges were underway – he was arrested in March 1938 and shot four months later.

As the purges receded, the war loomed. At this point Bakhtin's writing was, surprisingly, aided by a medical procedure: the amputation of his left leg below the knee in early 1938, which in fact led to a notable improvement in his general well-being. Accounts of Bakhtin's life sometimes give the impression that, after the 1920s, and in particular after his arrest and exile, he effectively gave up on public academic life, whether out of disgust or because he thought it wisest to keep his head below the parapet. No doubt Bakhtin made careful calculations when he needed to – leaving Saransk quickly, for example – but in general his activities are those of someone anxious to get back into the game. In exile, he had written a book and concluded a contract for its publication (although the book would not appear for another forty years). From 1938 onwards he made continual, albeit unsuccessful efforts to find work in Moscow. At the invitation of L. I. Timofeev of the Gorky Institute (which had just become an institute devoted to 'World Literature') he joined a newly formed research group on the theory of literature and delivered two of his most important papers on the novel there: 'From the Prehistory of Novelistic Discourse' (its original title was 'Discourse in the Novel') on 14 October 1940 and 'The Novel as a Literary Genre' (generally known by its later title, 'Epic and Novel') on 24 March 1941. 'World literature' and 'genre': these were two themes, prominent in Soviet critical discussion of the 1930s, which Bakhtin was happy to discuss. The idea that the evolution of and struggle among genres should be the focus of literary analysis had been central to his thinking since the early 1930s, and, as Katerina Clark has admirably detailed, the Soviet cultural authorities had been pushing the idea of 'world literature' (and the idea that Soviet literature would be its culminating point) from the mid-1930s onwards.[62] While pursuing this work Bakhtin found time to conduct research on and write up an entirely new project, although it had flowed from his interest in narrative, realism, and the chronotope. This project was his study of Rabelais and carnival culture, submitted to the Gorky Institute in 1940 as a doctoral dissertation.

But why was Bakhtin defending a dissertation on this topic, in 1946, when he would have been fifty-one years old? That had not been the original plan.[63] When Bakhtin mentioned the project in letters, it was as a book, not an academic dissertation, and correspondence between Bakhtin, Iudina, and various Soviet academics reveals there were several attempts to get it published (including one attempt to get the French Communist writer Louis Aragon involved) through the first half of the 1940s.[64] Although the original text was completed in the summer of 1940, Bakhtin continued to revise it, in some respects broadening its scope considerably; one set of proposed additions included Bakhtin's longest recorded discussion of Shakespeare's work. But every attempt failed, while Bakhtin's friends, Iudina in particular, worked to find some sympathetic examiners. In the end, it was reworked and resubmitted as a research dissertation in 1946.

In the year after the dissertation's original submission, however, the Soviet Union had been invaded by German forces. The war undoubtedly made arrangements more difficult, though, remarkably, Bakhtin was still asking for, and receiving, books he needed for research from his friends. His family, however, suffered grievously. His mother and two older sisters lived in Leningrad, and his youngest sister, Natalia, had, for unknown reasons, travelled from Moscow to Leningrad with her son at some point before the German siege took hold. In a letter to Zalesskii, written during the siege, Natalia described the terrible, frightening circumstances of the family: as her own health was declining and one sister was near death, she was filled with fear that 'I cannot endure', and with worry about her brother – 'we know nothing about them and cannot even imagine how they live'.[65] The mother and all three sisters would die of hunger in January 1942; Bakhtin's adopted sister, Nina, would die in a Leningrad hospital in 1944.[66] By the end of the war the only other surviving member of Mikhail Bakhtin's family was his brother, Nikolai, who was living in England and did not even know Mikhail was alive. Medvedev had been shot, Kagan had died of a heart attack, Voloshinov had died of tuberculosis in 1936, Pumpianskii had succumbed to disease in 1940, and Sollertinskii had died of a heart attack in 1944.

The friends who remained – Iudina, Zalesskii, and I. I. Kanaev – dedicated much of their time to Bakhtin's cause, in particular the cause of his book on Rabelais. After a good deal of manoeuvring and organising (in particular, to find sympathetic examiners), Bakhtin finally defended his dissertation, 'Rabelais in the History of Realism', in 1946. Again, the reference point was contemporary Soviet literary debate, about the nature of realism as a literary form or style. The defence itself was something of an event. All present were suitably impressed by the dissertation's seriousness and erudition, but some of them (who had, it seems, not actually read the dissertation, but only the examiners' reports) seemed to miss the point Bakhtin was making: they thought the modern, 'humanist' Rabelais was missing.[67] The director of the Institute, V. Ia. Kirpotin, had understood the quality of the dissertation and, as a consequence, had made an unusual arrangement – the dissertation would be assessed for two different possible degrees: the candidate's degree, a kind of preliminary doctorate, and the doctorate proper, which in Russia was like a German *Habilitationsschrift* (which qualified one for a full professorship).[68] The vote to accept the dissertation for the candidate's degree was 13 to nil. The vote to award the doctorate was, however, 7–6, although all three external examiners supported it. The vote was by no means split along 'party lines'; some of those who supported Bakhtin were long-standing Marxists and some who opposed him fairly traditional, unpolitical scholars.[69] The issue was kicked upstairs to the so-called Higher Attestation Committee, a slow-moving bureaucracy: other examiners read the dissertation, various addenda and amendments were asked for (and provided), and in the course of its drawn-out deliberations Soviet cultural policy took a decidedly reactionary turn.

In the end, Kirpotin's caution and canniness were justified – in 1951 the Commission settled on the candidate's degree only.[70]

Saransk: 1946–1961

In the meantime, Bakhtin had been invited to return to Saransk, the site of his abbreviated teaching experience in 1936–37. This time the stay would be longer and less stressful. Bakhtin assumed his post as a docent, teaching general literature at the Mordovian State Pedagogical Institute in 1947; ten years later the institute would become the Mordovian State University and Bakhtin would become the head of its department of Russian and foreign literatures. He taught regularly and uninterruptedly until a perfectly ordinary retirement in 1961. The aspirations to move to Moscow, to become part of the metropolitan intellectual community, seemed to have been surrendered. Bakhtin did not, as far as we know, engage further with events at the Gorky Institute. In his own way, however, he continued to respond to the strong currents of Soviet intellectual life. In 1950 a series of articles by, of all people, Josef Stalin (then still the leader of the Soviet Union) opened up discussion of linguistics in the Soviet Union, and Bakhtin tried to take advantage of the opportunity by composing an article on 'The Problem of Speech Genres'. The piece, researched from 1952 onwards and drafted in late 1953, made the customary genuflections to Stalin's article (although these were excised by Bakhtin's editors, so we don't know the details).[71] It may be the most purely 'linguistic' text Bakhtin composed, intervening in debates between various schools of linguistics in the Soviet Union, but it is also distinguished by a striking equanimity of tone and argument.

Was this equanimity something forced on Bakhtin, or a conclusion he reached on his own? It's hard to tell. Bakhtin's teaching and academic leadership at Saransk garnered an occasional mild criticism by reviewing authorities – not enough attention paid to Stalin's pronouncements, they thought in the early 1950s – but by and large he led an increasingly large department happily and successfully, teaching and lecturing on an exceptionally wide range of literary subjects: Russian and European literature, literary theory, classical literature, Chinese literature from 1952. Estifeeva, whose remarks on Elena Alexandrovna we noted earlier, claims that when Bakhtin had to make speeches on contemporary political topics (he had to at occasional joint sessions of the arts department with the department of Marxism-Leninism) his speeches 'were official and hardly different from the others. The past (the arrest and exile) still held him back'.[72]

Rediscovery, Rehabilitation: 1961–1975

Bakhtin might have shuffled off into a simple and peaceful retirement, but for a letter sent to him on 12 November 1960 from Vadim Kozhinov, a young scholar at the Gorky Institute, where Bakhtin had delivered his lectures and defended his dissertation. Kozhinov was writing on behalf of a 'group of young literary scholars' who wished 'to continue the work of your generation of Russian scholarship on literature'.[73] They had read the Dostoevsky book and had learned (recently, as it turned out) that its author was still alive: they wanted to make contact and, with his permission, write an article on him for the *Short Literary Encyclopedia*. Bakhtin responded almost immediately, and a series of letters were exchanged; in June of 1961 three of the young scholars – Kozhinov, Bocharov, and Georgii Gachev – made a pilgrimage to Saransk.

Kozhinov, Bocharov, and Gachev had great plans: they wanted to publish some of Bakhtin's unpublished material, including the dissertation on Rabelais. The plans were feasible because Stalin's death and the emergence of a more reforming leadership had led to the so-called Thaw, a brief period of liberalisation in intellectual life when previously unpublished and unpublishable work saw the light of day – the most famous would be Solzhenitsyn's *A Day in the Life of Ivan Denisovich* – and repressed figures were rehabilitated.

Nevertheless, it would take tactical nous, determination, and connections to revive Bakhtin's work. Kozhinov in particular seemed to possess all of these. He had decided that a move to publish the Rabelais study would be premature and that tactically it made more sense to revive Bakhtin by producing a new edition of the already published *Problems of Dostoevsky's Art* from 1929. In a number of reminiscences, Kozhinov has described the lengths to which he had to go to secure the publication of the new edition of Bakhtin's book. In the Soviet Union of the early 1960s, it required far more than the agreement of an editor to publish a book by a former exile: it demanded political pressure. Kozhinov composed a letter supporting the proposal, garnered signatures to it from the great and good of the Soviet literary intelligentsia, gave it to the publisher, and, when that failed to break the logjam, had the letter and signatures published (to the great consternation of those who had signed it as a 'private' letter).[74] By March of 1962 he had persuaded the Soviet publisher to issue a contract to Bakhtin; the completed book was sent to press a year later.[75] Even before that, however, the second stage of the plan was put into effect: in the summer of 1962 a letter signed by prominent literary critics (including the 'enemies' Ermilov and Shklovsky), demanding publication of Bakhtin's Rabelais study, appeared in the press. *The Art of François Rabelais and the Popular Culture of the Middle Ages and Renaissance* appeared in 1965.

Bocharov and Kozhinov then set about publishing Bakhtin's various essays, usually in abridged form, in Soviet journals: a section of 'Discourse in the Novel' in 1965, 'From the Prehistory of Novelistic Discourse' in 1967, 'Epic and Novel' in 1970, various other pieces in the early 1970s. As the work came out, Bakhtin's reputation blossomed, and the so-called cult of Bakhtin developed. As we mentioned at the beginning of this chapter, the reintroduction of Bakhtin to public life was neither smooth nor uncontentious. His work is often ambiguous, and the ambiguities made possible widely varying interpretations of both individual texts and his project as a whole.

Bakhtin's contribution to the clamour was to hand over an increasing number of unpublished works, a sort of living *Nachlass* (the term for the unpublished papers of a deceased scholar), and to meet with friends and well-wishers, even as his health steadily declined. In 1967, the conviction for anti-Soviet activity from 1929 was re-examined and formally reversed. In 1969, matters came to the point where he could no longer manage in the flat in Saransk; his next stay was arranged in a suitably bizarre manner. His champion and self-described 'chauffeur', V. N. (Vladimir Nikolaevich) Turbin, a teacher at Moscow State University, had one Irina Andropova in his class. Her father was Iurii Andropov, then head of the KGB and later to be the somewhat reformist General Secretary of the Communist Party and President of the Soviet Union. The daughter and Turbin met with the KGB head and somehow persuaded him to find Bakhtin a place in the Kremlin Hospital.[76] Thus the party bureaucracy that had originally persecuted him came to his aid late in life.

In 1970 the Bakhtins were moved to a home for the elderly in Klimovsk, south of Moscow. Bakhtin, through all this, continued to work, reading, researching, and filling his notebooks with drafts of ideas and arguments. In 1970, he became an 'author' of books and articles in a new way, when Viacheslav Ivanov made the first public claim for his authorship of the 'disputed texts'. Although he reportedly would confirm this version of events in private conversations, Bakhtin refused to sign any document affirming authorship. If Bakhtin was, as an article in an American magazine claimed, an international 'man of mystery', Bakhtin was doing his part to maintain the mystery.[77]

In December 1971, Elena Alexandrovna died, leaving Bakhtin in a depressed state. He would be moved two weeks later to the writers' colony in Peredelkino, where he would stay until, at the end of a long life, he was finally granted permission to live in Moscow in 1972. When he died in March of 1975, the collection of essays on the novel that, in translated form, would make him a theoretical master-thinker was about to be published.

Chapter 3

Context

Life – Context – Works: context is the middleman in this arrangement, providing the bridge between the author's life and the works he or she manages to compose in the course of it. In the present case, the life was extraordinarily difficult and the writings are ruins – often fragmentary, rarely polished, lacking an immediate audience. It's hard, therefore, not to conclude that context contributed to Bakhtin's works mostly by making it hard for him to write and by preventing him from producing as many finished works as he might have. The temptation is to regard context as only a *hindrance*, a worldly constraint on Bakhtin's inventive mind.

But context is the most ambiguous of ideas. It can vary dramatically in scale and structure, ranging from the quirks and random happenings of a biography to the large-scale structural forces at work in a particular historical period. A contextual reading can ground itself in the everyday circumstances of the author, in a contemporary clash of opinions or worldviews, or in the gender or class relations of a historical time and place. When the contextualised object is intellectual and cultural, context can mean other intellectual and cultural objects – 'influences', as they used to be called – as well as social and historical circumstances.

A subtler version of the 'hindrance' thesis would accordingly distinguish between a local, valuable context – the circle of 'unofficial' people who surrounded Bakhtin – and a larger, hostile one, consisting of the worldly conflicts and social struggles that defined imperial Russia and the Soviet Union. But we have to resist this account as well. For we must learn to think of social and political history as not just the storm that blows the intellect off course, but also the wind that fills its sails. And, happily, we can look for advice on the matter in Bakhtin's work itself, in which context and its relationship to words is an abiding concern. It is neatly summed up by a famous sentence in 'Discourse in the Novel':

> Every word smells of the context and contexts in which it lived its socially intensified life; all words and forms are filled with intentions. (DN 293/46)

Its socially 'intensified' life (*naprazhennoi*: it has also been translated as 'charged'): the point being that although context can appear as something solid and static – a set of fairly stable social circumstances, some commonly held views or assumptions, well-entrenched habits and practices – it may also be dynamic and conflictual, a situation in which the status quo is untenable and something has to give. As Bakhtin put it earlier in the essay, '[d]iscourse is born in dialogue, as a living reply within it' (DN 279/33). Context can be what demands and provokes a response, what makes the creative thought necessary in the first place.

While we're at it, let's draw on another sentence from 'Discourse in the Novel' relevant to the matter at hand:

> Every concrete discourse (utterance) finds the object at which it is directed always, so to speak, already spoken about, argued over, evaluated, shrouded by a mist that obscures it or, on the contrary, by the light of words already spoken about it. (DN 276/30)

Even with the confused metaphors (mist, light, arguments), the sentence reminds us that context also means thinking less about influences and more about inflections. Bakhtin does not create, *ex nihilo*, a theory of dialogism, of chronotope, of author and hero. He takes existing, competing ideas and refracts them, drawing them into new constellations with other ideas and giving them a philosophical shove in new directions. In fact, often his contribution to intellectual life consists precisely in taking an interesting idea from literary criticism or linguistics – free indirect discourse, for example – and making it the centrepiece of a philosophical argument. For sure, Bakhtin met storms of a violence and persistence that would have rendered many intellectuals mute. But, as we'll see, it was the drama of his time that motivated him to write in the first place, and his first recourse was to the words of others, which he could then inflect.

We can think of the drama as composed of three acts and an epilogue, each distinguished by a particular set of political and social tensions, which provoke a particular kind of response from Bakhtin. In the first act, extending from the late 1910s to the mid-1920s, the First World War and the political crises around it (in particular, the Russian Revolution of 1917) provoke a series of *philosophical* arguments, which Bakhtin drew on to craft his own response. In the second act, which takes place in the mid- and late 1920s, debates about Soviet culture take the form of arguments about the nature of *language*, in which Bakhtin becomes an active participant. In the 1930s and 1940s, when the Soviet Union has embarked on the path of building 'Socialism in One Country', arguments over the relationship of *literary writing* to social change and in particular the role of the novel in representing historical change take centre stage. The 1950s and 1960s, when the emergence of structuralist linguistics in the Soviet Union leads Bakhtin back to language, but in a more compromising spirit, constitute a kind of epilogue.

Philosophy: Influences and Options for the Young Bakhtin

What got the ball rolling? Bakhtin began to write seriously at the end of the 1910s – his first, short published piece is called 'Art and Responsibility', and it appeared in a Nevel' newspaper in 1919.[1] It would be an understatement to say there was, at the time, a great deal to write about. The First World War, unprecedented in its brutality, had just concluded and Russia was in the midst of the civil war that followed the 1917 revolution. In fact, Bakhtin, having been born in 1895, would have known Russia only as a place of continuous political ferment and social instability. He was living in Nevel´, after all, only because the civil war had made it too difficult to live in Petrograd.

'Art and Responsibility' didn't have a lot to say about all this: it was a plea for the mutual influence of art and morality. But when Bakhtin broached the larger issue, in the fragment 'Towards a Philosophy of the Act', he described the conflicts of the time in the most abstract terms possible. The crisis was not a consequence of politics, social division, or international rivalries: it was a 'crisis of the contemporary *act*' (TPA 54/50). A gulf or abyss, Bakhtin claimed, had opened up between 'the motive of the act and its product' (TPA 54/50), and as a result the act had become merely technical or instrumental. In his mind every act had to be 'responsible' (*otvetstvennyi*, a word that can also be translated as 'answerable'), which meant it had to be provoked by a unique sense of 'oughtness', a demand to act in conformity with the norms – political, scientific, or social – that applied in the given situation. When responsibility was lacking, the act itself fell apart, in the following terms: 'All the forces of responsible accomplishment pass into an autonomous domain of culture, and the act that has been separated from them sinks to the level of economic or biological motivation, it loses all its ideal moments: such is the condition of civilization' (TPA 55/50). In plainer language: the norms (rules, laws, customs) that should be part of the act become mere parts of an 'objective' culture (consisting of texts, works, images, etc.), while the act, now divorced from norms, is guided by something like self-interest, self-preservation or the desire for pleasure. 'Civilisation', in this context, is a problem; it's a way of describing a society gone wrong, one that has become mechanical and value-free, because 'culture' has somehow lost its way, become detached.

Philosophy and the Young Bakhtin 33

In their abstractness and opaqueness, these sentences are typical for early Bakhtin. But they are also characteristic of a much larger movement, echoing a horde of European intellectuals who understood the ongoing destruction and political upheaval of the time as symptoms of a deeper cultural crisis. Matvei Kagan, whom Bakhtin met in Nevel´ and who was destined to be one of his closest friends, had claimed that '[t]he revolution expresses the crisis of culture with unambiguous sharpness'.[2] His analysis was echoed by other Russians, such as, for example, the Symbolist writer Andrei Bely who understood the political revolution as the crest of deeper spiritual one.[3] The perception was by no means, however, unique to Russia. In Germany, Oswald Spengler's *The Decline of the West* (1918) had contrasted 'culture' with mechanical, soulless 'civilisation'. The claim that human activity was giving rise to an autonomous, lifeless culture, alienated from the energies that brought it into being, had found articulate expression in the work of Georg Simmel, whose 'The Conflict in Modern Culture' (1918), argued that 'life is always in a latent opposition to form [...] because cultural forms are conceived of as an exhausted soil which has yielded all that it can grow'.[4] In England, the lament took the form of the 'culture-and-society' tradition so brilliantly analysed by Raymond Williams: there was 'culture' on one hand, a narrow sphere of activity (literature, music, visual art, etc.) with the imprint of human creative effort; and society, on the other, dominated by machinery, mass production, and simple mass emotion.[5]

The vision is of a 'mechanical' reason, divorced from human ends and no longer the servant of human purpose. In a rare allusion to the First World War, Bakhtin compares the decay of human thinking ('cognition') to the development of technology. The cognitive act goes astray

> just as weapons are perfected in accord with their own inner law, which turns them from a reasonable means of defence into a terrible, deadly and destructive force. Everything technical, having been torn from a unique unity and delivered freely to the immanent law of its development, is terrifying; it can, from time to time, burst into the unique unity of life as an irresponsible and destructive force. (TPA 7/11–12)

The terms of the solution are evident from the terms of the complaint. One had to restore the unique unity of life and make development, both in cognition and technology, 'responsible' once more.

Defining this 'unique unity of life', however, was not straightforward, and 'Towards a Philosophy of the Act' spends a good many pages navigating its way between what are presented as complementary failures: Nietzsche-inspired *Lebensphilosophie* (life philosophy), on the one hand, and the rationalism of Immanuel Kant, on the other, which assumed that moral behaviour could be motivated by the exercise of reason alone. Bakhtin, however, saw a gap between the individual with will and the set of rules to which reason would lead you, because there is nothing that *compels* the individual to act in conformity with a moral rule or norm, and so the latter exists 'like a document without a signature, obligating no one to anything' (TPA 44/42). But despite his intense criticism, it's clear both from Bakhtin's earliest philosophical efforts and from his own testimony that it was the revised Kantianism of the late nineteenth and early twentieth centuries – the so-called Neo-Kantianism of the Marburg School, embodied in the philosophers Paul Natorp, Hermann Cohen, and Ernst Cassirer – that provided the framework and inspiration for his philosophical efforts. In the 1973 interviews, he confessed his 'passion for the Marburg School' (Conv 39/45). In Nevel´, his circle of intellectuals was known as the 'Kantian seminar'; when he presented an Introduction to Philosophy in lectures at Nevel´, the focus fell on 'Hermann Cohen, [Heinrich] Rickert, [Paul] Natorp, [Ernst] Cassirer' (Conv 215/261). The series delivered in Leningrad in 1924, for which we have Pumpianskii's notes, was also Neo-Kantian in form and substance.[6] His gymnasium friend Lopatto pointed to an early source for this inspiration when he claimed that Bakhtin's brother Nikolai had 'entered the cul-de-sac of Neo-Kantianism'.[7] And whether it was cause or effect, the man who was probably Bakhtin's closest friend in Nevel´, Matvei Kagan, was a Neo-Kantian philosopher trained by Natorp, Cassirer, and Cohen.

As we'll see, Cassirer became important to Bakhtin a bit later in his life, and Natorp's influence is hard to gauge. Hermann Cohen's writing, however, seems to have shaped Bakhtin's approach from the outset – 'he exercised an enormous influence on me', said Bakhtin, 'an enormous, enormous influence' (Conv 36/40) – and the influence was enduring. Cohen had produced a Kantian trilogy, parallel to Kant's original three critiques: a work describing the structure of scientific knowledge, a work accounting for the structure of ethics, and a work on the nature of aesthetic feeling.[8] We know Bakhtin read at least the last two of these, and throughout his career Bakhtin would treat scientific knowledge (cognition), ethics, and aesthetics as three different spheres, each with its own logic, in the Kantian manner. But it was Cohen's reworking of the relationship between Kantian philosophy and religion that seems to have grabbed Bakhtin's attention. Cohen believed that the 'ethical monotheism' of Judaism, as he called it, made a distinct and irreplaceable contribution to ethics, without which moral behaviour was inexplicable.[9] This contribution did not take the form of specific rules or maxims, such as those laid out in the Ten Commandments or the rest of biblical Jewish law – it had to do with the nature of the world and with what motivated us to act ethically. In his writing from the 1910s (precisely the period when Kagan was his student), climaxing in the posthumously published work *Religion of Reason Out of the Sources of Judaism*, Cohen examined the vision of the world and God's relation to it that was set out in the moral arguments and messianic evocations of the Hebrew Prophets. The central, constitutive insight of Jewish monotheism, Cohen argued, was not that there was only one god, but that God was unique.[10] To say God was unique was to say that God was not a part of the world, not in any respect substantial like the world, but stood in relation to it as its Creator. God 'is the *originative principle of activity*' and '[c]reation is God's primary attribute', according to Cohen.[11] But this creation is not a once-and-for-all event, concluded with the creation of human beings as in the book of Genesis; it is renewed through God's continuous relation to humans, which is called 'revelation' in the Jewish tradition. Through revelation, which in Judaism takes the form of study of the Torah and prayer, humans are made into rational beings. 'Rational', not merely 'intellectual', for reason is whole, complete, in Cohen's view, '[o]nly when reason becomes moral reason [. . .] only when the interest in the cause is supplemented by the interest in the *purpose*'.[12] Thus '[t]he correlation of God and man, as established by creation and revelation, fulfills its meaning only through the addition of moral demands'.[13] Ultimately, belief in the uniqueness of God, the distinctive innovation of Jewish monotheism, leads to the understanding of human history as a striving for universal justice and a universal human community bound by love. In Cohen's telling, God's holiness is entirely moral, and the task of humanity is to emulate it.

Bakhtin had encountered some of Cohen's writing directly and some of it through the mediation of Kagan, who had made a lengthy conspectus of Cohen's *Religion of Reason* in the early 1920s. It would shape his work in three fundamental ways. First, it established earthly existence as what Bakhtin called 'ethical reality'. In Cohen's account, monotheistic religion replaced the world ruled by myth, in which humans were the plaything of divine forces, with a world in which human beings took actions for which they were morally responsible. This sense of the world as a moral space would be taken up by Bakhtin enthusiastically.

This first claim was connected to a second one, according to which the world was a scene of constant 'becoming'. This did not mean merely that time rumbles along; it is not a reference to what one Cohen scholar has called '[t]he and-so-on of time'.[14] Cohen had argued that the world was temporal, that it witnessed actual historical events, precisely because it was orientated to a Messianic future, a future community governed by justice and love for one's fellows. Existence was, you could say, a project or task, and that is why it continually unfolded or 'became'. Bakhtin's close friend Kagan was particularly interested in this aspect of Cohen's argument, and his essays from the late 1910s and the early 1920s are largely devoted to analysing, in the words of one title, 'How Is History Possible?'[15] So far as Kagan was concerned, it was Judaism that, while not exactly making history possible, made humankind conscious of its historical vocation. In his essay 'Judaism and the Crisis of Culture', history depends first and foremost on '[t]he overcoming of the burden of fate by labour and work', which ensures a world that is 'not completed, unfinished [*nezavershen*], and open'.[16] Historical culture, however, is constantly threatened by pantheism and mythology, which root the world in ancestors, fate, and the past. 'The task of history in this respect is the task that emerges with the history of European humanity; a task that is in essence Jewish.'[17] For Cohen and Kagan, Judaism's gift to humanity is history itself.

The unfinishedness of the world, the need to recognise it as becoming, would become a central feature of Bakhtin's theory: it would provide him with a sense of history complementing the personal sense of responsibility that characterised ethical reality. But there was one more feature of Cohen's philosophy that made itself at home deep in the recesses of Bakhtin's writing: the idea that ethical feeling came from the relationship of *I* and *other*. We'll discuss that in detail in the Works section of this book. For now, we should consider, in general terms, how these religious elements fit into Bakhtin's writing as a whole. For, in fact, since Bakhtin emerged as a figure in the 1960s, there has been no shortage of scholars clamouring for him to be acknowledged as a great religious thinker. But they had a different religion in mind.

In his early philosophical fragments, 'Towards a Philosophy of the Act' and its extension, 'Author and Hero in Aesthetic Activity', Bakhtin speaks of Christ and Christian ethics, not of Moses or the Prophets. When describing the ethical world in the former text, Bakhtin calls it 'the world in which the event of Christ's life and death, as something factual and meaningful, was accomplished' (TPA 16/19), pointing to the Christian Messiah rather than Jewish Messianism as that which structures our world. The notes we have of Bakhtin's lectures and discussions explicitly devoted to religion in 1924–25 – a 1924 lecture titled 'The Problem of Grounded Peace', a 1924 comment on someone else's lecture, and a 1925 presentation – similarly take their bearings from Christianity: there is the 'abyss' between *I* and *other* for the Christian, the insistence that 'the true being of the spirit begins where confession begins', and there is 'the problem of the *incarnated* God' (Lect 209/331, 209/332).

Nor should one limit Christian influence to those passages that explicitly invoke Christ or Christian belief. Ruth Coates has pointed to certain grammatical tics in 'Towards a Philosophy of the Act' – Bakhtin's frequent recourse to the Russian prefixes *ot-* (meaning 'moving or falling away from') and *samo-* (meaning 'self') – as evidence of a subtle Christian critique of modern culture, in which 'a falsely conceived autonomy is bound up with the notion of pride'.[18] The false autonomy typical of modern culture is, Coates believes, a consequence and emblem of the Fall. And when Bakhtin begins to discuss authors and heroes, in works we will analyse in the next section, there are ideas that seem to have Christian resonance if not roots (I will point them out where they occur). We know that the 'circle' from Nevel´, once reformed in Leningrad, sometimes discussed theology and religious texts, and that Bakhtin attended meetings of the Religious-Philosophical Society, led by the theologian A. A. Meier, in the 1910s and thereafter.

In short, there are Christian themes and motifs sprinkled throughout the work – the issue, as with all the influences we discuss in this chapter, is their relative weight and significance. For it is a big leap from the acknowledgement of some Christian material to the claim, common among some of Bakhtin's most assiduous followers in Russia, that Bakhtin is essentially a Christian, or even specifically a Russian Orthodox philosopher. Among the things one must leap over to draw this conclusion are many of Bakhtin's concepts (with no clear Christian significance), most of his literary analyses, and indeed the vast majority of his works, which include little or no reference to Christianity and which are used, with great profit, by students, critics, and scholars with no Christian interests or religious commitments. The Bakhtin scholars who nevertheless make this leap have strategies for dealing with these problems. They may point to 'an everyday intuition' of Russian Orthodox 'ecclesiasticalness' (belief in the church as a spiritual organism), which is 'grafted onto the Russian person from childhood' and which Bakhtin must therefore share.[19] They may simply skip over the apparently secular works of the 1930s, focusing on the early philosophy and parts of Bakhtin's Dostoevsky book. Or, most dramatically, they may simply use the idea of 'Bakhtin in a mask' to uncover what they see as the hidden religious substance of apparently secular arguments, as when the Bakhtin scholar L. A. Gogotishvili explains that when Bakhtin is discussing a stylistic phenomenon that interested him – indirect and free indirect discourse – he is actually talking about God: 'The creaturely world can – in keeping with the distinctive features of Bakhtin's thought as a whole – be interpreted as the indirect or quasi-direct speech of God'.[20]

The point is not to dismiss the work of Bonetskaia (the one emphasising Russian intuition) and Gogotishvili, both of whom are brilliant, erudite scholars of Bakhtin and whose commentary is full of insight and interest. The point is that we have to be alert to a tendency that has shaped our image and understanding of Bakhtin: the tendency to see him as an aloof, spiritual figure, pursuing his research with blithe disregard for the world around him. It's an image that has been fostered by critics who wish to make Bakhtin an icon of Russian spirituality, a Christian Orthodox spirituality that they believe embodies a genuine Russia, surviving underneath the carapace of Soviet rule. And it's not just the image of Bakhtin that is at stake. For one of the people who thought Bakhtin symbolised an authentic Russian spirit was the postgraduate and later academic Vadim Kozhinov, who had helped rediscover Bakhtin and get his works into publication. Kozhinov was a literary scholar, of course, but also a leading figure in the right-wing Russian nationalist or Slavophile movement, hostile to malign 'Western' influence in Russia and to Jewish influence in particular.[21] He was also an editor of much of Bakhtin's work and, as we will see below, it's not clear that he was always able to separate his Russian nationalism from his scholarly editing.

One can acknowledge the presence of religious ideas, Christian and Jewish, in Bakhtin's work, however, without resorting to these kinds of extravagances. Bakhtin's other discoverer and editor, the late Sergei Bocharov, did as much when he observed that while Bakhtin inherited problems and ideas from religious philosophy, he did not himself become a religious philosopher. Speaking of Bakhtin's philosophical work, he commented: 'This is not religious philosophy – Bakhtin did not write that; it is aesthetics, but concluded in theological terms; aesthetics on the border with religious philosophy, but without crossing that border.'[22] Religious philosophy was not the only discipline occupying the border of Bakhtin's work: as we'll discuss below, Marxist ideas also trod that ground, as did ideas from linguistics and literary criticism. In fact, one of the most interesting features of Bakhtin's work is the way in which philosophical, social scientific, literary, and religious ideas are artfully combined, such that religious notions can serve secular purposes and vice versa. Religion is not blind faith in Bakhtin; it has, to use the words of Cohen, a 'share in reason'.[23] In the present case, ideas from Cohen and Christianity were brought in to fill what Bakhtin thought was a gap in ethics.

'Towards a Philosophy of the Act' assumes that the existing faculties of reason – aesthetics, politics, science – will perform their assigned tasks, making a case for the appropriate norms in their fields. But the existence of these norms on its own is not enough to create ethical action – something else must be added to fill the gap. That something is not, however, another set of distinctively 'ethical' norms – Bakhtin believes there is no such thing – but 'oughtness', the spark that sets the moral machinery in motion. 'Oughtness' compels one to realise the value one holds, to do the thing one knows is the right thing, to make the art one has the urge to make, and so forth. But this 'oughtness' is not the highest *value*, or a meta-value – it is, rather, what unites all values with acting subjects. Bakhtin will therefore say that there are no 'moral, ethical norms' because the 'ought does not have a determinate and specifically theoretical content' (it is not the content of a proposition, a rule or law; TPA 5/10). The ought 'is a certain orientation of consciousness, the structure of which will be phenomenologically disclosed by us' (TPA 6/10). How is this orientation generated? That will be the problem Bakhtin must solve.

But not in this text. The introductory section of this fragment will conclude with a largely unfulfilled promise:

> The first part of our investigation will be devoted to an examination of precisely the fundamental moments of the architectonics of the actual world, not as it is thought, but as it is experienced. The following part will be devoted to aesthetic activity as an act, not from within its product, but from the point of view of the author as a responsible participant in living <?> actuality – to the ethics of the artistic work. The third part is devoted to the ethics of politics and the final one to that of religion. (TPA 54/50)

Art, politics, religion: these are the three spheres in which Bakhtin would have articulated his ethics. Although the implication is that each sphere has its own ethics, as we will see below, it was their mixing, their interpenetration, rather than their separation, that became the distinguishing feature of Bakhtin's writing. What will emerge over time and under the influence of a number of European and Russian writers is a theory of culture in which art is political, the political is religious, the religious is artistic, and so on.

Language: Soviet Struggles over Literary Criticism in the 1920s, and Bakhtin's Linguistic Turn

Art, politics, religion: Bakhtin never finished the work he outlined at the end of his first philosophical effort, but this triad would furnish the framework for the many, many texts that followed its abandonment. The separate elements did not come into play simultaneously or systematically, and their amalgamation in Bakhtin's works often resulted in some highly unstable compounds. But you can see how Bakhtin's writing is pulled this way and that by their concerns, as if each pole of the triad had a kind of magnetic force.

The magnetic force came from the society around Bakhtin. The Bolshevik revolution had been political, but it unleashed expectations and energies that were not simply political, expectations of a new culture and new historical beginnings, and energies bent on making the kinds of art this new world would require. Some thought art would be the handmaiden of politics, providing cultural ballast for an essentially political cause. Others thought politics would be the handmaiden and that the essence of the revolution was cultural, artistic, or religious. In an essay titled 'On the Religious Crisis of Contemporaneity', Kagan claimed that 'in essence the crisis is a religious phenomenon',[24] while in a letter to his wife from the same period (1924) he was even more explicit, telling her that he now 'understand[s] profoundly the religious essence of the truth of the atheism that comes from historical materialism'.[25] A notorious poem by the Symbolist Aleksandr Blok, first read in 1918, seemed to fuse all three elements in a single vision of revolutionary 'worldwide conflagration'. It followed the path of a revolutionary wind in Moscow, in whose wake twelve young Bolshevik soldiers are marching, while 'ahead of them – with bloody banner / Unseen within the blizzard's swirl / Safe from any bullet's harm [. . .] Ahead of them – goes Jesus Christ'.[26] Christ, leading Bolshevik soldiers, in a Symbolist poem: religion, politics, and art fused into a single hymn to the revolution.

Bakhtin was making his own fusions in the 1920s. He was using religious philosophy, theories of art, and Neo-Kantian and other contemporary philosophy to devise a theory that would tell us how ethical reality, and through it, responsibility, could be established in the society around him. The various sources intersected in what became Bakhtin's signature argument: 'oughtness', that missing ingredient of responsibility, depended on our recognising the fundamental distinction between *I* and *other* (sometimes *I-for-myself*, the *other-for-me*). That 'certain orientation of consciousness' he had spoken about was summed up in this distinction, on which all else depended. According to Bakhtin, the fundamental error of the modern age is to think of humanity as subdivided into discrete individuals, who then may bridge the gap between each other by either empathising with one another or meeting on the ground of impersonal reason. On the contrary, Bakhtin argued, every individual experiences their own individuality, their feelings, sensations, thoughts, words, and so on as an *I* in a manner absolutely distinct from the way they experience the feelings, sensations, thoughts, and words of *others*. Acknowledge the distinction, Bakhtin claims, and responsibility will follow in its wake.

Bakhtin had not arrived at this philosophical insight on his own, through some remarkable feat of personal introspection – he'd been busy reading.

The problem of 'other minds' – how could we know them? could we even assume they existed? – had already become a set-piece in European philosophising.[27] A. I. Vvedenskii, for example, chair of the philosophy department at Petrograd University and a teacher Bakhtin claimed he had studied with, had discussed the issue at length in his 1915 book *Psychology without Any Metaphysics*. Mental phenomena, Vvedenskii argued, could only be directly perceived by the one experiencing them. '*We do not actually perceive*', he went on to say, '*the mental phenomena of others, but only those bodily processes that accompany them.*'[28] We don't see joy or grief, we see laughter or tears, and draw the appropriate conclusions (or, you could say, we see people behaving in a certain way that we understand as 'laughter' and 'tears', as behaviour that expresses something, thereby attributing to them inner feelings and thoughts). In fact, Vvedenskii concludes, belief that there *are* other minds, somehow analogous to our own, is in the end a metaphysical assumption that can't be proved.[29] You can't *know* there are other minds – you have to decide whether you will assume there are other minds or not.

Bakhtin's early writing ran along the same lines: oughtness is not something you can establish theoretically and the distinction between *I* and *other* that underlies it is not something you can *prove* like the Second Law of Thermodynamics or the previous existence of dinosaurs. As 'a certain orientation of consciousness', oughtness was something one 'disclosed phenomenologically'. That meant we could reveal the structure of *I* and *other*, demonstrate that it was always at work in our consciousness, by showing how the distinction shaped our perception of every human thought, feeling, or action. That also meant that Bakhtin had been drawing on another important philosophical source, the phenomenology of Edmund Husserl, in which consciousness had an 'orientation' [*ustanovka*], and where that orientation was something 'disclosed' or revealed by phenomenological analysis.

Husserl's phenomenology, first articulated in his *Logical Investigations* (published in 1900–1901 and first translated into Russian in 1909), proceeded from the conviction that in order to understand the world around us, we had to examine very carefully how we experienced the various objects of that world.[30] A phenomenologist, for example, will observe that when we apprehend an object visually, we do not see the whole object, but only a certain side of it (in fact, a set of shapes and colours that we interpret as representing the 'side' of something three-dimensional): we infer the 'rest' of the object from what we see. When we see a certain interplay of changing shapes and colours, we understand it as an object in motion. That doesn't mean we don't actually see objects or motion, it means that this is how we see objects, this is what it means to 'see' an object or to see something in motion. Husserl's point, in making these claims, was that we couldn't go about making judgements about the world, including scientific judgements, until we understood how we had constituted that world to begin with, how, in experience, we turned raw sensations into objects, movement, and so on. To disclose the distinction between *I* and *other* phenomenologically, therefore, was to show that whenever we perceived, discussed, or acted on human thoughts, feelings, and behaviour we automatically classified those phenomena as belonging to the *I* or to an *other* and they became different sorts of thoughts or feelings, different 'objects' in our consciousness, depending on the classification.

But although Bakhtin claimed the distinction was phenomenological, he almost immediately introduced a cultural element into the distinction. For no sooner had he introduced the *I/other* distinction, a distinction with ethical significance, then he drew an analogy between it and the distinction between 'authors' and 'heroes' (meaning characters or protagonists) in fiction and poetry. This was not an illustration or application of the idea of *I* and *other*, but part of its very constitution. The analogy first appears in the short fragmentary section of 'Towards a Philosophy of the Act' in which Bakhtin introduces the distinction between *I* and *other*, and there it is justified by the claim that 'the world of art, [...] by virtue of its own concreteness and its permeation by emotional-volitional tone, is the closest of all the abstract cultural worlds (in their isolation) to the single and unique world of the act' (TPA 61/56). In the much longer fragment, 'Author and Hero in Aesthetic Activity', he expounds the analogy at great length, in a somewhat muddled way that will become a pattern later on. For although Bakhtin implies that 'authors' and 'heroes' are built on the basis of the *I/other* distinction, as an extrapolation of it into the realm of written prose, in fact the description of how the *I* and *other* differ and of how they relate is made almost entirely on the basis of authors and heroes, so that the *I* and *other* end up having aesthetic qualities built into them from the outset.

The theoretical consequences of Bakhtin's analogy were dramatic: it's fair to say it was the starting point or spark for every major Bakhtinian insight, which will be discussed in the following chapter. But drawing art, religion, and ethics together in this way also had an immediate practical consequence: it drew Bakhtin directly into the maelstrom of 1920s Soviet literary debate, where art, politics, and religion were already being thrown together in surprising and inventive combinations.

In the wake of the 1917 revolution, the most pressing concerns of the Bolsheviks and the Soviet government were the creation of an effective government structure, the establishment of new institutions, and fighting the civil war that would conclude only in 1921. Nevertheless, from the outset the governing party was acutely aware that the struggle for hearts and minds was only just beginning and that literature would play a significant role. State interventions took three forms. First, there was direct repression of intellectuals and intellectual organisations deemed hostile to the regime: almost immediately certain journals and newspapers were shut down, intellectuals were arrested (and deported), and when the government established the publishing house Gosizdat and a literary bureau Goslit, it in effect created an administrative apparatus for control of the printed word. Second, the government itself established the People's Commissariat of Enlightenment, *Narkompros*, which sponsored new research institutions, reorganised the inherited ones, and created a series of literary and academic journals. There were, finally, halting attempts to frame a government policy on the kind of literature and literary criticism most conducive to Soviet culture.

The Communist Party had been, for most of its existence, a relatively small organisation and most activists focused on political or economic questions. There were exceptions, like A. V. (Anatolii Vasil'evich) Lunacharskii, who was appointed to lead the Commissariat of Enlightenment (and who would become a crucial supporter of Bakhtin later on), and A. K. (Aleksandr Konstantinovich) Voronskii, who edited a Party literary journal from the 1920s, but not many of them. The 1920s witnessed, therefore, not a coherent Soviet cultural project led and staffed by Party intellectuals, but something of a free-for-all, in which a wide range of writers and intellectuals, with varying degrees of closeness to the Party, jostled for position, forming groups and leading cultural movements that would claim to represent the way forward for Soviet, or perhaps Russian culture (this could be contrasted with the so-called Red Vienna of the same period, where the ruling Social-Democratic Party pursued a number of cultural initiatives guided by a more or less coherent Party policy).[31] Their arguments were addressed to other intellectuals, occasionally to the citizenry at large, and frequently to the Party's leadership, which did not itself have a coherent position on literary matters. Leon Trotsky's *Literature and Revolution*, published in 1923, argued that '[t]he domain of art is not one in which the Party is called upon to command': it could lead and encourage, but it should not be issuing instructions on how to write (although a 'watchful revolutionary censorship' was available for anyone explicitly opposing the revolution).[32] A Central Committee resolution in June 1925, 'On Party Politics in the Field of Artistic Literature', made clear that no single group outside the Party would be allowed to dictate the terms of cultural debate. The Party leadership might have wanted to direct literary culture in such a way as to strengthen its social and political hand, but it could not do so on its own and it was not entirely clear, in any case, what that direction would be. As a result, from 1917 until 1927 there was a remarkably vibrant and substantial debate over not just literature, but the social and political role of culture more widely – a debate that would draw to a close when the government, now led by Josef Stalin, decided to intervene suddenly and dramatically in 1928.

The lines of debate and the groups involved did not form distinct sets: there could be quite traditional intellectuals, supporting a rather metaphysical concept of the poet, who nevertheless supported the Soviet government – Andrei Bely is an example – and there could be fully paid-up members of the literary avant-garde who not only opposed the regime in theory but actively conspired against it in practice – Viktor Shklovsky, Formalist theorist and Socialist-Revolutionary agitator, comes to mind. Nevertheless, for our purposes one can divide the groups and positions into four categories, some more coherent than others.

The 'modernists' consisted of writers of quite different stripes and styles, who nevertheless want literary culture to move along the tracks set down before the revolution, many believing that literary culture constitutes an alternative source of moral and social authority. Many of these writers were active in the literary movements that preceded the revolution, such as the Symbolist (Viacheslav Ivanov, Bely, Aleksandr Blok) and Acmeist (Nikolai Gumilev, Anna Akhmatova, Osip Mandelstam) movements in poetry. So far as the Soviet government was concerned, this group represented a traditional intelligentsia whose wings had to be clipped: they bore the brunt of the government's most repressive measures, which included shutting down their journals, the forceful exile of more than 200 intellectuals on the so-called Philosophers' Ships in 1922, and even murder (of, for instance, Gumilev). They were not, however, necessarily hostile to the regime, although some made no secret of their disdain. The range of positions can be illustrated with the contrasting examples of the Symbolist Valerii Briusov, who joined the Bolshevik Party, worked in its organisations, and wrote in its journals; the playwright and novelist Mikhail Bulgakov, who remained fiercely hostile to the Bolsheviks and became a target of Party criticism in the mid 1920s, but nevertheless survived; and the poet Boris Pasternak, who accepted the revolution as a historical fact and navigated its currents as best he could. A representative organisation of this group would be the Free Philosophical Association of St Petersburg (*Vol'fila*), the meetings of which Bakhtin attended. Its representative journals might be *Novaia Rossiia*, shut down by the government in 1926, and *Russkii sovremennik*, an explicit nod to Pushkin's *Sovremennik*, launched and closed in 1924. If there was a shared critical stance, it would be belief in literature itself as moral authority and source of philosophical insight. Stylistically, the work had the density and linguistic experiment generally associated with European modernism.

The 'avant-gardists' were distinct from the modernists: they had been issuing manifestoes calling for radical cultural transformation, and publishing poetry in daring but flimsy pamphlets, since 1912. In critical thought, they were mirrored by the Russian Formalists, whose literary theory identified art with formal experimentation and estrangement in a series of essays published during the First World War. Some avant-gardists believed the Bolshevik political revolution was unlikely to lead to anything culturally significant, while others thought it was analogous to the cultural revolution they were leading in the sphere of art. In 1924, the poet Vladimir Mayakovsky teamed up with the Formalist critic Osip Brik to form the Left Front in Arts and to publish a journal *LEF*, which was to represent artistic avant-gardism as the only correct means of cultural and social revolution. A new society, in their minds, could not be shaped by means of a conservative form of art: the pages of *LEF* were littered with calls for poets to create new language forms in the cause of revolution.[33]

The 'proletkultists' enthusiastically backed the political revolution and thought its complement was a fully 'proletarian culture'. They agreed with the avant-garde that Soviet literary culture had to make a dramatic break with the past, but had an entirely different vision of the break itself. In practice, proletarian culture meant either writing by people from proletarian families or writing that addressed the proletariat (in what they felt was the appropriate style). It would represent working-class interests, as understood by the Bolsheviks, and would provide a new stratum of intellectuals loyal to the Soviet project. Lenin, however, was sceptical from the beginning, while Trotsky made clear in *Literature and Revolution* that he was wholly unpersuaded by their arguments.[34]

The final group can be called, anachronistically, 'critical realists' (the name is drawn from the writings of Georg Lukács, the Hungarian Marxist critic who, after he immigrated to the Soviet Union in 1933, became an eloquent spokesperson for this position in the 1930s). These intellectuals and writers believed the Soviet Union was best served by inheriting and developing the great humanist tradition of nineteenth-century European writing. They could call on the authority of both Marx and Lenin, because the former had written admiringly of Balzac, the latter of Tolstoy. In the 1920s, this stream was best represented by a Soviet initiative, the journal *Krasnaia nov'* (*Red Virgin Soil*), founded in 1921 with the explicit backing of Lenin, Natalia Krupskaia (his wife), and the writer Maksim Gorky. The journal, edited by Aleksandr Voronskii, would publish a range of work and would be the Party's vehicle for bringing on board the so-called fellow-travellers of the revolution, intellectuals of talent who were neither opposed to nor wholly committed to the revolutionary cause.

Battle was joined, arguments were made, work was published, and, in the end, some of the participants ended up in positions of power, some were exiled, shot, or imprisoned, and others retreated into as much obscurity as they could manage, working away at projects unlikely to attract controversy. It was characteristic of the period that an intellectual, say, Voronskii, could be given the prestigious job of editing *Krasnaia nov'* in 1921 and then find himself dismissed and disgraced in 1928, or that the Proletkultist Leopold Averbakh could celebrate victory over Voronskii in 1928, only to find himself attacked and dismissed by 1932 (and executed in 1937).

Bakhtin was hardly on the front lines of this furious struggle: he had moved to Leningrad in May of 1924 and would stay there until his term of exile began in March of 1930. He participated in the many informal circles and discussion groups that dotted the city, several of which were hosted by his friends from Nevel'. His own sympathies do not align him precisely with any of the above charted groups, but as a fairly traditional intellectual, inspired by Neo-Kantian philosophy and taking his bearings from the Symbolists – Viacheslav Ivanov's work was the starting point for his group's discussions of Dostoevsky – he sits closest to the modernists.

He was not on the front lines, but neither was he unaffected by what was going on around him. One of the most persistent myths of Bakhtin criticism is that he located himself above the fray, that he was devoted to what he would call 'the ultimate questions' (religious questions, questions about the meaning of life, etc.) and so uninterested in getting his hands dirty in the struggles and disputes of the fallen, secular world. It's an attitude summed up in a famous intervention by the critic Sergei Averintsev, who, in an article appearing just after Bakhtin died, claimed the worst thing one could do was 'drag Bakhtin into the dualism of arguments between circles', because '[t]he essence of Bakhtin's position always consisted not of "against" but of "for"'.[35] Don't tell us Bakhtin was for the avant-garde and against realism, Averintsev is telling us, or vice versa – Bakhtin had no dog in that fight. But if we look at what Bakhtin was writing in the 1920s (and much later), it's clear he was more than willing to get involved in the 'dualism of arguments between circles', more than willing to take a stand against others. In 1924 he was against the theory of Russian Formalism and he explained why in the long critical essay, 'The Problem of Form, Content, and Material', intended for, but never actually published in, the modernist journal *Russkii sovremennik*. The critique's target was the central claim of Formalist theory: that the essence of art was the deformation, the breaking up and distorting, as Viktor Shklovsky had put it, of language.[36] Poetic language, they claimed, was language that had been made strange and difficult, in which the sounds of language, its syntax, its morphology were intentionally distorted, so as to draw attention to itself, muddying the window on reality, so to speak. Against this theory, Bakhtin marshalled the forces of Neo-Kantian aesthetics. Language, he argued, provided neither the content nor the form of verbal art; it was simply the 'material', in much the same way that marble could be the material of sculpture. Art was a reshaping not of this bare material, but of 'content', that is, of objects already given shape by our everyday cognitive and ethical-practical thought. 'Art creates a new form as a new value relation to what has already become reality for cognition and the act' (PFCM, 279/287). The elements of Pushkin's poem 'Remembrance' are 'the city, and night, and remembrance, and remorse, and so on' (PFCM, 296/304), not the words 'city', 'night', and so forth.

When Bakhtin did finally publish something, his book *Problems of Dostoevsky's Art* in 1929, he presented himself as a mediator between the warring factions. The book opened with the claim that neither a 'narrowly formalist approach', nor a 'narrowly ideological approach' could do justice to Dostoevsky's 'revolutionary innovation in the field of the novel as an artistic form' (PDA, 276/4). Bakhtin was trying to split the difference between Formalism, which was under constant attack for ignoring the ideological role of literature, and those – Proletkultists among others – who wanted only ideological cheerleading from literature. He would split the difference by making stylistic features central to his analysis, by making particular forms of literary language the focus, while at the same time describing style as a manifestation of specific social relationships. Bakhtin would downplay the philosophical and political views expressed by Dostoevsky's characters in favour of an analysis of the style of their language, but that analysis would reveal that the work was 'internally, immanently sociological' (PDA 276/3-4), sociological at a level more profound than express opinions. The effectiveness of Bakhtin's strategy can be gauged from the fact that many years later, when this Dostoevsky book was rediscovered by Slavists working in America and Europe, Bakhtin was taken to be a somewhat renegade or dissident member of the Formalist school.

The strategy would be repeated in Bakhtin's next major work, the book (printed as an essay) 'Discourse in the Novel', which opens with a quite similar claim:

> The leading idea of this book is to overcome the divide between an abstract 'formalism' and an equally abstract 'ideologism' in the study of artistic discourse, to overcome it on the ground of a *sociological stylistics* for which form and content are unified in the word when it is understood as a social phenomenon, social in all the spheres of its life and in all its moments, from the sound image to the most abstract layers of meaning. (DN 259/10)

Bakhtin had decided to fight Formalism on its own territory, to give language itself priority, but through a different conception of language. He took, in effect, the sharpest of linguistic turns, visible to all in the page turn from Part One to Part Two of *Problems of Dostoevsky's Art*. It was the works of Medvedev and Voloshinov, particularly the latter, that helped or prodded Bakhtin to change course, to shift his attention to 'the stylistics of genre' and the study of discourse, instead of works Bakhtin secretly wrote. Let's take a moment to see how Voloshinov ended up being a scholar of linguistics and how that might have fed into Bakhtin's own turn to language.

Excursus: Voloshinov's Linguistic Turn

In 1922, Voloshinov moved from Vitebsk to Petrograd in order to complete the university education he had suspended at the time of the revolution.[37] Originally training to be a lawyer, he now enrolled in ethno-linguistic studies, completing his degree work in 1924. In the following year, as we pointed out in the previous chapter, he joined ILIaZV, one of the new Soviet academic institutions, where he would work as a postgraduate and a researcher until its dissolution in 1930. Formally a student of literature, he seemed to move steadily towards linguistic topics, perhaps under the influence of L. P. (Lev Petrovich) Iakubinskii, a linguist at ILIaZV with literary interests and an early contributor to Russian Formalism.

From all the available evidence, Voloshinov read and otherwise absorbed an extraordinary range of writing about language, about literary style, and about formal linguistics. He was lucky: the 1920s were a moment of exceptional openness and ferment in Soviet linguistics; new, radical ideas about the discipline – including the then revolutionary ideas of Ferdinand de Saussure – were being introduced and discussed; new institutions, like ILIaZV, were being created as centres of research; and linguists were being drawn into the process of remaking a society (many of them became involved in language planning projects, such as the creation of writing systems for oral languages). From his official records at ILIaZV and the references in his published works, we know Voloshinov came into contact with works of the new structuralist linguistics inspired by Saussure, with the Romantic, aesthetic conception of language advanced by Benedetto Croce, Karl Vossler, and Leo Spitzer, with the phenomenological writings of Husserl, Franz Brentano, and Russia's own Gustav Shpet, with the pragmatic theories of Karl Bühler, and with Ernst Cassirer's magisterial *Philosophy of Symbolic Forms*, a recasting of Neo-Kantianism as a theory of different kinds of symbol.[38] All of the above would feed into Voloshinov's evolving ideas about language. The last two figures, however, would be crucial.

Bühler was one of a number of writers in the early twentieth century pressing for a pragmatic conception of language – that is, a conception of language as communicative activity (rather than an autonomous system), involving one person saying something to another.[39] Bühler had described the act of speech as composed of three elements: a sender, a receiver, and an object or state of affairs. Every communicative act thus had three dimensions: the expressing of something by the speaker, the appeal to or influencing of the listener, and the representation of a state of affairs. This so-called organon model of communication was described in an article of 1922, 'The Essence of Syntax', which Voloshinov translated into Russian during his time at ILIaZV. With this in mind, it appears that, in his first contribution to philosophy of language, the 1926 article 'Discourse in Life and Discourse in Poetry', Voloshinov overlaid Bühler's model of the utterance with the author/hero categories Bakhtin had been deploying.[40]

In that article, Voloshinov claimed that every piece of discourse was organised around the tripartite relation of the speaker (Bühler's 'sender'), the hero (Bühler's 'state of affairs'), and the listener (Bühler's 'receiver'). The two schemes he was combining, Bakhtin's and Bühler's, were not a perfect fit. The speaker and the 'author' could be conflated easily enough, but Voloshinov had to turn Bakhtin's 'hero' into the topic of discourse, and the listener was something outside Bakhtin's scheme altogether (he would, beginning in the 1930s, make it part of his set-up, eventually christening this figure the 'addressee'). The phenomenological business Bakhtin had emphasised, the difference between the experience of one's own feelings or speech and that of *others*, was skipped over.

But just as Bakhtin spent more time on authors and heroes than ordinary, everyday *Is* and *others*, so Voloshinov only briefly discusses his scheme for 'discourse in life' before moving on to 'discourse in poetry'. While Voloshinov's ostensible model for language is the local, personal interaction – he asks us to imagine a couple sitting together in a room and one saying 'So!' – he is at pains to describe the context of this interaction not in terms of a particular time and place, but in terms of the shared 'social evaluations' that make understanding possible, even in this everyday situation.[41] For social evaluations are mobile: they can be expressed in words and are therefore easily transposed into a literary work, in which authors, heroes, and listeners do not share a physical space. The communicative act is structured by the triad of speaker, listener (addressee), and topic/hero, but the relationships are established by social evaluations that are expressed in the vocabulary, style, and tone of the particular utterance. In this way, Voloshinov manages to aestheticise Bühler's organon model of communication, to make it useful as a tool for 'sociological poetics' (the subtitle of the essay is 'On Questions of Sociological Poetics').

Voloshinov does not mention Bühler in the essay, which is conspicuously lacking in references. He also doesn't mention Ernst Cassirer, though it is clear from some of the discussion that he had read at least the first volume of Cassirer's *Philosophy of Symbolic Forms*.[42] When Voloshinov began to prepare his book-length study, *Marxism and the Philosophy of Language*, in 1927–28, Cassirer was slated to play a major role. In the outline of the work Voloshinov submitted to ILIaZV, Cassirer is described as the philosopher who has discovered that the spheres of culture and the sphere of life, which Bakhtin had found hopelessly distant from one another, came together in the world of symbols and more specifically in the practice of language. Cassirer's philosophy demonstrated that

> the form of the sign and its meaning (symbolic form) is common to all fields of cultural creation, uniting them. Such is the systematic place of discourse according to the doctrine of the Neo-Kantians (see Cassirer's book, the *Philosophie der Symbolischen Formen*, 1925, the fundamental Neo-Kantian work on the philosophy of language) [...] By means of *the inner forms of language (semi-transcendental forms, as it were)* movement and historical becoming are being introduced into the petrified kingdom of transcendental-logical categories.[43]

What this mouthful amounts to is the claim that the forms of language can mediate between the forward movement of 'historical becoming' and the 'transcendental-logical' categories, that is, the abstractions of culture, science, and so forth. It could do this because language was, as Voloshinov put it, 'semi-transcendental'. On the one hand, the 'inner forms of language' (a term Cassirer had inherited from Wilhelm von Humboldt) made it possible for people to relate as *I* and *thou* (through the pronoun system), to locate themselves and the objects of their world in time and space, to make meaningful thought possible. On the other hand, language only existed in the form of discrete utterances and it had a history of its own, its forms changing over time. Bakhtin had claimed that in art, which depended on the author's ability to endow heroic 'life' with form, one found a place where culture and life were synthesised. Voloshinov, with his borrowing from Cassirer, seemed set to raise the stakes with a bolder claim: language itself could accomplish this synthesis, perhaps with particular force in the forms of literature.

What literature brought to this project was a set of techniques that related the author to the hero linguistically. When Voloshinov reported on his research for *Marxism and the Philosophy of Language*, he also included an outline for an accompanying article on 'The Problem of the Transmission of Alien Discourse'.[44] The article would focus on what had become a fashionable topic in European literary and linguistic study: how a literary text conveyed the speech of its characters. European literature of the nineteenth and twentieth centuries had developed a rich repertoire of styles for representing the speech of *others*, which now included not only direct quotation but also indirect discourse and so-called free indirect discourse. In these forms, Voloshinov saw a way of discussing the author and hero as a relationship manifest in literary language, which often combined the perspective of the author with the words of its heroes. The article never made it into print, but its content became the final chapters of *Marxism and the Philosophy of Language*.

In fact, Cassirer ended up being relegated to a footnote in the published book, and the philosophy of language Voloshinov actually describes is not, in its details, Cassirerean.[45] It's not because Voloshinov grew disenchanted – in the early 1930s he was making a translation of the *Language* volume of Cassirer's *Philosophy of Symbolic Forms*. But the significance of Cassirer, in any case, had been less the details of his philosophy of language than the role he assigned to the philosophy of language, and to symbolic forms themselves, in the scheme of things. For symbolic form in general – which, in his three-volume study, would encompass not only language, but also myth, religion, and science – embodied, in his words, an 'original formative power'.[46] Its different configurations (in science, myth, language, etc.) were united by their productivity and creative spontaneity, that is, by the fact, that they did not simply copy the world but played a part in creating and shaping it. In Cassirer's view, the path taken by natural science showed us how a symbolic form would gradually penetrate and organise reality for us (in the way that scientific symbols, although many of them don't 'copy' anything, nevertheless reveal the lawlike constitution of the universe), while the evolution of myth towards monotheism gradually sharpened our practical and creative power. In the posthumously published fourth volume of the *Philosophy of Symbolic Forms*, Cassirer concluded with the declaration that 'every symbolic form works towards the transition from "nature" to "freedom"'.[47] In this way, symbolic forms served as the media in which historical becoming took place.

The Russian Formalists had insisted that the value of literature depended on its manipulation of language. Bakhtin had at first resisted this, arguing that language, as the mere material of literature, was distinct from its value-laden content. Voloshinov, however, showed Bakhtin he could thread the needle by making language the bearer of content and by thinking about manipulations of language as a matter of 'style', as a way of encoding relationships between an author and a hero. As Galin Tihanov has shown, Bakhtin was only willing to discuss language when language was able to embody the pressures and shape of the culture beyond it.[48] Voloshinov made that move possible: the road from philosophy to the study of literary style was paved by him.

* * *

Of course, once Bakhtin chose that road, he was bound to go his own way. In the notebooks he made while researching the Dostoevsky book, we find descriptions of the critical literature on Dostoevsky, extensive notes on Max Scheler's *Essence and Forms of Sympathy*, a résumé of Karl Vossler's article, 'Grammar and the History of Language', and a substantial series of excerpts from Leo Spitzer's book *Italienische Umgangssprache* (*Italian Conversational Language*). The quotations drawn from Spitzer are revealing: they focus on how conversational language is a compromise between what the *I* wants to say and what the *thou* is ready to hear. That is, Spitzer creates an account of language in which conversation serves as the model or paradigm, in which *I* and *other* have become moments of language, which is precisely what Bakhtin does when he rethinks language as 'dialogism'.

Bakhtin will overcome 'formalism' and 'ideologism' by moving into Formalist territory: *skaz*, parody, language itself. He doesn't abandon talk of authors and heroes entirely – it makes periodic returns in his writing – but for the most part he exchanges it for a relation that is at once analogous and different: the relationship between the 'novelist' (which is in actuality the novel itself as a unified whole) and its constituent styles of language. But in making this linguistic turn, Bakhtin is *not* exchanging philosophy for linguistics or literary criticism, because Voloshinov has helped him find a conception of language that endows the progress and evolution of language with philosophical significance. But while Bakhtin was making his linguistic turn, far more ominous turns were taking place in the Soviet Union.

Literature: Socialist Realism and Arguments about the Novel in the 1930s

Stalin and those in the Communist Party sympathetic to him had taken over the leadership of the Party at the end of 1927, a seizure of power that climaxed with the expulsion of Trotsky, his main rival, from the Central Committee. In 1928 the Soviet Union would embark on a dramatically new course, politically, economically, and culturally. Economically, the new leadership formulated and implemented the first Five-Year Plan as well as the collectivisation of agriculture (forcing all peasants to become members of collective farms, *kolkhozy*). Politically, a host of repressive measures was taken not only against hostile political opponents outside the Party, but also against rivals within the Communist Party and what was characterised by the Party as the 'prerevolutionary intelligentsia'. The first true Stalinist show trial, the Shakhty trial of 1928, was characteristic: engineers, that is, the technical intelligentsia, were accused of sabotage in coal mines. Internationally, the political line of the period was exemplified by the tactics of the German Communist Party (KPD), which, under instructions from the Communist International, attacked its Social-Democratic rivals, the German SPD, incessantly, treating them as in effect allies of fascism. There would be no compromise, no coordination, with anyone not wholly committed to the Bolshevik vision of revolution.

The cultural turn was in keeping with the above. The Soviet government had allowed for competition between the various literary groups claiming legitimacy after 1917, and had even gone so far as to institute its own relatively open journals, such as *Krasnaia nov'* and *Pechat' i revoliutsiia* [*The Press* and *Revolution*], where Formalists and their opponents might publish. In 1928, the government and the Party chose a favourite: the Russian Association of Proletarian Writers, RAPP, which was the institutional form of the Proletkult movement. The RAPPists had been currying the favour of the Soviet government and relentlessly attacking their rivals for a decade – suddenly they were put in the driver's seat of Soviet cultural policy. Voronskii, editor of *Krasnaia nov'* and critical realist (in our classification), was sacked and replaced by a Proletkult supporter, and RAPPists assumed the leadership of various literary organisations.[49]

There is no reason to suppose that the Party came to embrace the cause of proletarian literature after serious reflection on the nature of culture – RAPP was simply a club with which to beat the fellow-travelling intelligentsia. These new policies did not affect Bakhtin's writing in theoretical terms, but they were the direct cause of his arrest and exile: as an articulate, but uncommitted member of the intelligentsia, he was in the regime's crosshairs.

RAPP's pre-eminence was short-lived. Having done their destructive work, they were attacked in turn. A Party decree in April 1932 dissolved all existing organisations and established the Union of Soviet Writers as the leading organisation in literary studies. Over the next two years, the new organisation would establish a preferred form for literary prose: socialist realism. Socialist realism was, from the very beginning, caught between two aspirations: on the one hand, it was to be critical realism in the sense we discussed earlier – an artistic cognition of reality, which would show the actual workings of the social structure beneath surface appearances. It was analytic in aim. On the other hand, it was supposed to build support for the Soviet cause, being propagandistic in aim. The ambiguity gave rise to many debates in the 1930s, one of the most significant and well-known being the debate on Georg Lukács's entry for 'The Novel' in the *Soviet Literary Encyclopaedia*, discussed at meetings of the Communist Academy in December 1934 and January 1935. Lukács was the critic who could most energetically and subtly defend the critical realist position described above. A Hegelian Marxist, he believed that the successful literary work would penetrate the mystifying appearance of capitalist society by totalising its elements, revealing the profound interconnectedness that made capitalism systematic. The essence of capitalist ideology was fragmentation: to the naked eye, it appeared like a loose amalgamation of people and commodities, things made and bought, and people with varying responsibility for making them. The only way to reveal the true nature of capitalism was to join up the dots, to show how each detail of the system was intimately connected with the rest. In this respect, the novel shared the aspirations of the classical epic, but in a context where the totality, the integrated character of the society, was more difficult to represent, on account of the fractured, contradictory nature of capitalist society. Lukács argued that this was a matter of novelistic technique and method, so that an artistic understanding of capitalism could be had *despite* the class position of the writer. He, and those who agreed with him, were labelled the *voprekisty*, the 'despitists'.

Lukács would wage a struggle throughout the 1930s for the kind of critical realism he thought a Communist society required and against any attempt, in criticism or imaginative writing, to sacrifice realism at the altar of propagandistic 'Party-mindedness' [*partiinost'*]. Within Russia, his chief venue was the journal *Literaturnyi kritik* [*The Literary Critic*], which had been founded in 1933 as an explicitly Marxist critical journal, but one that would take a relatively independent line. A transcription of the discussion of 'The Novel' at the Communist Academy was published in the journal, and Lukács, as well as fellow critic Mikhail Lifshits, published a series of articles in the decade laying out his case, the most important of which were probably 'Narrate or Describe' in 1936 and the articles from 1936–37 that were eventually brought together in his book *The Historical Novel*.

In artistic terms, the case was clear. Prose writers should make sure that every detail of the text, whether it was a narrative event or a descriptive element, should play a determinate role in revealing the play and movement of social forces in the society represented. The antitheses of this kind of 'realism' were naturalism – too much empirical detail, without any particular purpose – and modernism, as exemplified in the stream-of-consciousness writing practised by James Joyce, John Dos Passos, and, in a different way, Marcel Proust. The latter's focus on subjective sensations and thoughts, without narrative direction, gave you a text that floated on the surface of reality, without ever digging deeper.

Bakhtin followed the debate on Lukács's article in the mid-1930s and read some of the material on the historical novel that was published in the late 1930s: direct references to Lukács and echoes of his argument are scattered throughout the long 'laboratory' text he composed in 1937–39, which has been named 'On the *Bildungsroman*' by Bakhtin's editors. But was Lukács simply a foil for Bakhtin or a genuine influence? It's tempting to simply counterpose Bakhtin to Lukács: the former the apostle of unfinishedness and becoming, the latter a lifelong devotee of totality and completeness. Matters are, unsurprisingly, more complicated. Galin Tihanov has described their trajectories and concerns as largely in parallel: an early interest in aesthetics, followed by a turn to cultural analysis, focused on the novel as the privileged bearer of modernity.[50] In this light, it makes sense to see Bakhtin's work on Goethe and the *Bildungsroman* as the moment when the two trajectories approach each other or even cross. For the work on Goethe and the *Bildungsroman* adopts much of Lukács's aesthetic: the aim of the *Bildungsroman*, achieved fully in Goethe's writing, is the assimilation of 'real historical time', and this historical time is successfully assimilated when it is manifested in details of time and space in the novel, when the abstract course of history is rendered in the concrete details of what Bakhtin will call a 'chronotope', a network of temporal and spatial references.

Bakhtin's final bloc of writing in this decade, his work on Rabelais and carnival, is also understandable as a response to context. As Katerina Clark has pointed out, in the 1930s Rabelais occupied one of the perches of world literature in the Soviet imagination: several translations of his work, with trade-sized print runs, came out in the decade.[51] Indeed, the opening gambit in Bakhtin's book on Rabelais was to insist that 'Rabelais's historical place in the ranks of the creators of modern European literature, i.e., in the ranks of

Dante, Boccaccio, Shakespeare and Cervantes is beyond any doubt'.[52] Soviet literary policy aimed to project Soviet literature as the heir, the fulfilment, of the great stream of modern European literature: Bakhtin, like many others, aimed to identify and characterise that stream. While his implicit and sometimes explicit promise to tie this heritage to the contemporary Soviet novel was probably not in earnest, Bakhtin's commitment to the idea of world literature – in fact, to European literature as world literature – was.

Was it all a clever pretence, though, Bakhtin just going along to get along (and to get published)? Not at all. Bakhtin could join the debate, a debate conducted in terms of Marxist theories of history, because his own conception of history as 'historical becoming' had a lot in common with the Marxist one.[53] The overlap should not be surprising. Bakhtin's sources for his definition of history and his belief in 'historical becoming' were, as we've said, in the first case Hermann Cohen, and in the second, Cohen's student and Bakhtin's friend, Matvei Kagan. Cohen was not a Marxist but a socialist – a 'Katheder-socialist' or 'socialist of the lectern', according to his opponents – who saw universal justice as the endpoint of human history, although he thought the route there was not the one Marx had chosen. Kagan had been a Russian Social-Democratic agitator, a Bolshevik, and his own philosophy of history made human labour the central creative force in the historical process, an idea borrowed from Marx.

But it's not just a matter of sources: from the 1920s onwards, Marxism provided the environment in which Bakhtin lived and was a major element of the intellectual atmosphere he breathed. He could work towards a sociological stylistics because he found so much of the work around him on the sociology of language interesting and persuasive. He could participate in debates about the nature of the novel and its representation of the historical world because, he, too, thought the novel should be representing the world as dense, thickly spatial and temporal, concrete, and at the same time as something on the threshold of radical transformation. In short, he could borrow from and align with Marxism without signing up for the political program in part or whole. Which, a sober view of the evidence suggests, is exactly what he did.

The 1950s and 1960s: Consolidation and a Quiet Life

The Second World War had produced a temporary alliance between Soviet Russia and the Allied forces of Western Europe and North America. Its end ushered in the period of the so-called Cold War between the Soviet Union and the capitalist countries of Europe and North America. Soviet cultural policy, unsurprisingly, took a sharp nationalist turn. 'World literature' rapidly lost its sheen; Russian national spirit quickly asserted itself in a series of direct interventions by the Party, embodied in the Central Committee resolution 'On the Journals *Zvezda* and *Leningrad*' and in speeches given by Andrei Zhdanov, the Party member in charge of ideology, from 1946 until his death in 1948. The new line criticised what it called 'cosmopolitanism' or 'kowtowing toward the West'.[54] Not only admiration for 'Western' literature, but also acknowledgement of Russian connections with or indebtedness to European culture generally, now or in the past, was discouraged. The change in Party policy could not have been more badly timed for Bakhtin, for 1946 was also the year in which he publicly defended his dissertation, a dissertation that opened with the claim that in the Soviet Union Rabelais was 'the least popular, least studied, least understood and valued of all the great writers of world literature'.[55] The next five years would be spent in a long struggle with the Stalinist bureaucracy, a struggle that ended with Bakhtin finally being awarded his degree, after much rewriting and adjusting.

There was another dramatic development, one that surprised people in the Soviet Union and beyond. In 1950, a series of pieces on Soviet scholarship in linguistics, presented in a question-and-answer format, appeared in the Soviet newspaper *Pravda*.[56] Their focus was on the relationship between Marxism and linguistics, and they were signed by none other than Josef Stalin. Whether Stalin actually wrote these pieces and whether the views expressed in them were his own, rather than the views of certain Soviet linguists, is a matter of dispute. But they signalled a sharp change in direction for Soviet linguistics, which had, since the late 1920s, been dominated by the linguistic framework of N. Ia. (Nikolai Iakovlevich) Marr (though Marr had died in 1934). Marr had been a severe critic of the mainstream of both the historical wing and the emerging structuralist wing of European linguistics. In its stead, he offered what came to be known as Japhetology, a linguistic doctrine that prescribed a universal set of stages for all linguistic development, a set of fundamental lexical roots shared by all languages, and the conviction that languages had a class basis.

Stalin cut the ground from under this doctrine. Was language part of the superstructure, and thus tied to the class conflicts of the base? (asked the very first question). 'No, it is not true', claimed Stalin, who went on to observe that the Russian language had served the bourgeoisie as well as the proletariat and that, like other languages, it served its society as a whole and had no class character. Marr was roundly condemned and his stranglehold over linguistics broken. The effect of this intervention was to revive the efforts of those Soviet linguists who had been working in the wake of the systematic, structural linguistics pioneered by Saussure (and who had been condemned as bourgeois during Marr's rise to power). The effect on Bakhtin was twofold and, in its own way, ambiguous. On the one hand, it clearly convinced Bakhtin that it was time to write about language again. Around 1952 he began work on the unfinished piece that would be called 'The Problem of Speech Genres', which was a critique of existing linguistics and an attempt to found a new dialogical linguistics based on the 'utterance' rather than the sentence. The preparatory materials include references to Stalin's intervention.[57] On the other hand, the linguists who were liberated, so to speak, by Stalin's intervention, were, to Bakhtin's mind, the leading representatives of a monological, idealist linguistics, a linguistics focused on a shared grammar and on the sentence.[58] His main opponent in the 'The Problem of Speech Genres' was in fact the linguist V. V. Vinogradov, who was appointed director of the Linguistics Institute of the Academy of Sciences directly after Stalin's articles had appeared. Vinogradov, whom Bakhtin had referred to twenty years earlier in 'Discourse in the Novel', represented a sophisticated version of the monological linguistics Bakhtin opposed. Stalin's intervention had made relatively open discussion of linguistic topics possible, but it also had put linguists Bakhtin disagreed with in the driver's seat.

Chapter 4
Works

Some Preliminary Observations

The complicated life and the complicated times have been described; it is time to get to the writing itself. But, as we've noted, the life and the times had repercussions not only for the content, but also for the form of the writing. Most writers who have *Cambridge Introductions* devoted to them leave behind a series of published works: books, essays, articles, transcripts of lectures, maybe some journalism. Bakhtin left behind one book published 'on time' (just after it had been written), one book published in revised form about twenty years after it had been written, and then a seemingly endless trail of not-quite-finished essays, half-finished essays, outlines for books and essays, and notebooks filled with material that might have become books or essays, had circumstances been different.

Another consequence of the complicated times was that when the notes, drafts, and outlines were finally published, they were, with one or two exceptions, chosen, shaped, edited, corrected, and given titles by someone besides Bakhtin, often with an eye on the still-existing regime of Soviet censorship. As a result, in the thirty years between Bakhtin's rediscovery (in 1961) and the disintegration of the Soviet Union (1991), Bakhtin's archive of unfinished, unpublished texts was gradually turned into a body of published work, but almost all the published work was in some way deformed or distorted, often very substantially. Many texts appeared in censored form, with lines, paragraphs, and pages excised from them, either because Soviet censorship required these excisions or because Bakhtin's editors decided that certain lines or paragraphs didn't represent the true Bakhtin, that they were mere 'camouflage' added by Bakhtin. Some texts were in effect composed by the editors, who took different works and melded them into a single new one or who took excerpts from Bakhtin's notebooks and created an artificial work out of them. As a result, the body of published work available to the English-language reader (or for the casual Russian-language reader) is in many instances compromised or unreliable, making careful and critical analysis of it more difficult than it should be. In order to do justice to

Bakhtin's work, we therefore have to begin with some table-clearing and table-setting, so that we understand what the work actually consists of. Below is a list of Bakhtin's published work, with a few notes designed to set the record straight. For this purpose, our definitive source is the Bakhtin *Collected Works*.

The order of the texts: Like many writers, Bakhtin moved from one theme or concern to another over the course of his life. But when he turned to a new topic – or a new angle on an existing topic (architectonics, dialogism, the novel, etc.) – he did not simply leave the old work behind. He'd return to Dostoevsky over and over again, he'd think about stylistics in the novel repeatedly, and carnival, having surfaced in 1940, would never really be submerged. So, instead of simply listing Bakhtin's works in strict chronological order, I've organised them in blocs, each of which includes the first work or works that mark a new angle and then all the works in which that theme or angle continues to play a major role. In a few cases, the placement is debatable, but for the most part it is straightforward and the result is, I hope, a clearer and more useful picture of Bakhtin's *oeuvre*.

Titles in italics or quotation marks are Bakhtin's (often, they are a phrase or title scribbled on the front of a notebook). All other titles have been assigned by Bakhtin's editors. Texts with an asterisk have not, at the time of writing, appeared in English translation. In each case, I list the location of the English translation first and then the location of the authoritative text in Russian. Bibliographical details for the published collections of English and Russian texts cited in this list are provided at the end.

List of Bakhtin's Published Works

Philosophical texts (author, hero, art, responsibility, the nature of the human sciences): 1919 onwards

'Art and Responsibility'. 1919. A one-page article, originally published in *Den' isskustva*, 13 September 1919, 3–4. *Art and Answerability*, 1–3; Russian *Collected Works, Vol. 1*, 5–6.

Towards a Philosophy of the Act. Date estimated at 1921–23. Long fragment. Introductory section for a large work of ethical philosophy. *Towards a Philosophy of the Act*, trans. Vadim Liapunov (Austin: University of Texas Press, 1993); Russian *Collected Works, Vol. 1*, 7–68.

Author and Hero in Aesthetic Activity. Probably around 1924 but could be as late as 1927. Long fragment. Further section and elaboration of the above philosophical work. *Art and Answerability*, 4–256; Russian *Collected Works, Vol. 1*, 69–263.

'On Issues in the Methodology of the Aesthetics of the Verbal Artwork: 1. The Problem of Form, Content, and Material in Verbal Art'. 1924. Usually known by its subtitle alone. Draft of an article, allegedly scheduled to be published in the journal *Russkii sovremennik*. *Art and Answerability*, 257–325; Russian *Collected Works*, *Vol. 1*, 265–325.

Lectures and Comments by M. M. Bakhtin in 1924–1925 from Notes Taken by L. V. Pumpianskii. The notes include: an outline of a series of lectures on 'Hero and author in artistic creation'; notes of six lectures Bakhtin gave on Kantian philosophy; two contributions to discussion; notes to a lecture Bakhtin gave on the philosophy of religion, titled 'The Problem of Grounded Peace'. As appendix in Susan M. Felch and Paul Contino (eds.), *Bakhtin and Religion: A Feeling for Faith* (Evanston, IL: Northwestern University Press, 2001), 197–221; Russian *Collected Works*, *Vol. 1*, 326–42.

'Contemporary Vitalism'. 1926. This is the sole instance of a 'disputed work' where there is clear evidence of Bakhtin's authorship (a signed declaration from the credited author, I. I. Kanaev, that Bakhtin was the actual author). In F. Burwick and P. Douglass (eds.), *The Crisis in Modernism: Bergson and the Vitalist Controversy* (Cambridge: Cambridge University Press, 2010), 76–97; *Chelovek i priroda* 1(1926), 33–42.

*'Towards Philosophical Foundations for the Human Sciences'. 1940–43. Short, but very significant philosophical statement. Russian *Collected Works*, *Vol. 5*, 7–10.

Rhetoric, to the extent that it is something false ... 1943. *Slavonic and East European Journal* 61, 2 (2107), 202–15; Russian *Collected Works*, *Vol. 5*, 63–70.

'The Man in the Mirror'. 1943. *Slavonic and East European Journal* 61, 2 (2107), 216–17; Russian *Collected Works*, *Vol. 5*, 71.

On Questions of Self-consciousness and Self-evaluation. 1943–46. *Slavonic and East European Journal* 61, 2 (2107), 218–32; Russian *Collected Works*, *Vol. 5*, 72–79.

Working Notes from the 1960s and Early 1970s. Early 1960s–74. The contents of four notebooks and occasional single sheets, covering a wide range of topics. Extracts from these notebooks became 'Towards a Methodology of the Human Sciences' and 'From Notes Made in 1970–71'. *Speech Genres and Other Late Essays*, 132–72; Russian *Collected Works*, *Vol. 6*, 371–439.

Bakhtin does literary criticism: 1923 onwards

*Notes on Lectures by M. M. Bakhtin on the History of Russian Literature, taken by R. M. Mirkina. From roughly 1923 to 1927. Covers a wide range of topics, from Turgenev and Tolstoy to Akhmatova, Blok, and Futurism. Russian *Collected Works, Vol. 2*, 213–427.

*'A Lecture on Mayakovsky'. Notes for a lecture in 1926–27. *Dialog Karnaval Khrontop* 2 (1995), 111–14.

'Tolstoy the Dramatist: A Preface'. 1929. Introduction to a volume of Tolstoy's dramatic works, written after Bakhtin's arrest. In Gary Saul Morson and Caryl Emerson (eds.), *Rethinking Bakhtin* (Evanston, IL: Northwestern University Press, 1989), 227–36; L. N. Tolstoy, *Polnoe sobranie khudozhestvennykh proizvedenii* [*Complete Works*], *Vol. 11* (Moscow: Gosizdat, 1929), iii–x and reprinted in the Russian *Collected Works, Vol. 2*, 176–84.

*Tolstoy, as Dramatist: working notes. 1928. Notes for the above. Russian *Collected Works, Vol. 2*, 205–12.

'The Ideological Novel of Tolstoy: A Preface'. 1929. In Morson and Emerson (eds.), *Rethinking Bakhtin*, 237–57; L. N. Tolstoy, *Complete Works, Vol. 13* (Moscow: Gosizdat, 1930), iii–xx and reprinted in the Russian *Collected Works, Vol. 2*, 185–204.

*'*The Lay of Prince Igor* in the History of the Epic'. 1940–41. Russian *Collected Works, Vol. 5*, 39–41.

*'Mariia Tudor'. 1954. Russian *Collected Works, Vol. 5*, 298–303

*The Problem of Sentimentalism. 1958–59. Russian *Collected Works, Vol. 5*, 304–5.

*'Characteristics of Chinese Literature and Its History'. Notes for lectures in the 1950s. In A. D. Eremmev et al. (eds.), *Esteticheskoe nasledie i sovremennost'*, *Vol. 1* (Saransk: Izdatel'stvo Mordovskogo universiteta, 1992), 5–12.

Lectures on the History of Foreign Literature: Antiquity, the Middle Ages. (from the notes of V. A. Mirsky). Note from lectures at the university in Saransk from 1958 to 1959. Saransk: Izdatel'stvo Mordovskogo universiteta, 1999.

Works on Dostoevsky (dialogism as 'polyphony'): 1929 onwards

Problems of Dostoevsky's Art. 1929. The first version of the Dostoevsky book. There is no English translation, but most of the book is preserved in *Problems of Dostoevsky's Poetics* (below). (Leningrad: Priboi, 1929); reprinted in the Russian *Collected Works, Vol. 2*, 5–175.

*'Towards a History of the Type (Generic Variety) of Dostoevsky's Novel'. 1940–41. First text in which Bakhtin links Dostoevsky to carnival. Russian *Collected Works, Vol. 5*, 42–44.

'1961. Notes'. Notes made while Bakhtin prepared a revision of the Dostoevsky book for the Italian publisher Einaudi. Opening is translated as second half of 'The Problem of the Text in Linguistics, Philology and the Human Sciences', in *Speech Genres and Other Late Essays*, 118–31 and remainder as 'Towards a Reworking of the Dostoevsky Book', an appendix to *Problems of Dostoevsky's Poetics*, 283–302; Russian *Collected Works, Vol. 5*, 329–60.

*'Dostoevsky. 1961'. Revision notes following those from the preceding entry. Russian *Collected Works, Vol. 5*, 364–74.

*'Notes 1962–1963'. Notes made when Bakhtin was revising the Dostoevsky book for the Russian edition. Russian *Collected Works, Vol. 5*, 375–78.

*Additions and Amendments to Dostoevsky. 1961–63. Notes made when revising the Dostoevsky book for new editions (detailed amendments, instead of general critical and philosophical discussion). Russian *Collected Works, Vol. 6*, 301–67.

Problems of Dostoevsky's Poetics, trans. Caryl Emerson (Manchester: Manchester University Press, 1984); Russian, Fourth edition (Moscow: Sovetskaia Rossiia, 1979 [first publication, 1963]); reprinted in the Russian *Collected Works, Vol. 6*, 5–300.

*'On the Spiritualists (on the Problem of Dostoevsky)'. Early 1960s. Russian *Collected Works, Vol. 6*, 368–70.

The novel in stylistic terms (dialogism as heteroglossia): 1930 onwards

'Problems in the Stylistics of the Novel'. 1930. Single-page plan for a book. Russian *Collected Works, Vol. 3*, 6.

'Discourse in the Novel: On Issues in the Stylistics of the Novel', 1930–36. A short book (or long essay), generally known by the title alone. English translation is of an early, abridged version of the essay. *The Dialogic Imagination*, 259-422; Russian *Collected Works, Vol. 3*, 9–179.

'From the Prehistory of Novelistic Discourse'. 1940. Lecture delivered at the Gorky Institute in Moscow. Its original title was 'Discourse in the Novel' and it was retitled when published in Russia in 1975. *The Dialogic Imagination*, 41–83; Russian *Collected Works, Vol. 3*, 513–51.

*From the Prehistory of Novelistic Discourse (Saransk). 1967. Material added for the publication of the above in a Saransk collection. Russian *Collected Works, Vol. 3*, 552–53.

*'Discourse in the Novel: On Issues in the Stylistics of the Novel. Theses.' 1940. Russian *Collected Works, Vol. 3*, 554–56.

*'Multilanguagedness, as a Presupposition of the Development of Novelistic Discourse'. 1940. Russian *Collected Works*, Vol. 5, 157–58.

*'On the Stylistics of the Novel'. 1944–45. Russian *Collected Works*, Vol. 5, 138–40.

'Questions of Stylistics in Russian Language Lessons in Middle School'. 1944–45. 'Stylistics in Teaching Russian Language in Secondary School', *Journal of Russian and East European Psychology* 42, 6 (2004), 12–49; Russian *Collected Works*, Vol. 5, 141–56.

*'Language in Artistic Literature'. 1954. Russian *Collected Works*, Vol. 5, 287–97.

The novel in plot and narrative terms (Bildungsroman, chronotope, historical time, and contemporaneity): 1937 onwards

'The *Bildungsroman* and Its Significance for the History of Realism'. 1937. A long (35 pp.) outline for a book contracted for publication. The English translation is of a shorter version of this outline, amalgamated with some sections of 'On the *Bildungsroman*'. *Speech Genres and Other Late Essays*, 10–19; Russian *Collected Works*, Vol. 3, 181–217.

*On the *Bildungsroman*. 1937–39. So-called laboratory text, an extensive preparatory version of the *Bildungsroman* book. The second half of this draft text was reworked by Bakhtin in the early 1970s as the 'Forms of Time and of the Chronotope' essay. Sections of it were incorporated into 'The *Bildungsroman* and Its Significance in the History of Realism', *Speech Genres and Other Late Essays*, 19–59; Russian *Collected Works*, Vol. 3, 218–335.

'Forms of Time and of the Chronotope in the Novel'. 1937–38, conclusion added in 1973. The second half of the *Bildungsroman* draft, reworked. *The Dialogic Imagination*, 84–258; Russian *Collected Works*, Vol. 3, 341–511.

*'On the Emotive and the Familial-Biographical Novel'. 1937–39. Russian *Collected Works*, Vol. 3, 337.

*'On Questions of the Theory of the Novel'. 'On Questions of the Theory of Laughter'. On Mayakovsky. 1940–45. Russian *Collected Works*, Vol. 5, 48–62.

*On Flaubert. 1944–45. Russian *Collected Works*, Vol. 5, 130–37.

'The Novel as a Literary Genre'. 1941. Lecture delivered at the Gorky Institute in Moscow. Retitled 'Epic and Novel' in 1975, which is also the title of its English translation. *The Dialogic Imagination*, 3–40; Russian *Collected Works*, Vol. 3, 608–43.

*Theses for M. M. Bakhtin's Lecture 'The Novel as a Literary Genre'. 1941. Russian *Collected Works*, Vol. 3, 644–45.

*Appendix: The Concluding Words of M. M. Bakhtin at the Discussion following the Lecture 'The Novel as a Literary Genre'. 24 March 1941. Russian *Collected Works, Vol. 3*, 646–54.

*'On Questions in the Theory of the Novel: The Problem of Dialogue, of the Letter, and of Autobiography'. 1941. Another 'laboratory text', probably written in preparation for the 1941 lecture (although it ranges beyond it in topic). Russian *Collected Works, Vol. 3*, 557–607.

*'Problems in the Theory and History of the Novel'. Russian *Collected Works, Vol. 3*, 655–60.

*Appendix: The Novel. Russian *Collected Works, Vol. 3*, 661–67.

Works on Rabelais (popular-festive culture and the novel): 1938 onwards

'Satire'. 1940. Written as a commissioned encyclopaedia entry for volume 10 of the *Soviet Literary Encyclopedia*, which was never published. In Ilya Kliger and Boris Maslov (eds.), *Persistent Forms: Explorations in Historical Poetics* (New York: Fordham University Press, 2016), 369–91; Russian *Collected Works, Vol. 5*, 11–38.

François Rabelais in the History of Realism. 1940. A book, submitted as Bakhtin's doctoral thesis to the Gorky Institute. Preparatory materials for this version are listed directly below. Materials for the revision of the thesis (it was revised continually until 1950, and then again for publication in 1965) are listed in chronological order. Russian *Collected Works, Vol. 4 (1)*, 11–505.

*Notebooks for 'Rabelais'. 1938–39. Draft materials. Russian *Collected Works, Vol. 4 (1)*, 605–75.

*Sketch for a Conclusion. 1938–39. Russian *Collected Works, Vol. 4 (1)*, 677–80.

'Rabelais and Gogol (the Art of the Word and the Popular Culture of Laughter)'. 1940, revised 1970. In Henryk Baran (ed.), *Semiotics and Structuralism* (New York: International Arts and Sciences Press, 1977), 284–96; Russian *Collected Works, Vol. 4 (2)*, 517–22.

*On Questions of Historical Tradition and of the Popular Sources of Gogolian Laughter. 1940–45. Russian *Collected Works, Vol. 5*, 45–47.

'Additions and Amendments to "Rabelais"'. 1944. A long, somewhat ruminative set of thoughts and observations on the topics of the thesis, including some substantial discussion of Shakespeare, tragedy, and sentimentalism. This material did not make it into the revised thesis. Translated as 'Bakhtin on Shakespeare: Excerpt from "Additions and Changes to *Rabelais*"', *PMLA* 129, 3 (2014), 524–37; Russian *Collected Works, Vol. 4 (1)*, 681–731.

66 Works

*Menippean Satire and its Significance in the History of the Novel. 1944. Russian *Collected Works, Vol. 4 (1)*, 733–49.

*The Problem of the Continual Epithet. Russian *Collected Works, Vol. 4 (1)*, 751–52.

*Tales about Animals. 1944. Russian *Collected Works, Vol. 4 (1)*, 753.

*'The Work of Rabelais and the Problem of Popular Culture in the Middle Ages and Renaissance (Additions and Amendments to the Edition of 1949–1950)'. Russian *Collected Works, Vol. 4 (1)*, 517–601.

The Work of François Rabelais and the Popular Culture of the Middle Ages and Renaissance. 1965. (Moscow: Khudozhestvannaia literatura, 1965). Translated as *Rabelais and His World* (Bloomington, IN: Indiana University Press, 2009); reprinted in Russian *Collected Works, Vol. 4 (2)*.

Review of L. I. Pinsky, *Shakespeare's Dramaturgy – Fundamental Principles*. 1970. Russian *Collected Works, Vol. 6*, 440–50.

Reply to a Question from the Editors of *Novyi mir*. 1970. In *Speech Genres and Other Late Essays*, 1–9; Russian *Collected Works, Vol. 6*, 451–57.

Speech genres, utterances, and metalinguistics: 1953 onwards

'The Problem of Speech Genres'. 1953–54. *Speech Genres and Other Late Essays*, 60–102; Russian *Collected Works, Vol. 5*, 159–206.

Archival notes for the work 'The Problem of Speech Genres'. Russian *Collected Works, Vol. 5*, 207–86.

Dialogue. 3 pp. 1952?
Dialogue I – The Problem of Dialogical Speech. 10 pp. 1952.
Dialogue II. 23 pp. 1952. These notes include quotations from 'Discourse in the Novel', as if Bakhtin were revising it.
Preparatory materials. 27 pp. 1952–53.

*Language and Speech. 1957–58. Four-page notebook draft on philosophical significance of the language/speech distinction. *Dialog Karnaval Khronotop* 34 (2001), 23–31.

'The Problem of the Text'. 1959–60. *Speech Genres and Other Late Essays*, 103–18 (the remainder of the English text is taken from '1961. Notes'); Russian *Collected Works, Vol. 5*, 306–26.

Bibliographical details for collections of Bakhtin's works in English and Russian

The Dialogic Imagination, trans. Caryl Emerson and Michael Holquist (Austin: University of Texas Press, 1981).

Art and Answerability, trans. Vadim Liapunov and Kenneth Brostrom (Austin: University of Texas Press, 1990).
Speech Genres and Other Late Essays, trans. Vern W. McGee (Austin: University of Texas Press, 1986).
Sobranie sochinenii [*Collected Works*], Vol. 1: *Philosophical Aesthetics of the 1920s* (Moscow: Russkie slovari, 2003).
Collected Works, Vol. 2: *Literary Studies from the 1920s* (Moscow: Russkie slovari, 2000).
Collected Works, Vol. 3: *The Theory of the Novel (1930–1961)* (Moscow: Iazyki slavianskikh kul'tur, 2012).
Collected Works, Vol. 4 (1): *François Rabelais in the History of Realism* (1940), *Materials for the Book on Rabelais* (1930s–1950) (Moscow: Iazyki slavianskikh kul'tur, 2008).
Collected Works, Vol. 4 (2): *François Rabelais and the Popular Culture of the Middle Ages and the Renaissance* (1965), 'Rabelais and Gogol (the art of discourse and the popular culture of laughter)' (1940, 1970), Commentary and Notes (Moscow: Iazyki slavianskikh kul'tur, 2010).
Collected Works, Vol. 5: Works from the 1940s to the beginning of the 1960s (Moscow: Russkie slovari, 1996).
Collected Works, Vol. 6: *Problems of Dostoevsky's Poetics* 1963, Works of the 1960s and 1970s (Moscow: Russkie slovari, 2002.)

Some challenges, stemming from the above

Besides untranslated works, there are two significant differences between the works listed above and the existing corpus of English-language translations:

1. Some works were translated on the basis of Russian editions that we now know were defective. The texts in which these differences are most substantial are:

   'Author and Hero in Aesthetic Activity': there are several excisions (marked by an ellipsis in the English translation), each of which amounts to between one and three pages of text.
   'The Problem of Form, Content, and Material': the work's third introductory paragraph is missing, as is any indication that it was the first of a two-part series.
   'Discourse in the Novel': The English translation lacks the first page and a half of text (an introduction to the work), the final page and a half of text (its conclusion), various lines and paragraphs throughout the text, and the majority of the text's footnotes (which documented Bakhtin's reliance on German scholarship in particular).

'The Novel as a Literary Genre' ('Epic and Novel'): the opening paragraph is missing, the last paragraph has been severely abridged, and numerous lines and short paragraphs throughout the body of the text are missing.

'From the Prehistory of Novelistic Discourse': lines and paragraphs throughout are missing.

2. A number of works in English were made from texts that we now know were put together by editors, as composites of different texts.

'The *Bildungsroman* and Its Significance in the History of Realism': This text had two components. The opening section, roughly the first ten pages, is taken from the outline for a book with this title that Bakhtin prepared for a publisher in 1937. The remainder of the text was extracted from the long series of notes and drafts now titled 'On the *Bildungsroman*'.

'Towards a Reworking of the Dostoevsky Book'. This text is in fact the latter half of a notebook with the title '1961. Notes'.

'The Problem of the Text in Linguistics, Philology and the Human Sciences.' This text was a composite: its first half was a text now known in Russian as consisting of the work 'The Problem of the Text'; its second half was the first half of the notebook called '1961. Notes'.

'Towards a Methodology of the Human Sciences', 'From Notes Made in 1970–1971': These collections of notes and observations were extracted from four notebooks and some additional pages Bakhtin filled between the early 1960s and 1974. They were presented originally as collections authorised by Bakhtin himself; however, we now know that Bakhtin did not have anything to do with the selection and combination of extracts, which was probably the work of Vadim Kozhinov, one of Bakhtin's editors. As a consequence, not all of 'From Notes Made in 1970–71' are in fact from 1970–71. In the *Collected Works*, the four notebooks and the additional single sheets have been published as 'Working Notes from the 1960s and Early 1970s'.

The Concepts and Arguments

The table is set. In what follows, I present the reader with a systematic account of Bakhtin's most valuable ideas, an account that will make these ideas useful, while making the reader aware of the ambiguities and rough edges that characterise each of them. The divisions roughly correspond to the sections in the foregoing bibliography. In each case, I begin by describing how and where the idea(s) in question emerged in Bakhtin's writing. I then provide an exposition, defining the concept in detail. This is usually followed by a critique of the concept, in which I focus on possible objections to it and its ambiguities. I conclude each section with a summarising definition of the concept in question.

Author, Hero, Art, Responsibility

Exposition

Bakhtin's career begins with a claim that is, strictly speaking, phenomenological. It concerns how we perceive human feelings, ideas, and expressions in relation to the world around us. His claim is that there are two radically distinct modes of perceiving them: we perceive our own feelings, ideas, and expressions – the ideas, feelings, and expressions of an *I* – in a way absolutely distinct from the way we perceive the feelings, ideas, and expressions of *others*. One's own feelings and thoughts are experienced as a stream, something relentlessly pushed forward by life, by our needs, goals, and intentions, whereas those of *others* appear to us as expressed and embodied (we don't think the thoughts of others, but interpret them from their embodiment in words, gestures, bodily movement, facial expressions, and so on). As Bakhtin put it in 'Towards a Philosophy of the Act', there is a 'principled architectonic difference between my own singular uniqueness and the uniqueness of any other – aesthetic or actual – human being, between the concrete experiencing of myself and the experiencing of an other' (TPA 73/66). Bakhtin first mentions this 'architectonic' difference in this fragment, and he also makes clear that it's the acknowledgement, the recognition of this difference that makes ethics possible: an ethics that abstracts from this difference, that assumes the world is composed of homogeneous persons, will stall at the very beginning.[1] But Bakhtin goes into much greater detail about this distinction in the later fragment, 'Author and Hero in Aesthetic Activity'.

There Bakhtin distinguishes between the perspective of the *I-for-myself* and the *other-for-me* along three axes: differences in the experience of space, the experience of time, and the experience of meaning and value. The discussion of space starts in an interesting place: Bakhtin asks us to imagine 'a human being before me who is suffering. The horizon of his consciousness is filled by the circumstance that makes him suffer and by the objects which he sees in front of him' (AH 25/106). But *I* see a series of things he cannot:

> thus, the one suffering does not experience the fullness of his own external expressions, he experiences it only privately, in the language of internal sensations, he does not see his own muscles tensed by suffering, the whole plastically finished posture of his own body, the expression of suffering on his own face, he does not see the clear blue sky against the background of which his suffering external image is delineated for me. (AH 25/106)

The example of the suffering person is not lightly chosen. For the distinction between the way the suffering *I* perceives their feelings and the way someone outside them perceives them turns out to be central to Bakhtin's ethical philosophy. One acts ethically – 'responsibly', to use his preferred term – not as the simple result of identifying or empathising with someone who is suffering, not because you can internalise their *I*-experience of suffering, but as the result of what Bakhtin calls a 'return to myself, to my own place outside the one suffering' (AH 26/107): 'When I empathize with another's suffering, I experience it precisely as *his* suffering, in the category of the other, and my reaction to it is not a cry of pain but a word of comfort and the act of helping.' (AH 26/107). Ethical behaviour comes not from some Golden Rule or the universalising of one's self-regard ('do unto others as you would have them do unto you'), but from one's distance from others, a distance which for Bakhtin is the precondition of human concern and love.

As we pointed out in the previous chapter, this idea is not original to Bakhtin, but something he probably drew from either Hermann Cohen's writings, or a summary of Hermann Cohen's writings written by his friend Kagan. In *Religion of Reason Out of the Sources of Judaism*, Cohen argues that observation of another's suffering is not an inert experience, not an empirical observation made with a theoretical interest, because 'I make of it a question mark for my whole orientation to the moral world'.[2] In the words of the Cohen scholar Hartwig Wiedebach, Cohen 'describes compassion as an *active* feeling which engenders ethical responsibility'.[3] In 'Towards a Philosophy of the Act', Bakhtin will repeatedly claim that one's unique position in being is not something you can know or learn about – it is not a matter of 'knowledge' – but something you come to recognise or acknowledge. How? Bakhtin's mention of the suffering *other* points to one possible route. Following in Cohen's footsteps, he believes that compassion with another is what turns the merely different individual into someone distinctively *other* (what Cohen will call a Thou). But there will be another route as well, which Bakhtin explores at much greater length: verbal art, or literature.

The spatial distinctions between experience of one's *I* and experience of *others* are complemented by temporal ones, the most obvious being that

I cannot picture my own death or see my own life as an articulated whole. As for meaning, Bakhtin has in mind the meaningfulness, the significance of a person's actions. For the *I*, the act needs

> only the goals and values that govern it and give it meaning. My act-performing consciousness, as such, poses only the questions: for what, to what end, how, is this correct or not, is it necessary or unnecessary, should it be done or not, is it good or not, but never the questions: who am I, what am I, and what am I like? (AH 139/206–7)

Or, to put it more concisely, for the acting consciousness, 'its act needs no hero' (AH 139/206).

We perceive the acts of *others*, their behaviour and life course, very differently. Bakhtin notes that I come to know 'a considerable portion of my own biography from the alien words of people close to me [...] [w]ithout the narratives of others my life would not only lack fullness and clarity of content, but would also remain internally dispersed, lacking the value of *biographical unity*' (AH 154/218-19). Because 'my I-for-myself cannot *narrate* anything', we must rely on *others* to give our life a coherence and shape (AH 155/219). This may include, among other things, the delineation of a 'character', the production of 'the whole of the hero as a determinate personality' (AH 174/234). That character may be relatively stable or may change, and it is the narrating *other* who can tell the story of that change, by drawing together the acts of a person and the circumstances of their life. Bakhtin calls this process of narrating an *I*'s life *zavershenie*, a somewhat ambiguous term which has been variously translated into English as consummation, finalisation, completion, and finishedness. The point is that when we perceive human action and expression from outside, it can acquire a narrative wholeness and formal integrity it cannot generate for itself.

Hero, narration, character: even in this brief account it's clear that Bakhtin is talking less about our everyday perception of the human lives of others than about the way these lives are put together and represented in certain kinds of writing. Bakhtin will occasionally pause to tell us that authoring is just an extrapolation of othering, as when he claims that the 'excess of vision' that one has in relation to *others* is 'the bud in which form slumbers and from which it unfolds like a blossom' (AH 24/106). But the brief pauses cannot disguise the fact that Bakhtin's account of the way meaning is comprehended by the *other* is a discussion of literature, not everyday situations, elaborated in analyses of genres like biography, lyric poetry, novels, saints' lives, and so on. And if we look back for a moment, we'll remember that the initial announcement of the architectonic of *I* and *other* – found near the end of the fragment

'Towards a Philosophy of the Act' – actually follows an analysis contrasting authorial and heroic vision in Aleksandr Pushkin's poem 'Parting'.

Bakhtin's claim is that the central feature of literary writing, the feature that makes it literary, as opposed to scientific, political, and so on, is the relation it creates between 'author' and 'hero'. An author will first draw on the substance of a hero's consciousness – not only its particular values and perspectives, but also that forward-moving orientation that is part of the *I-for-myself*. The author then returns to its own place, its position outside the hero (its 'outsidedness' – *vnenakhodimost'*, Bakhtin calls it) and uses that perspective to aesthetically 'consummate' the life of the hero, to make whole what was only forward motion, to draw together expression and environment, to make sense of a life which, from the inside, appears dispersed and without coherence. The author, according to Bakhtin, thereby saves the hero by transforming its actions, characteristics, development over time, outward appearance, and relationship to its environment into elements of a self-contained and self-sustaining whole, a 'beautiful givenness' (AH 19/100), as he calls it. Bakhtin will resort to a number of contrasts and metaphors in order to describe this transformation. He will, for example, say that when the life of the hero is consummated by an author, its timing acquires a rhythm: '[t]he actual, fateful, risky absolute future is overcome by rhythm' (AH 117/189). Like music, the pace and emphases of a life can be seen as 'immanent', as part of its internal structure – in narrative, as the pacing and progress of a story – rather than a mere reaction to contingent needs and circumstances. He will also invoke the contrast of form and content: forward-directed life, aimed at the achievement of particular ends, is content, while the author is a 'uniquely active form-giving energy' (AH 8/91). In fact, for Bakhtin the author is not so much the individual who composes the text as the structure and shape of the composition itself, the form of the work.

There is a series of metaphors, however, that are more than metaphors. When speaking of rhythm, Bakhtin allows himself to call it 'an embrace of and kiss on the valued, embodied time of the mortal life of an other' (AH 120/192) and he will elsewhere characterise the author's activity as 'aesthetic love' (AH 11/94) (the latter term borrowed from Hermann Cohen).[4] He'll define artistic objectivity as 'artistic *kindness*' (AH 200/256) and define the artist as someone who not only leads their own life, but also 'loves it from without – where life is not for itself, where it is turned outward and needs an activity beyond its own meaning and place' (AH 191/248). The aesthetic work, by virtue of its drawing together an entire life, an entire hero, warts and all, successes and failures, and making it beautiful and lovable, redeems the necessarily fallen life of its hero. The parallel between the artwork and the religious notion of salvation and redemption is clinched when Bakhtin claims, almost in passing, that '[t]he divinity of the artist lies in their attachment to a supreme outsidedness' (AH 191/248), making art into the human correlate of the divine love for humankind. The correlation works both ways: art must become God-like to embody divine love, and God must become author-like to do the same: 'even God', Bakhtin remarks, 'had to incarnate himself in order to be merciful, to suffer and to *forgive*' (AH 129/198).

This is precisely the place where those, like Bocharov, who claim Bakhtin's work is 'aesthetics on the border of religious philosophy' have the strongest case.[5] Artistic activity seems to depend on religious faith in a 'supreme outsidedness', on the idea that the world as a whole and its human inhabitants in particular are objects of divine love, which is in its turn loaned out to authors. The nature and direction of that love, furthermore, may be shaped by Christ's teaching, for whom, as Bakhtin puts it, 'the I and the other are counterposed: absolute sacrifice for myself and mercy for the other.' (AH 56/133). In this particular respect, Bakhtin's version of the *I/other* distinction may, as Ruth Coates has observed, be grounded in the traditions of Russian Orthodoxy, which contrast the kenotic version of the *I*, which humbles itself before the *other*, with the autonomous or self-sufficient version of the *I* that pridefully imagines it has no need of an *other*.[6] But does this mean that L. A. Gogotishvili is right to claim that '[t]he ethical reality of Bakhtin' is part of an 'exclusively religious consciousness', which is 'lodged in Christianity'?[7] Not at all, and not only because what religion there is seems to come from at least a couple of different religions. Most of 'Author and Hero' is about authors and heroes, about how literary form captures and transforms life, without any kind of faith or belief coming into it. God may sit on the sidelines and offer encouragement and advice, but she never actually takes the field. For there the battle is between art and life, or sometimes between different kinds of art, not between faith and secularism.

Critique

Bakhtin's early writing about art is complex and fragmentary, raising many questions it cannot answer. There are two we should focus on.

The first is whether the phenomenological analysis of our experience leads to the split between the *I-for-myself* and *other-for-me* Bakhtin describes. After all, the whole project of this aesthetics depends on the notion of an *I* that requires the finalising, completing activity of an *other*. In Bakhtin's description, the *I* is constantly dispersed and on the move, a creature of goals and desire-directed action, whose satisfactions are necessarily brief and disappointingly earthly. It's the *other*/author who can make this creature whole, by narrating its life. The *I-for-myself* cannot narrate anything; all narration is the prerogative of the one who sees me as *other*.

There is good reason to doubt this account. It may do as a description of a particular historical experience of subjectivity: there may be historical moments in which a particular group of subjects feels dispersed, perhaps buffeted by the randomness of their own desires. But philosophical arguments over the last few decades have stressed the degree to which an *I*, simply to constitute itself as a subject at all, has to have some narrative framework for its own life.[8] Narrative is not an alien addition to the *I-for-myself*, but an essential part of it.

The second concerns the assumption that the study of literature should be grounded in philosophical aesthetics. Should we think of literary art as grounded in some inevitable phenomenological situation or as a cultural-historical phenomenon, the purposes and boundaries of which are shaped by the socio-historical world around it? The critic Raymond Williams pointed out that 'literature' and 'culture' took on the kind of baggage Bakhtin assigns them – the redemption, through form-giving, of a world torn apart by short-term practical action – in the wake of capitalist industrialisation. Before the early nineteenth century, literature was the domain of 'good writing' and printed knowledge in general, with no particular preference for the imaginative: it included the cognitive and the ethical, in Bakhtin's terms.[9] Similarly, culture was the tending of human faculties rather than a specific kind of activity. It was when capitalism and the creation of factory work seemed to strip the human from labour that imaginative writing took on a striking new significance. Terry Eagleton, in his study *The Ideology of the Aesthetic*, argued that the very category of the aesthetic, as it emerges in eighteenth-century Germany, takes on the force and importance it does because it appears to address so many of the central worries of class-divided societies, 'freedom and legality, spontaneity and necessity, self-determination, autonomy, particularity and universality, along with several others'.[10] Reading 'Author and Hero', it's hard not to think that Bakhtin is deriving his description of our experience of *others* from his account of literary art, rather than – as he claims – the reverse. But while Bakhtin is very interested in the history of literary forms, he is not ready to think of the aesthetic itself as having a history. At least not yet.

Summary

'Author' and 'hero' stand for two intersecting dimensions of a literary work. The hero is the thoughts and actions in the work understood as guided by knowledge, ethical considerations, and practical interests – that is, as elements of life. The author is the form of the work itself, which takes those actions and thoughts and reinterprets them as embodied in particular people, with particular surroundings, as part of a life story, and in a specific time and place. By virtue of this reinterpretation, these same thoughts and actions become interesting aesthetically: we understand them as interesting by virtue of what they contribute to a narrative or a literary description rather than by virtue of what they mean for the heroes or characters themselves. Because of authorial form, a sequence of actions that is tragic or unsettling in life may nevertheless be meaningful or satisfying as a narrative.

Dialogism as Polyphony

Exposition

The idea of 'dialogism' makes its debut in Bakhtin's 1929 study of Dostoevsky, where it appears as a peculiar and interesting form of the author/hero relationship. The first half of that book, as we have already noted, looks like a continuation of the work Bakhtin had been doing earlier in the decade. Dostoevsky's 'revolutionary innovation in the novel as an artistic form' (PDA 276/4) is the 'polyphonic novel', distinguished by what looks like a levelling or equalisation of the roles of author and hero. In the ordinary novel, Bakhtin claims, the hero is part of the world that the author represents and the hero's discourse – the words it speaks, whether quoted or rendered indirectly – is likewise a part of that represented world, an element in the author's grand design. By contrast, in Dostoevsky's writing the hero appears 'as if the hero were not the object of authorial discourse, but the bearer, fully valued and endowed with rights, of his own discourse' (PDA 5/7–8). 'In his works', Bakhtin says

> we do not find the unfolding of a multiplicity of fates and lives in a single objectified world, illuminated by a single authorial consciousness, but the combining of a *multiplicity of consciousnesses with equal rights and with their own worlds,* preserving their unmergedness, in the unity of a single event.[11]   (PDA 6/8–9)

Bakhtin notes that this distinctive trait of Dostoevsky's heroes has been acknowledged, albeit unknowingly, in the critical literature on Dostoevsky. For time and again, critics will argue with Dostoevsky's heroes, treating their ideologies not as character features, but as independent ideological positions with which one can and should engage.

The idea of dialogism and of the dialogical novel will evolve continuously from this point onwards in Bakhtin's writing, so it's important to distinguish the core idea of the dialogical from the specific 'polyphonic' form it has in Dostoevsky's novels. Dialogism will refer to any situation in which a unit of discourse (word, sentence, paragraph, speech) or an otherwise expressed idea has what Bakhtin calls 'dual directedness' (PDA 185/105): it is directed simultaneously at two different goals; it is meaningful in two different dimensions.[12] The author/hero relationship Bakhtin had discussed earlier manifested this dual directedness in embryo: the space, time, and events of a plot were interpreted simultaneously as elements of the 'life' of the hero (directed, therefore, at the hero's own goals, aspirations, and so on) and as elements of the authorial form of the work (directed, in this respect, at the work as an artistic whole: playing a distinctive role as part of a plot, as an element of an evolving character or of the world depicted in a text). In the polyphonic novel heroes partake of the same systematic ambivalence, but the scales are reweighted. What a hero does and says means something to the hero and means something within the literary work, but the literary work (embodying the authorial perspective) no longer dominates the hero, so that it appears as if the hero is on equal terms with it: the hero 'knows' it is part of a literary work and can address not just other characters within the work but the readers of the work as well. It's this apparent autonomy of the heroes that makes novels polyphonic.

But the independence of the heroic voice is not what it seems. After all, if you get into a political or philosophical debate with one of Dostoevsky's heroes – with Alyosha in *Brothers Karamazov* or Raskolnikov in *Crime and Punishment* – you are turning their discourse into something cognitive or ethical: you want to show it is right or wrong, morally correct or not, and so forth. But Bakhtin had insisted that Dostoevsky's 'revolutionary innovation' was a matter of the novel's 'artistic form', so if he's giving the voices of his heroes equal rights, this shouldn't be a matter of liberating them from the constraints of art, but of some different conception of art, a different idea of what it means to represent a hero's discourse artistically. Just how different this conception is can be gauged by a striking change in Bakhtin's vocabulary: the discourse of the heroes represented in Dostoevsky is described as – in fact, praised for being – *nezavershennyi*, *un*finished (perhaps 'unfinishable') or *un*consummated, which is the exact opposite of the *zavershennost'*, the finishedness, that authors gifted to their heroes in the 'Author and Hero' essay.

While it may look like the author is simply retiring from the scene in Dostoevsky's work, leaving the heroes to get on with their lives, in fact the author is even more active than it would be in an ordinary, 'monophonic' novel. When describing the 'artistic atmosphere' that the author creates in order to shape a hero's discourse, Bakhtin offers the following revealing description:

> Not a single element of such an atmosphere can be neutral: everything must touch the hero to the quick, provoke him, interrogate him, even polemicise with him and taunt him; everything must be addressed to the hero himself, turned toward him, everything must feel like *a discourse about someone present*, like the discourse of a "second" and not a "third" person.   (PDA 64/70)

The claim is vivid, but paradoxical. For while Bakhtin describes what is happening as if the author were a voice, a participant in a conversation – provoking, interrogating, and addressing the hero – the author does not exist as a voice here but as an 'atmosphere'. And, as it turns out, for the most part the author in Dostoevsky will not provoke the hero by actually speaking. As Brian Poole has shown in an article describing the book's sources, Bakhtin was heavily influenced by the German critic Herbert Spielhagen, who argued that novelists should avoid narrators who speak to their readers or comment on the action, that novels should show and not tell.[13] If there is a dialogical relationship between author and hero in Dostoevsky's works, it isn't generally visible in anything resembling an actual dialogue: what taunts and interrogates the hero is not the language of a speaker, but what Bakhtin will call the artistic atmosphere, or the author's '*scheme for discourse*' (PDA 63/70). The author of the polyphonic novel is not Dostoevsky or some narrator within the text: it is the very form of the text – its structure, its atmosphere, its plot.

Just how this amorphous author taunts the hero can be illustrated with a well-known passage from Dostoevsky's *Crime and Punishment*. Raskolnikov, the hero, has just received a long letter from his mother, who tells him that their financial woes are at an end, because Raskolnikov's sister Dunya (or Dunechka) has decided to accept the generous offer of the well-off Mr Luzhin to marry her, even though neither loves the other. Raskolnikov has just come from a session at the pub with Marmeladov, who has explained to him how his daughter Sonia has become a prostitute. After he has read the letter, Raskolnikov's mind is racing, and he runs outside and mutters to himself for several pages. The following is a brief excerpt of his reaction:

> ... Mother, well let her be, God bless her, that's how she is; but what about Dunya? I know you, Dunechka, my dear! You were going on twenty when we saw each other last: I already understood your character then. Mother writes that 'Dunechka can endure much'. I know she can!

> I knew it two and half years ago, and for two and a half years I've been thinking about that, precisely about that, that 'Dunechka can endure much'. If she was able to endure Mr Svidrigailov [a previous employer who tried to seduce her, KH], with all the consequences, then indeed she can endure much. And now they imagine, she and mother, that one can also endure Mr Luzhin, expounding his theory about the advantage of wives rescued from destitution by their benefactor husbands, and expounding it almost the moment they first met. Well, suppose he just 'let it slip', though he's a rational man (in which case maybe he didn't let it slip at all, but precisely meant to explain it then and there), but Dunya, what of Dunya? The man is clear to her, and she'll have to live with this man. She could eat only black bread and wash it down with water, but she would never sell her soul, she would never trade her moral freedom for comfort; she wouldn't trade it for all Schleswig-Holstein, let alone Mr Luzhin. No, Dunya was not like that as far as I knew her, and ... well, of course she's no different now! What's there to talk about? [...] And even if Mr Luzhin was made entirely of the purest gold, or a solid diamond, she still would not consent to become Mr Luzhin's lawful concubine. Then why has she consented now? What's the catch? What's the answer? The thing is clear: for herself, for her own comfort, even to save herself from death, she wouldn't sell herself; no, she's selling herself for someone else! For a dear, beloved person she will sell herself! That's what our whole catch consists of: for her brother, for our mother, she will sell herself! [...] Do you know, Dunechka, that Sonechka's lot is in no way worse than yours with Mr Luzhin?[14]

There are taunts at three different levels in this passage, and Raskolnikov responds to all of them. First, he taunts himself, insofar as he is asking questions (notionally addressed to his mother and sister) and then answering them. Second, he is taunted by the letter itself, which demands a careful and probing analysis: Raskolnikov lets us know that he understands the full and unpleasant import of the sentences 'Dunechka can endure much' and 'let it slip'. We read the letter (it is itself several pages long in the text) and Raskolnikov reads it alongside us, so to speak: he appears here not as a character merely reacting to the letter, but as a reader interpreting it, much as the reader of *Crime and Punishment* might interpret it. Finally, he is taunted by, and responds to, the events of the plot: Raskolnikov draws the parallel that the text asks us to draw, between the actions of his sister Dunya and those of the prostitute Sonia, whose story has conveniently preceded the arrival of this letter. Conveniently: because in this narrative, events take place in order to provoke or enlighten Raskolnikov. They are part of the 'scheme for discourse'.

Plot events exist 'to put the human being in different situations, which reveal and provoke him, to bring people together and make them clash' (PDA 276-77/100). You could say that the events of the plot are *addressed* to Raskolnikov and that he responds to them with discourse: quite a lot of discourse, as it happens (his response to the letter takes several pages). Addressed not only in the sense that they seem designed to provoke his thoughts (he learns of Sonia's fate so that he can make the comparison with Dunya's), but also in the sense that the events of the plot are continually mediated by people speaking or writing within the novel: Sonia's fall is related to Raskolnikov by Marmeladov in the pub, and Dunya's is conveyed through his mother's letter. Bakhtin will claim that in Dostoevsky's writing all events are filtered through the consciousness of the characters, and what this means in practice is that events are recounted from within the discourse of others, by means of sub-narratives (letters, stories, etc.) embedded within the larger one. As Bakhtin puts it, the hero 'does not think about phenomena, he speaks with them' (PDA 237/189). The hero's voice is 'fully-valued' when it is put on the same level as the narrative, when events are somehow converted into the same discursive stuff as the voice.

Can you design an entire plot around this kind of thing? On this question Bakhtin is somewhat sketchy. The 1929 version of the book on Dostoevsky does not, like the later version (the one translated into English) have a long chapter on Dostoevsky's debt to carnival and Menippean satire. In its place there is a very short chapter, in which Bakhtin tries to describe the kind of plot that makes polyphonic novels possible. For the most part he describes this plot form, which he calls 'the adventure plot', by contrasting its emphasis on 'eternal human nature' (PDA 99) with the rigid social determinism of the traditional European novel. In the 'social-psychological, quotidian, family and biographical novel', Bakhtin says, social and familial identities 'constitute the hard all-determining basis of all plot relations' (PDA 98). The adventure plot used by Dostoevsky, conversely, is mere 'clothing that dresses the hero', creating opportunities for what 'would be unpredictable and unexpected' (PDA 99). In the former, 'heroes, as heroes, are generated by the plot itself' (PDA 98); in the latter, '[t]he authentic bonds begin where the plot ends, having fulfilled its secondary function' (PDA 277/100).

To some extent, the problem is simply insuperable. Bakhtin wants the polyphonic novel to synthesise two fundamentally distinct modes of expression: dialogue, with its give-and-take, responsive structure, on the one hand; and narrative, with its chronological, successive structure, on the other. But he makes matters harder for himself by identifying the very idea of narrative, of a logical, ordered succession of events with the 'monological novel' – apparently the European norm – and then digs himself in even deeper by identifying this monological narrative, governed by 'plot-pragmatic connections of an objective or psychological order' (PDA 7/10) with a scientific, objectifying worldview, with 'the ideological work of modernity' (PDA 82/79). If narrative is an inherently monological form, in which scientific causality binds one event to the next, then it's hard to see how it can be dialogised.

Bakhtin could not find a way out of the corner he had painted himself into, which required a less 'scientific' concept of narrative (a concept like Roland Barthes's, for example, according to which narrative events are bound not by causality, but by a 'relation of solidarity', a 'confusion of consecutiveness and consequence' that seems to compel one event to follow from another, to ensure that 'the struggle' leads to 'a victory', for example, although struggles don't 'cause' victories).[15] Of one thing, however, he was certain: that, however these narratives worked, they pushed the hero into an uncomfortable place, in which the stakes were high but the way forward unclear. In Dostoevsky, Bakhtin argues, 'the communion of this *I* with *another* and with *others* takes place directly on the ground of ultimate questions, bypassing all intermediate and local forms' (PDA 280/240–41). Ultimate questions, which seems to mean questions not couched within a particular way of life, but questions that put an entire way of life in play, that potentially upend the hero's understanding of himself and his world. In 1929, Bakhtin was better at emphasising the high stakes than at figuring out how these questions could be embodied in a narrative, but it's clear that he kept working at it. *Problems of Dostoevsky's Art* spends fifty pages or so trying to define the author/hero relationship in Dostoevsky, but Bakhtin continued to gnaw away at the problem, in notes prepared for the revision of the book first in the 1940s, and then again in the 1960s (when he had been invited, first by the Italian press Einaudi and then by a Soviet publisher, to prepare a revised edition), and finally with the revised *Problems of Dostoevsky's Poetics* from 1963.

In a notebook composed in the 1940s, Bakhtin noted '[t]he absence of inner space (of the *intérieur*) in Dostoevsky. All action, all events are accomplished *on the threshold*.'[16] While in everyday life we are surrounded by the 'warm and dense masses of the world', Dostoevsky puts his heroes on 'the narrow space of the threshold, a boundary, where it is not possible to settle in, find comfort'.[17] The threshold was literal – foyers, landings, doorframes – and metaphorical: in 1963, he would claim that Dostoevsky 'always represents the human being *on the threshold* of a final decision, at the moment of *crisis*, at an unfinishable – and *unpredeterminable* – turning point for his soul' (PDA 61/71).

The identification of the threshold and the moment of crisis with 'unfinishability' [*nezavershennost'*] is crucial for two reasons. First, because it reminds us that Dostoevsky's heroes don't become autonomous by being left to get on with their lives, but by virtue of narratives that push them into a corner. In this text, unfinishability takes the place of 'becoming', standing for the orientation to the future that characterises literary work.

Second, because this sense of crisis will turn out to be the thread that binds Part One of the Dostoevsky book – 'Dostoevsky's Polyphonic Novel' – with Part Two of the book, 'Discourse in Dostoevsky'. Let's borrow one more quotation from the early 1960s:

> The hero in Dostoevsky takes part in the world dialogue *completely*, with his entire being: by means of his discourse, his act, his face, eyes, body, by means of every gesture, by means of his silence, even by means of his death (by suicide). The heroes in Turgenev *live*, realize their social and individual fate (which fully consummates them), and they also, *incidentally*, argue. For Dostoevsky's heroes their whole life and fate is dissolved into argument, into the dialogical position they occupy.[18]

'Their whole life and fate is dissolved into argument': for in the end, the crisis or threshold experience of Dostoevsky's heroes will find its most precise and vivid expression in the language they use.

Problems of Dostoevsky's Art is the moment at which Bakhtin, taking his cue from Voloshinov, makes a linguistic turn: he takes a project in aesthetics, focused on the relationship between author and hero, aesthetic form and 'life', and reworks it as a project in literary stylistics. The turn is made in two steps: a short, initial foray in Part One and the plunge taken in Part Two. The heroes Bakhtin described in 'Author and Hero' were bodies located in space and time, inhabited by spirit and soul. But in Part One of the 1929 book the hero is redescribed as *'pure voice'* (PDA 53/63). 'Voice' is an intermediate or syncretic concept in Bakhtin, capturing both the bodily presence of the hero-as-other and the hero's conversion into something linguistic. In Part Two, Bakhtin will argue that the shaping of these voices, their emergence in a prose text, depends on the creation of a distinctive literary style.

The style will be named 'double-voiced discourse': speech that is at once directed towards its own object (the living speech of a hero, cognitive or ethical in intent) and somehow redirected by the work of an author. Two 'voices', authorial and heroic, in a single line of discourse. The concept is metaphorical in two respects. First, of course, in describing the distinctive speech manner of the hero, or the distinctive ideological position of the hero (it is never clear which) as 'voice'; second, in describing the literary reworking or refracting of that heroic language as the addition of a second authorial voice. The metaphors imply that this particular style embodies or represents some kind of conversation between author and hero, even though, as we shall see, for the most part only the hero speaks.

Dostoevsky's prose will be distinguished by its extensive and elaborate use of this double-voiced discourse; in fact, its invention is what specifically constitutes his 'revolutionary innovation in the novel as an artistic form'. Bakhtin will cash out the claim in a series of detailed analyses of the speech of Dostoevsky's heroes: Devushkin in *Poor Folk*, Golyadkin in *The Double*, the Underground Man from *Notes from the Underground*, Raskolnikov in *Crime and Punishment*, Alyosha in *Brothers Karamazov*. In each instance, Bakhtin demonstrates, very persuasively, that the discourse of the hero is constantly marked, thrown off course, even distorted by 'the intense anticipation of another's discourse' (PDA 205/137). Characters will constantly anticipate objections, answer defensively to an imagined interlocutor, strive to justify their position or worldview with a little too much vigour, as if they were constantly under threat. Their language will take shape, in Bakhtin's wonderful phrase, as words with 'a sideward glance' (PDA 205/137), as words that are never sure of themselves, because they embody 'the whole life and fate' of the one uttering them. The sense of crisis is manifested as a constant lack of sureness, a constant sense of an author that provokes and questions, a constant need to justify.

But here's an interesting thing. Bakhtin describes these speeches as examples of 'hidden polemic', 'hidden dialogue', 'the word with a sideward glance' (PDA 199/127) and the descriptions seem wholly justified, for these examples of discourse actually do sound as if the speaker were aware of an imaginary other, an authorial presence that constitutes the invisible half of a conversation. But at the very beginning of Part Two, Bakhtin lumps this kind of style in with what look like very different kinds of speech. 'There exists', he says, 'a group of artistic-speech phenomena that at the present time have begun to attract the special attention of investigators. These are the phenomena of stylisation, parody, *skaz*, and dialogue.' 'All these phenomena', Bakhtin claims, 'despite the essential differences among them, share one common feature: discourse in them has a twofold direction – towards the referential object of speech, as in ordinary discourse, and towards *another's discourse, towards someone else's speech*' (PDA 185/105).

The investigators Bakhtin had in mind were the Russian Formalists. Boris Eikhenbaum had been fascinated by the comic play with language typical of *skaz*, the use of a distinctively 'oral' narrator, often a foolish, comic, digressive narrator.[19] Iurii Tynianov, another Formalist, had focused attention on parody, the comic mocking and exaggeration of a style of speech (and he had plenty of material, as Soviet Russian writers had been producing parodies at an impressive rate in the 1920s).[20] Bakhtin was making a daring raid on their territory, claiming that parody, *skaz*, and stylised language were fundamentally akin to Dostoevsky's hidden dialogues, all species of the same genus, 'double-voiced discourse'. It's a proposal he fleshes out in the first twenty-odd pages of Part Two of the book (titled 'Types of Prosaic Discourse') and which receives its boldest expression in a notoriously elaborate table that lays out the possible range of literary styles (PDA, 199/127). At one end of the table, we find the single-voiced discourse of an ordinary narrator, describing a world and its events, and at the other, the 'active type' of double-voiced discourse, which finds its paradigmatic expression in the looping, uncertain language of Dostoevsky's hidden dialogues. In between: what are implicitly the passive types of double-voiced discourse – stylisation, parody, *skaz*, and so on – which, so to speak, bask in the reflected double-voiced glory of their Dostoevskian cousins. Viewed in retrospect, you can see that Bakhtin is mapping out the territory he will occupy in 'Discourse in the Novel', in which parody and stylised language will become the exemplary actors in dialogism, rather than extras, as they are here. But did the classification actually make sense? We'll consider that below.

Nevertheless, there are two respects in which the polyphonic dialogism of Dostoevsky's work differs from the 'novelistic' dialogism Bakhtin will describe in the 1930s. The double-voicedness of Dostoevsky's heroes does not entail any stylistic differentiation of their language. In the later, revised version of the text, Bakhtin inserted a passage noting that '[in] Dostoevsky's multivoiced novels, for example, there is significantly less language differentiation, that is, fewer styles of language, territorial and social dialects, professional jargons and so forth, than in the work of many writer-monologists – Lev Tolstoy, Pisemsky, Leskov, and others' (PDP, 182/211). It also is clear that Dostoevsky's dialogical novels don't necessarily feature dialogues *between* heroes – the critical feature is the way in which a hero's speech is dialogically provoked by the narrative as a whole and the way in which the hero, as a consequence, seems to address the reader directly, just as the author might.

Critique

Problems of Dostoevsky's Art was the only book Bakhtin managed to publish near the time it was written, and it immediately provoked critical reactions. Some of these were vulgarly party-political, complaints that Bakhtin had not aligned Dostoevsky clearly enough with a particular political tendency. But to the extent there was a common point of worry, it was over the central claim that Dostoevsky's novels were composed of multiple voices with 'equal rights'.

If this was truly the case, then, the reasoning seemed to go, there could be no authorial position that unified the whole. A review in the Soviet journal *Oktiabr*, therefore, argued that Bakhtin had been taken in by appearances – he had failed to discern, behind the multi-voicedness in Dostoevsky's works, 'a *unified* class voice'.[21] The converse position was argued by A. V. Lunacharskii, the former Commissar of the Enlightenment, who, in a long and serious review, admitted the claim of multivoicedness, but said its logical consequence was that Dostoevsky's novels had no overarching unity, each novel was like 'an orchestra not only without a conductor, but also without a composer, whose score could be performed'.[22] The idea of heroes with equal rights sounded appealing, but it wasn't clear what it could actually mean.

When Bakhtin came to revise the book for republication in the early 1960s, he therefore knew that he needed 'to deepen the analysis of the specificity of dialogue and the position of the author in the polyphonic novel (the latter more than anything else has called forth objections and misunderstandings)'; the revision notebooks are accordingly littered with discussions of the 'position of the author'.[23] In 1929 the issue was Dostoevsky's revolutionising of the form of the novel; in the 1960s, with another thirty years of philosophising to draw on, he turned Dostoevsky's achievement into the index of a much larger question, the question of what it meant for human consciousness to be autonomous in the first place. You needed an active author to represent the consciousness of a hero, Bakhtin argued, because no human consciousness could be fully autonomous on its own to begin with. Human consciousness lived on the border with other consciousnesses, that is, its very existence depended on interaction with others, so its representation could never be a mere passive description of it. 'I am conscious of myself and I become myself only when revealing myself for another, through another, and with the help of another' (61N 287/343). Because a person has 'no inner sovereign territory' (61N 287/344), there is, strictly speaking, nothing to represent before or outside of the author's attempt to engage the hero dialogically.

As Bakhtin's editor, Sergei Bocharov, has observed, 'in striving to make precise and to strengthen his idea about the (unusual for a classical novel) freedom of the hero in relation to the author in Dostoevsky, MMB relied on the key opposition "personality – thing"'.[24] Bocharov was thinking in particular of a short piece Bakhtin wrote in the early 1940s, 'Towards Philosophical Foundations for the Human Sciences', which explored the difference between '[k]nowledge of the thing and knowledge of the personality' (TPhFHS 7). There Bakhtin contrasted knowledge of the 'dead thing' (TPhFHS 7), exemplified by natural science, which could be more or less precise, with knowledge of a 'personality', for which the idea of precision was wholly inappropriate. The human sciences, sciences that aimed to understand and interpret human actions and language, aimed for penetration and depth, for a richness of understanding that depended in large part on being able to see through the eyes of the one whose actions or language you were seeking to understand. The object of such sciences was not natural being, but *'expressive and speaking* being' (TPhFHS 8), which demanded a unique method and approach.

In many respects Bakhtin was echoing what had become the common sense of the social sciences, sociology and anthropology in particular. You can't analyse a human action without knowing what it means or what is intended by it. If you see someone raising a hand, the bare physical action is not a 'fact' for the social sciences: you need to know if they are hoping to be called on in class, waving to a friend, asking someone to stop, threatening someone, and so on. In short, the action needs to be made meaningful, and you do this by supplying a social context and an intention. It was this that made sociology, in Max Weber's famous phrase, 'a science concerning itself with the interpretative understanding of social action', which assumes that for all action 'the acting individual attaches a subjective meaning to his behavior'.[25]

Of course, Weber knew that the subjective meaning an individual attached to their behaviour was not necessarily the same as the meaning it had for society in general: actions had unintended meanings, just as they might have unintended consequences. But Bakhtin limited the force of subjective meaning in a different way. He had, as we've seen, insisted that understanding 'expressive and speaking being' depends on acknowledging a fundamental distance between *I* and *other*, a distance between the one who understands and the one whose actions and language are understood. The distance was necessary for being to express anything at all, in Bakhtin's view, because from within the consciousness of the one acting, actions were not invested with a settled meaning, but with desire, with forward movement, with a drive to accomplish something. It was, ironically, the *other* or author, who, by virtue of their distance, could endow action and words with subjective meaning, and to the extent that the *I* managed this, it was because it borrowed or learned the meaning of its external action or expression from the *others* around it.

This might explain why in 'Towards Philosophical Foundations for the Human Sciences', Bakhtin speaks of the 'significance of sympathy and love' in the relation between knower and known and claims that '[w]hat is important here is the secret and the lie (rather than the error)' (TPhFHS 7). For, in a sense, knowledge of a personality is an ethical and a cognitive achievement at the same time. To ascribe a combination of settled traits to a person is to make them a stable 'character'; by contrast, to treat the person as a 'personality' is to assume they are permanently on the move, a spontaneously developing and evolving being that changes either partially or dramatically in response to the others around them. From this point of view, the truth of a personality is not a property or a characterisation that one could determine, but its free and spontaneous development, which is made possible by an environment of supportive (but perhaps also probing, interrogating) *others* or authors. The reality of subjectivity, what needs representing, is this development, and that is why what looks like Dostoevsky's constant interrogation of the heroes is in fact the 'objective-realistic, sober, prosaic depiction' (PDA 277/101) of their personalities. In this context, we can also understand precisely what Bakhtin means when he claims in 'Towards Philosophical Foundations for the Human Sciences' that 'self-discovering being' is 'free' and that human spirit 'discloses itself freely for our act of cognition' (TPhFHS 8). Freedom does not have its familiar liberal meaning here – it is not what Isaiah Berlin called 'negative liberty', the 'area within which a man can act unobstructed by others'.[26] Freedom is the condition when *I* and *other* have a relationship that allows each to disclose or discover itself, which means not to uncover something already there, but to move further in its quest to understand its place and justification in the world. It's therefore a condition of the hero's freedom that there is an author there to provoke and interrogate it (but not to demean it): the hero only has 'equal rights' or 'full value' in the presence of such an author.

But, of course, there are many different ways for a personality to tread life's narrow path, and Dostoevskian personalities did not take the usual one. They did not evolve along the lines of the classic European scheme of *Bildung* (formation), in which the ardent youth gradually learns the way of the world and settles down to a modest, but satisfying bourgeois existence. They did not learn the value of compromise or about the need to damp down one's aspirations. In Bakhtin's view, their personalities developed only by virtue of crisis situations, brought on by extreme circumstances (murder, as in *Crime and Punishment* or *Brothers Karamazov*), by their lack of grounding and status in the society around them (as in the Underground Man or the poor clerk in *Poor Folk*), or by fear of public judgement. It is not, significantly, sympathy and unconditional love that prompt these heroes to dialogical self-doubt. And, even more significantly, the crisis situation is not designed to lead the hero to some resolution or reconciliation, to a sense of equipoise or resignation – the uncertainty and discomfort is the desired endpoint. The self-consciousness of the Dostoevskian hero, Bakhtin says, 'lives by virtue of its unfinishability, its unclosedness and its indeterminacy' (PDA 53/63).

The language in which Bakhtin describes this heroic spirit – 'unfinishability', 'indeterminacy', and so on – disguises the continuity in his thought. The unfinishedness that characterises the consciousness of Dostoevsky's heroes and the style of their language is what we had earlier described as 'becoming', triggered by a Messianic conception of history. As we'll see, the motive force for this becoming shifts and morphs as Bakhtin thinks more deeply and extensively about the novel. In *Problems of Dostoevsky's Art*, it is crisis, the experience of the threshold, that drives language forward. In the early 1930s, it will be the power of heteroglossia that accomplishes this. In the later 1930s, it will be the future that pulls language towards it.

For the time being, however, this becoming depends on the most extreme pressure on the discourse of the hero, whose 'whole life and fate is dissolved into argument'. The events of the plot cannot furnish a solid background, a valued or interesting way of life for the action of the hero: they have to taunt him, so that his path within the text becomes a kind of test. Who conducts the test? You could say 'the author', but what Bakhtin means by 'author' is not anything like a person or speaker – it is the invisible form of the work, which is not a recognisable voice in the same sense as a character or hero might have a voice. By calling the form of the work, including its plotting and narrative structure, 'author', Bakhtin wanted to make clear that the 'artistic, structural elements of the novel' of the work were somehow caught up in a dialogue, that they did not create a solid background of certainties within which the heroes would conduct themselves.

That uncertainty is clearly captured in the many 'hidden dialogues' and 'words with a sideward glance', and 'words with a loophole' Bakhtin analyses in *Problems of Dostoevsky's Art*. Raskolnikov, as we pointed out in our example above, creates dialogues with imagined interlocutors, anticipates the reactions of others, and even anticipates the reader's interpretation of events. Is it also captured by parody, stylisation, and *skaz*? In these speech phenomena, there are no imaginary interlocutors or anticipations; they are what happens when 'the author [uses] an alien discourse for its own purposes, by inserting a new intention into a discourse that already has and preserves its own referential intention' (PDA 189/111). Such styles may have, as Bakhtin claims, 'two intentions, two voices' (PDA 189/111), but the sense of uncertainty and crisis is absent. The authorial voice, which would be the critical, satirical note we find in parody or the exaggeration of certain features we find in stylisation, does not provoke or interrogate, does not elicit a reaction from discourse of the hero (the discourse being stylised or parodied). If you parody a way of speaking or endow your narrator with some strange quirks and verbal tics (as happens in *skaz*), the way of speaking or the narrator doesn't find itself pushed onto some existential precipice. Given how little these newly enlisted forms contribute to the overall project of Dostoevsky – crisis, unsureness, ultimate questions – it's not surprising that in the many analyses that follow Bakhtin's classification of styles there is relatively little discussion of parodic discourse, of stylisation, or of *skaz*.

If anything, Bakhtin gives us good reason to think that *skaz*, parody, and stylisation *wouldn't* be adequate vehicles of crisis. Stylisation focuses on an established style, understood as 'the sum total of devices in an alien form of speech, precisely as the expression of a particular point of view' (PDA 189/112). *Skaz* should be understood, Bakhtin says, as 'an *alien voice*, a socially defined voice, bearing a series of points of view and evaluations that the author needs' (PDA 192/115). Parody can be aimed at 'an alien socially-typical or individually characterological manner of seeing, thinking and speaking' (PDA 194/118). In other words, these kinds of double-voiced discourse work in precisely that thicket of 'intermediate and local forms' that Dostoevsky bypasses for the ultimate questions. If there is an authorial intention here, it's aimed at social questions, historical questions, questions of character, not at the 'ultimate questions.' Bakhtin would have to rework and reorientate his theory to make sense of these phenomena; which, indeed, was his next step.

Summary

Dialogical writing is, on the one hand, a matter of style – the nervous hidden dialogue, words with sideward glances that constantly anticipate the reactions and judgements of an (imaginary) interlocutors – and, on the other hand, the relationship between 'author' and 'hero', between narrative frame and heroic action and speech. In a dialogical novel, the events of the plot don't follow a purely causal logic, but seem guided by the project of provoking, testing, and interrogating the hero. In this way they make the discourse of the hero 'fully valued' and the hero itself autonomous.

Dialogism as Heteroglossia

Exposition

Bakhtin was sent into exile in the 1930s, and he reacted by producing what might be his most interesting, well-known, and important work, the long essay 'Discourse in the Novel'. He had started making plans to elaborate and broaden his study of Dostoevsky almost as soon as it was published in 1929. On 25 March 1930 – four days before leaving for Kustanai – Bakhtin composed a plan for a book, in six chapters, titled *Problems in the Stylistics of the Novel*.[27] The book was going to make the claim for a distinctive 'stylistics of the novel', which it would explain in its opening chapters and cash out in a final chapter devoted to analyses of the modern French, German, and Russian novel. It divided up the kinds of 'artistic prosaic discourse' in much the same way the Dostoevsky book had done: direct discourse, objectifying discourse, and both an active type and a 'conventionalising type' of double-voiced discourse. There would be chapters on the types of authorial and heroic discourse, on the different ways of representing the speech of others, and on how various 'semantic-stylistic unities', that is, different styles from extra-literary sources such as letters, could be incorporated into the novel yet subordinated, made to serve the 'stylistic unity of the novel as a whole'.[28]

The eventual book on stylistics – for 'Discourse in the Novel' in fact described itself as a book, not an essay – would look very different. Maybe just as importantly, it would *sound* very different: militant and energetic, combining dramatic theoretical claims about the nature of language with enthusiastic political cheerleading for the dialogical novel, which appears as the genre that would make modern life modern and free us permanently from every form of authoritarianism. It is worth listing the differences between this book and Bakhtin's book on Dostoevsky before elaborating on them:

1. The linguistic turn is completed. The dialogical relationship that defines Dostoevsky's prose is between author and hero, although Bakhtin will often classify both author and hero as voices. In 'Discourse in the Novel', dialogism is a purely stylistic affair: the author becomes the 'higher stylistic unity' of the novel while the heroes morph into the novel's constituent 'socio-ideological languages' or 'styles'. Also, dialogism is no longer something that only happens in literature, but is a constitutive but unrecognised feature of language as such.
2. In the study of Dostoevsky, the opposite of the dialogical novel is the monological novel. In 'Discourse in the Novel', the opposite is 'poetry' and, later in the book, authoritative discourse and myth.
3. Poetry and myth aren't simply problems – they are enemies, hostile forces that must be overcome in a large-scale cultural struggle. The opposition between them and the novel is now politicised, so that monological culture is allied with forces of socio-ideological centralisation (i.e., the state), and dialogism is allied with a democratic popular culture originating in the Middle Ages.
4. The monological perspective is no longer identified with modernity and science. Dialogism and the novel now occupy that space: they date their

90   Works

>   flowering to the Renaissance, are considered equivalent to science, and
>   have become the advance cultural forces of modernity. As a consequence,
>   monologism is redefined as something distinctly *un*modern, as a residual,
>   antiquated form of authority, the ultimate source of which is ancient myth.
> 5. It is no longer the frazzled, uncertain hero, plagued by the ultimate
>   questions, that drives everything forward and renders it unfinalisable. That
>   role is now taken up by 'heteroglossia', which embodies an endless
>   'historical becoming'.
> 6. The paradigm of the dialogical is now precisely those forms of double-
>   voiced discourse, parody and stylisation, that were deemed weaker versions
>   of dialogism in the earlier work.

The how of this change is easier to pin down than the why. Was the new, political tone a reaction to Bakhtin's arrest and exile and to the increasingly deadly grip of Stalinism in Soviet life? Was it in some way a response to the horrific situation around him – as Kustanai reeled from the deadly combination of collectivisation and famine? It's hard not to conclude that the urgent tone reflected a desperate world. But many of the changes noted above seem to be rooted in what Bakhtin had been reading, either in the early 1930s or as a kind of delayed reaction to material in the 1920s. The footnotes to the text reveal he had read rather a lot: German critical works on technical features of the novel; a good deal of Russian Formalism; some sociology of language; and works in aesthetics and the philosophy of language, in particular Gustav Shpet's work and the volume of Ernst Cassirer's *Philosophy of Symbolic Forms* devoted to 'Language'.[29] The footnotes: of which only a few are found in the English translation, because it is based on a heavily edited version of the text from which most of the references had been removed (including nearly all references to German sources and some to French ones), making Bakhtin sound more original, and intellectually stranded, than he actually was.[30]

'Discourse in the Novel' starts out boldly. It does not ask us merely to focus attention on some new and interesting phenomena in artistic prose. Instead, it claims that we have completely failed to understand the style of the novel, and that we have failed because we do not understand language in general. To grasp the distinctive achievement of the novel, to understand in what precise way '[t]he novel is an *artistic* genre' (DN 269/23), we therefore need a new, dialogical philosophy of language. Nor is this new philosophy of language only relevant to literary criticism, for the novel is the advance guard of 'a radical revolution in the fates of human discourse: the fundamental liberation of cultural-semantic and expressive intentions from the power of a single and unified language, and, as a consequence, the loss of a feeling for language as myth' (DN 367/122). The novel has made possible a new relationship with language, has enabled us to participate in what Bakhtin will later call the 'third dimension of language; a new mode in the life of language'.[31] But if we do not grasp what the novel does, we're in danger of being left behind.

What stands between us and this new mode in the life of language is a false conception of language, the conception of language as a shared system of forms that individuals then deploy. In that conception, 'style is understood as *the individualisation of a common language* (in the sense of a system of common linguistic norms)' (DN 264/16). To see style as the idiosyncratic practice of a particular writer, reflecting their individual subjectivity, is to think of language as a reservoir of neutral forms from which the speaker or author selects at will. Bakhtin believes that poetic language, in theory and practice, treats language as if it were that kind of reservoir. But language, Bakhtin argues, is not organised that way. The writer does not choose from a reservoir of forms, each carrying a meaning (and a series of possible relationships to other forms). What the writer faces is an internally riven linguistic world, fractured by differences of linguistic form and habit, a world Bakhtin calls 'heteroglossia'. It's defined in the following famous paragraph:

> The inner stratification of a single national language into social dialects, group mannerisms, professional jargons, generic languages, the languages of generations and age-groups, the languages of political tendencies and parties, the languages of authorities, the languages of circles and passing fashions, the languages of socio-political days and even hours (every day has its own slogan, its own vocabulary, its own accents): this inner stratification of every language at every given moment of its historical existence is a necessary prerequisite for the genre of the novel – by means of social heteroglossia and the individual multivoicedness that grows on its ground the novel *orchestrates* all its themes, the whole objective, meaningful world represented and expressed in it. (DN 262–63/15).

'The active literary consciousness', Bakhtin claims, 'always and everywhere (in all the historical literary epochs known to us) finds "languages", rather than language. It is confronted by the necessity of *having to choose a language*' (DN 295/48). The novel, therefore, does not speak directly, as though language was transparent, but 'orchestrates' its themes. But perhaps we can tweak this metaphor and think of the novel as the conductor of the orchestra (rather than the composer of the piece), who does not express themselves directly, by playing an instrument, but through the coordination and organisation of those who are playing. As Bakhtin puts it a few pages earlier, '*the style of the novel is its combination of styles; the language of the novel is a system of "languages"'* (DN 262/15).

These are provocative, fascinating claims. On their basis Bakhtin will develop a very new idea of dialogism, one that looks quite different from the idea of dialogism in his book on Dostoevsky. In 1929, the double-directedness of dialogical prose was generated by heroes in a state of permanent crisis, whose interaction with the novel's form 'takes place directly on the terrain of ultimate questions, bypassing all intermediate and local forms'. Five years later, it is precisely those intermediate and local forms, the forms that populate heteroglossia, that furnish the basis for dialogism.

But the idea of heteroglossia, the idea that a national language is stratified into social dialects, group mannerisms, and so on, was neither new nor original to Bakhtin. It had been a continuous theme in Soviet linguistics in the mid to late 1920s and early 1930s. Linguists who worked at or were associated with ILIaZV, where Voloshinov worked, had become particularly interested in social dialects (dialects defined by social rather than geographical criteria) and similar phenomena such as professional jargons[32] Bakhtin would have been aware of the work either directly or through Voloshinov (Zhirmunskii's *National Language and Social Dialects* and Iakubinskii's 'On Dialogical Speech' are cited in his footnotes). Forty years later, the study of social and class dialects would become a crucial movement in Europe and North America, under the rubric of sociolinguistics. The American linguist William Labov would, in the 1960s, conduct studies of class differences in the English spoken in New York City and of the variety of English spoken by African Americans in other US cities.[33] Other sociolinguists would map variations in pronunciation, vocabulary, syntax, or forms of address onto differences in social class, racial classification, gender, age, and other social variables. But sociolinguistics also had a political point, captured in the title of Labov's famous article, 'The Logic of Nonstandard English': it proved that nonstandard varieties of the language, often spoken among groups with little political or social power, were not lazy or error-ridden, but just as systematic and rule-governed as 'standard' English.[34]

Bakhtin's sociolinguistic insights point in a somewhat different direction. It would be a mistake to think of heteroglossia as the division of a particular national language into smaller 'systems', or, conversely, as a simple multiplication of language systems. The issue for Bakhtin isn't how many language systems we have to choose from, how many codes or grammars there are to use; the issue is whether we should think of language as a code to begin with. Bakhtin tries to make this clear early on: 'Language at every moment of its development', he says, 'is stratified not only into linguistic dialects in the strict sense of the word (by means of formal linguistic makers, for the most part phonetic), but also – and this is the most important thing for us – into socio-ideological languages: languages of social groups, professional languages, generic languages, the languages of generations, etc.' (DN 271-72/25). A socio-ideological language is not supposed to be a dialect with social instead of geographical boundaries; it's a different kind of beast altogether.

What kind of beast can be made clear by looking at Bakhtin's examples of the novelistic orchestration of heteroglossia. Let's look first at an astonishingly direct, even vulgar example: in Turgenev's *Fathers and Sons* some characters say *princhip* (with a soft 'ch') and others say *printsip*. As Bakhtin notes

> The different pronunciations of the word 'principle' in this instance are a marker of the differentiation of separate cultural-historical and social worlds: the world of noble-landowner culture of the 1820s and 30s, educated in French literature and distant from Latin and German science, and the world of the *raznochinets* intelligentsia of the 1850s, where seminarians and doctors, educated in Latin and German science, set the tone. (DN 357/112)[35]

Thus, a relatively minor stylistic detail is made to stand for a dramatic socio-ideological difference – it represents a larger worldview, the perspective of a social class in nineteenth-century Russia. 'In the novel', Bakhtin claims, 'the formal markers of languages, manners and styles are symbols of social horizons' (DN 357/111). These socio-ideological languages are not just different ways of speaking: they are also different ways of seeing the world and acting within it.

But we are still missing something crucial in Bakhtin's conception. Let's examine another passage, also taken from Turgenev (italics, Bakhtin):

> *Matvei Ilych's suavity of demeanor was equalled only by his stately manner.* He had a gracious word for everyone – with an added shade of disgust in some cases and deference in others; he was gallant, 'un vrai chevalier français', to all the ladies, and was continually bursting into hearty resounding laughter, in which no one else took part, as befits a high official.[36]

The narrator is speaking, describing the character of Matvei Ilych Koliazin, a scion of the landowner culture just mentioned. But the narrator is using the socio-ideological language or style of the culture itself in the narration, describing Matvei Ilych in the words he would use to describe himself. And yet, even in this small quotation, one can also see that the novel is ironising this language, questioning the words and manner in which members of this social class portray themselves. In 'Discourse in the Novel', the novelist always stylises, parodies, or ironises the language being appropriated. Just as the melody played by a single instrument sounds very different when it is complemented by the lines played by other instruments in an orchestra, so the distinctive social dialect used in a novel sounds different when it is 'subordinated to the higher stylistic unity of the whole' (DN 262/15). The coexistence of the original significance or 'directedness' of this style and the second, ironising 'directedness' it acquires in the novel is what Bakhtin calls 'double-voiced discourse'.

But there is a paradox at work here. For while you might assume that stylising or ironising a language variety would weaken it, render it less persuasive or compelling, a central plank in Bakhtin's argument is that this novelistic treatment makes language more powerful, that it thereby allows the language of a novel to tap into fundamental social forces. Double-voiced discourse in the novel

> draws its energy, its dialogised ambivalence, not from individual disagreements, misunderstandings, or contradictions (even if these are tragic and profoundly grounded in individual fates); in the novel this double-voicedness is deeply rooted in an essential socio-linguistic heteroglossia and multilanguagedness. True, in a novel heteroglossia is basically always personified, incarnated in individualised images of people with individualised disagreements and contradictions. But in this case contradictions between individual wills and minds are immersed in social heteroglossia and given new meaning by it. Contradictions among individuals are now only the rising crests of the spontaneous forces of social heteroglossia, spontaneous forces which play through them and force them to be contradictory, which saturate their consciousnesses and words with their own essential, historically creative, heteroglossia. [...] The inner dialogicity of authentic prose discourse, which grows organically from a stratified and heteroglot language, cannot be essentially dramatised or dramatically completed (genuinely ended), it cannot be completely encompassed within the bounds of a direct dialogue, a conversation between people, it cannot be conclusively separated into sharply demarcated replies. This prosaic double-voicedness is prefigured in language itself (in both authentic metaphor and myth), in language as a social phenomenon, historically becoming, socially stratified and torn up by this becoming. (DN 325–26/79–80)

We can ask – we should ask – whence this force comes. From the above paragraph it looks like it is partly a matter of scale and numbers – an individual voice is reconceptualised as representing a social voice (not Matvei Ilych, but the landowner class of which he's a member), while individual disagreements stand for social ones. And, indeed, when Bakhtin speaks of the 'socially contradictory historical becoming of language' (DN 330/84), it sounds as if using social languages allows one to tap into the dynamism of social life, a dynamism described here in unmistakably Marxist terms.[37] Bakhtin incorporated the insights of Soviet linguists – why not admit he incorporated some of the accompanying social theory?

There is no good reason not to, but, at the same time, there is something else going on here. To say that historical becoming is bound up with social contradictions is to place oneself right inside the Marxist conception of history, according to which social contradictions – contradictions between classes, or between the forces and relations of production – are the motor force of history itself. Nevertheless, the force of socio-ideological languages does not come primarily from their contradictory insertion into social heteroglossia. We know this because, according to Bakhtin, a novel does not have to actually represent those contradictions in order to infuse its language with the force of historical becoming. One of the great misunderstandings surrounding dialogism is that it refers primarily to a dialogue between or among styles within a novel. Bakhtin's talk of a 'system' of styles and some of his concrete analyses naturally lead us to think of dialogism as the collision of different languages within a single work. But any dialogue between languages in a work is secondary to, in fact a by-product of, the more fundamental dialogical relationship, which is between the novel as a whole and any single constituent style. For each constituent style or language of the novel takes its meaning from the interplay between 'the subordinate stylistic unity which it is an immediate part of' – a social dialect, professional jargon, urban vernacular, or whatever – and the 'higher unity of the whole work', that is, from how the novel stages, ironises, or represents that style (DN 262/15). It would be possible, therefore, to write a dialogical novel in a single style, provided that style was distanced and ironised, just as, in the study of Dostoevsky, it was possible for a single heroic voice to be represented polyphonically by an author.

A socio-ideological language, represented in a novel by some kind of double-voiced discourse, embodies the force of historical becoming, even if it is the only such language in a novel. Figuring out what this means and how it would even be possible, however, puts us in a rather awkward position, because the more rigorously we explore the issue, the clearer it becomes that Bakhtin's terminology, the talk of 'dialogism' and 'double-voicing', is at once insightful and misleading. 'Double-voicing' and 'dialogism' focus our attention on the ironic structure, the dual directedness of the speech that interests Bakhtin, the way in which it means more, or differently, than it intends.

But are there actually two voices in any meaningful sense? We have just reminded ourselves that dialogism does not entail a dialogue between *different* socio-ideological languages or voices. But calling the interaction between the 'higher unity' of the novel as a whole and its constituent styles 'double-voiced discourse' is also a problem: if the novel is the work as a whole – the work as a narrative structure, a system of characters, a rendering of atmosphere, and so on – it is hard to see what's gained by calling it a second 'voice', as it never speaks, but simply frames and organises the voices within it. But there's a final step to take: even the *first* voice in Bakhtin's scheme – the socio-ideological language in the novel – isn't a voice on its own, independently of its inclusion in a novel. Because what Bakhtin calls double-voicing isn't the addition or the synthesis of two voices but the condition of all voice, of all style, to begin with. Recall that, according to Bakhtin, 'Dostoevsky's hero is not an image, but a fully valued discourse, *a pure voice*' (PDA 53/63) and that it becomes a fully valued pure voice only because it is taunted and provoked by the novel as a whole (in a different sort of novel the speech of a hero wouldn't, presumably, qualify as a voice at all). Likewise, in the novel, it is only by virtue of a novel's framing narrative and structure, only by virtue of the way a novel provides a context for certain words, that there is a style, a socio-ideological language in the first place.

In what sense, then, does the double-voicedness of the novel draw its energy from heteroglossia? How is it 'deeply rooted in an essential socio-linguistic heteroglossia and multilanguagedness'? At several points Bakhtin describes this energy with the Russian word *stikhiia*, meaning a spontaneous or elemental force. And midway through 'Discourse in the Novel', he tells us, with a certain gravity and emphasis, that 'the central problem for a stylistics of the novel can be formulated as *the problem of the artistic representation of a language, the problem of the image of a language*' (DN 336/90). To make an image of a language is to take the rough materials of speech and give them the form of a 'socio-ideological language'. The rough material itself is described with a term borrowed from Husserl, the idea of 'intentionality'. According to Husserl, all mental acts are intentional in character: we do not just think, we think 'about' something, we don't perceive blankly, we perceive 'something', desire 'something', and so on – there is always something outside that is intended, aimed at, by our mental activity. Language is similarly intentional in the sense that it is always aimed at what is beyond it: at states of affairs, at the behaviour of others, at people's beliefs, at social bonds, and so on. Bakhtin accordingly explains that 'we always put forward the referential-semantic and expressive, i.e., intentional, moment as the force that stratifies and differentiates a common literary language' (DN 292/45). It's the shared intentional aspect of all language that makes it possible to 'put such methodologically heterogeneous phenomena as professional jargons, social dialects, worldviews, and individual works in a single series' (DN 292-93/45-46).

But intentionality in ordinary life is, you might say, practical and interested, it's the force of language directed towards specific and context-laden ends. The novelist's task, in Bakhtin's theory, is to reshape these ordinary and varied intentional acts into a language that is socio-ideological. We've already mentioned one element of this transformation: making formal linguistic markers – aspects of phonology, vocabulary, syntax, and grammar – the 'symbols of social horizons' (and note the terminology: 'social horizons', which describes how a worldview looks from the inside, from the perspective of an *I* – like a horizon in front of you). But the novelist's job isn't just to pin certain perceptible features of the signifier onto language-in-use, leaving us with the linguistic equivalent of a butterfly collection. A novel must take that bare intentionality and turn it into an ideological project, by which Bakhtin means a consistent, articulate position, which could govern one's 'whole life and fate' and which would guide one's behaviour as an ethical task, a project aimed at the future. For this reason, the image of a language that appears in a novel is supposed to include not just elements of speech drawn from actual usage but speculative elements as well, what Bakhtin calls 'the free creation of moments in the spirit of a given language which are, however, completely alien to the empirical facts of that language' (DN 336-37/91). For Bakhtin, in keeping with the linguistic philosophy of Humboldt and Cassirer, languages evolve and develop according to an inner form that binds external features to a spirit or ideology.

'Behind every utterance in a genuine novel', Bakhtin remarks, 'one senses the spontaneous force of social languages with their inner logic and their inner necessity' (DN 356/110). How is that logic revealed and represented? In part through the 'free creation of moments' and in part via the same means as in Dostoevsky's prose: through the re-purposing of plot, so that its events test the hero's consciousness and discourse. 'The plot of a novel', Bakhtin argues, 'must organise the disclosure of social languages and ideologies, an exhibition and testing of them: the testing of a discourse, a worldview and an ideologically grounded act [...]' (DN 365/119). Plot and context – attaching an utterance to a character and to a situation – reveal the consequences, often unintended, of speech acts, thereby making the reasonable sound absurd or pompous and the foolish sound wise and prudent. Plot is the defining element of that higher unity of the work that determines the place and consequently the tone of the styles that are used within it. 'The idea of testing the hero and its discourse is perhaps the most fundamental organising idea of the novel'

(DN 388/144), Bakhtin notes, but it is remarkable how little attention this claim has been given. For what Bakhtin calls double-voiced discourse is in effect a kind of testing and exhibiting: by stylising and ironising forms of language, novels interrogate the ideologies they embody, which reveals their limits but also their potential, forcing them to respond and evolve, to, as Bakhtin puts it, 'become'. The novel aims at an 'image of the language': 'an *image* – and not a positivistic empirical given of the language' (DN 356/110). The image will endow language with historical becoming, a becoming that is hidden and spontaneous in everyday life.

That historical becoming should, at this point, acquire such a central position in Bakhtin's argument is a little surprising. He had not seen his principal immediate source for the idea, the philosopher Matvei Kagan, for several years and the concept is entirely absent from his book on Dostoevsky. Hermann Cohen, the philosopher who had formulated the idea in its original form (passing it on to Kagan), was seemingly distant from Bakhtin's thoughts at the time (though Cohen is briefly discussed in the 1928 book *The Formal Method in Literary Scholarship*, written by Bakhtin's friend Pavel Medvedev).[38] It's as if Bakhtin had stored away Kagan and Cohen's terminology and finally decided it was time to dust it off and put it to use. As to what prompted the retrieval, we don't actually know, given that Soviet history cloaked almost everything Bakhtin did for five years in the darkness of exile.

But just as the rediscovered keepsake can become one's most treasured possession, so Bakhtin became enamoured of the concept he had recollected, not just using it but expanding and elaborating on it for the next ten or fifteen years. While Bakhtin will examine the novel from a number of different angles in the 1930s and 1940s, its central feature will be its ability to embody, in 1930-36, 'the unique event of the heteroglot becoming of the world' (DN 331/85), in 1941, the 'unfinished process of the becoming of the world' (NLG 30/633), in 1946, a kind of being defined by its 'unmadeness in principle, its unfinishedness and unfinishability in principle'.[39] To represent a history that moves forward, animated by a Messianic future, becomes the novel's *raison d'être*.

Critique

A text as ambitious and complex as 'Discourse in the Novel' is bound to raise many questions. We will focus here on three fairly obvious ones: Is poetry always, and by its nature, monological? Does the novel have the power Bakhtin ascribes to it? Is heteroglossia a fact of everyday language, or something that only exists in novels?

Poetry as the Enemy

'Discourse in the Novel' opens with the claim that critics have not been able to understand the style of the novel because 'all the categories of contemporary stylistics and the very conception of poetic artistic discourse that lies at their heart are not applicable to novelistic discourse' (DN 261/14). The analysis of style in literary art had been so overwhelmingly orientated to poetry – to rhythm and metre, to euphony and prosody, to figurative language – that it could not see the art of prose, could not see how literary prose manipulated its language.

Bakhtin's text is supposed to remedy this problem: it will show us precisely why 'the novel is an *artistic* genre' and how we must understand language in order to grasp the art of novelistic style. Fair enough, one might say. But Bakhtin continues to push at poetry and goes on to make somewhat more extravagant claims, in which the problem is not critical ideas based on poetry, but poetry itself. In the following chapter of the text, 'Heteroglossia in the Novel', he will say that '[i]n poetic genres in the narrow sense, the natural dialogicity of discourse is not exploited artistically' (DN 285/38) and, more drastically, that 'the language of the poetic genres, when it approaches its stylistic limit, often becomes authoritarian, dogmatic, and conservative' (DN 287/40). Style in poetry, Bakhtin argues, assumes a language that is everywhere a direct expression of its author; presumably Bakhtin is thinking of a controlling lyric voice here. The complexity of poetry comes from rhythm and euphony, from figurative language that does not touch on heteroglossia, from language understood as a complex system of meanings, but of meanings that lie, so to speak, on a single plane.

These claims led to immediate objections, particularly in the Anglophone literary world, where readers and critics could point to a wide range of poets, past and present, who were more than interested in using the social languages around them. Hadn't even the fairly conservative T. S. Eliot planned to give his multilingual poem 'The Waste Land' a different title, 'He Do the Police in Different Voices'? Wasn't Bakhtin's account a caricature of poetry?

One could point to places where Bakhtin obviously qualified his case. When he accused poetic language of being authoritarian, he added a footnote in which he admitted that '[w]e are always characterising, of course, the ideal limit of the poetic genres' (DN 287n12/40n24). When Bakhtin chooses to illustrate dialogism and double-voicedness, one of his leading examples in this essay and elsewhere is Aleksandr Pushkin's *poem* 'Evgeny Onegin'. In preparatory notes for an article on the poet Vladimir Mayakovsky, he claimed that '[o]ne of the most important historical tasks of such epochs is to close the scissors of prose and poetry, to eradicate the too sharp divide between them', insisting that Mayakovsky's contemporary, familiarising poetry did just that.[40] Bakhtin may have been identifying an ideal of poetry, to which, however, many poems do not adhere. You can use Bakhtin's critical ideas in the analysis of poetry – many have done so – although it seems to be the case that in doing so you admit that the poems in question are not, in Bakhtin's terms, purely poetic.[41]

The ultimate source of this odd situation is the state of literary-critical discourse in Russia and the Soviet Union in the first three decades of the twentieth century. The Russian Symbolist poets had invested a great deal in the idea that the language of poetry was self-contained and distant from everyday language. One of their number, Viacheslav Ivanov, wrote that 'modern poetry is the first vague reminiscence of the holy language of high priests and magi', a comment Bakhtin alludes to when claiming that poetry could be dogmatic and conservative.[42] When Russian Formalists like Shklovsky and Iakubinskii rebelled against this conception, they nevertheless retained the idea that literary criticism should focus its efforts on understanding the distinctive qualities of 'poetic language' (thus the Formalist organisation in Petersburg was the Society for the Study of Poetic Language: OPOIaZ). In the first of the Russian Formalist anthologies, Iakubinskii argued that it was only in poetry, for instance, that sound in language acquired an 'autonomous value', where it 'focuses attention on itself'; in practical language this distinctive property of language was simply ignored.[43] Indeed, the avant-gardist poets of the time themselves claimed over and over again, in endless manifestoes, that in their poetry 'language must be first of all *language*', as if they did no more than exploit the bottomless potential of 'the word as such'.[44]

In short, Bakhtin was justified in arguing that, in Russia at least, the artful use of language was equated with poetry, and that this equation blinded critics to the possibility of a different kind of art, embodied in novelistic discourse. To be literary was to traffic in poetic images, poetic tropes, poetic play with sound. Novels might do interesting things with plot, but their discourse was only artistic, 'focus[ing] attention on itself', when it mimicked or borrowed the techniques of poetry. Claiming that actually existing poetry conformed to Symbolist and Formalist theory was a step Bakhtin didn't have to take explicitly, because he had already made Formalist philosophy of language the theoretical superstructure of a larger cultural formation, the '*forces for the unification and centralisation of the verbal-ideological world*" (DN 270/24). Thus, Formalist (and what came to be called structuralist) philosophy of language, the project of a 'unified language' (a standardised form of the national language), and actual poetry ended up walking hand in hand in Bakhtin's essay, united by their common cause.

But poetry turned out to be a temporary foe. Its centralising tendencies are anatomised at some length in the first two sections of 'Discourse in the Novel'. Then, when Bakhtin gets down to the nitty-gritty of analysing the forms of double-voiced discourse and dialogism, poetry disappears almost entirely: when Bakhtin discusses centralising forces, their cultural expressions are 'authoritarian discourse', 'officialness', and, in the final chapter of the book, myth. Nor does poetry make a later return – in the 1930s and 1940s, its role is taken over by 'official' seriousness (in the works on Rabelais) and by epic (in the talks on the novel). As far as one can tell, once Formalism ceased to be a force, poetic language ceased to be a concern.

The Force of the Novel

I mentioned earlier that 'Discourse in the Novel' marks a change not only in the substance of Bakhtin's argument, but also in its tone. The text is militant, enthusiastic, a testament to the power of the novel and not just an analysis of it. The enthusiasm starts on the second page (the first page of the abridged English translation), when Bakhtin complains that stylistics ignores not only the 'great historical destinies of artistic discourse', but also 'the social life of discourse beyond the cloistered artist, in the open spaces of public squares, streets, cities and villages' (DN 259/10-11). It continues when Bakhtin opposes the forces of verbal-ideological centralisation to 'social and historical heteroglossia (the centrifugal, stratifying forces)' (DN 272/26n), hosted first and foremost in the parodic language of popular culture, setting up a confrontation of high and low that will support the contrast of unified, authoritative language on one hand and novelistic dialogism on the other. He'll contrast the pale dialogue of rhetorical discourse with the dialogism that is 'made fruitful by a profound connection with the language-stratifying forces of historical becoming' (DN 325/79). And before Bakhtin launches into his history of the novel as a form, he'll insist that what is at stake in the novel is 'a radical revolution in the fates of human discourse'. Throughout the text, Bakhtin will contrast critical concern with petty trends and literary fashions with a focus on this radical revolution, the great historical destinies embodied in generic change.

Bakhtin has certainly drawn interest from critics who find his technical tools original, but it's the promise that novels do great things that draws the critical crowds. But do they? Is the emergence of novelistic prose as important as Bakhtin claims, and is the prose itself as powerful? The simple answer is: of course not. If there has been a radical revolution in human discourse, and if it took place in, say, the eighteenth and nineteenth centuries, it's embodied in a number of a social and political developments – the democratising revolutions of the time; the emergence of a political 'public sphere' embodied in periodicals, newspapers, and clubs; the creation of mass printing and public education systems – rather than just the stylistic inventiveness of the novel. However, Bakhtin will provide an idea that makes the leading role of the novel more plausible: the argument, hazarded in the 1941 talk-turned-essay, 'The Novel as a Literary Genre', that '[i]in epochs when the novel is dominant, almost all the other remaining genres are to a greater or lesser degree "novelised"' (NLG 5/611). 'They become', Bakhtin goes on to say, 'freer and more flexible; their language is renewed thanks to extraliterary heteroglossia and thanks to the "novelised" layers of literary language; they are *dialogised*; furthermore, they are permeated by *laughter, irony, humour*, and elements of *self-parody*; finally – and this is the most important thing – the novel introduces *problematicity*, a specific semantic *unfinishability*, and *living contact with unfinished, becoming contemporaneity* (the unfinalised present) into them.' (NLG, 7/612). Bakhtin argues that the ironising tendencies of the novel, its focus on the socio-ideological, its emphasis on the historical becoming of the world, establish themselves as features of public discourse more generally, artistic and non-artistic. Is there, then, a more general 'novelisation' of public discourse beginning in the second half of the eighteenth century, the moment when novelisation, Bakhtin believes, takes hold 'particularly forcefully and clearly' (NLG 5/611)?

If the issue is the introduction of 'unfinished, becoming contemporaneity' into the public world, there is little doubt about it. The intellectual historian Reinhardt Koselleck has probably explored this particular question, whether and when perceptions of time and history changed, in the most detail. Like Bakhtin, he points to the 'second half of the eighteenth century' as the decisive moment when '[t]ime becomes a dynamic and historical force in its own right'.[45] In Germany, the shift is christened with a striking lexical change: the waning use of *Histoire*, which is pushed out by 'the collective singular form of *Geschichte*, which since around 1780 can be conceived as history in and for itself in the absence of an associated subject or object'.[46] History, not histories: the process is singular and unified. But the notion of history as a unified and dynamic process also alters the relative weights of past, present, and future. '[L]ived time was experienced as a rupture, as a period of transition in which the new and the unexpected continually happened'; but this continually new was not happening *to* people – it was conceived of as the result of human will and action.[47] In his study of nationalism, *Imagined Communities*, Benedict

Anderson made a related case, arguing that the contemporaneity of novels and newspapers fostered a sense of a common national space (and a common national history) to which all citizens belonged.[48] In this new historicised world, the time of the present took its bearings from the future: the present was the time in which one determined the future and one's acts were to be judged by their future consequences. In the famous words of Friedrich Schiller, 'World history is the world's tribunal' – the future made its judgement on the present. A future that in shape and function looks very much like the one proposed by Cohen and Kagan.

Heteroglossia: Novelistic or Everyday?

Bakhtin insists that the novel draws its force from 'social heteroglossia', and that the double-voiced discourse of the novel is 'made fruitful by a profound connection with the language-stratifying forces of historical becoming'. At the same time, he admits that it is in novels that socio-ideological languages are made, that 'linguistic markers become symbols of social horizons'. So which is it? Is heteroglossia the ordinary state of language transposed into novels or an artefact of the novel itself? Or can one resolve the ambiguity by means of some fancy Hegelian footwork, as when Bakhtin says, late in 'Discourse in the Novel', that '[h]eteroglossia "in-itself" becomes in the novel and thanks to the novel heteroglossia "for-itself"' (DN 400/155)?

When heteroglossia is used as a critical term in literary criticism, the default interpretation seems to have been that heteroglossia is simply there in the language, that the concept is the overdue recognition of actual linguistic diversity, which might then be reflected in novels with an interest in the multiple styles and dialects of modern life. But the term has attracted a more intense and probing scrutiny in sociolinguistics, where it has played a significant role in that discipline's rapid evolution from its insistence that social dialects (like African American Vernacular English) are just as systematic as 'standard' forms of language to its rejection of the idea of language as a system or structure in the first place. What's interesting from our point of view is the way in which heteroglossia has been conceived of less and less as a given and more and more as a process through which 'styles' or socio-ideological languages are constituted as such.

Traditionally, the division of a language into 'the languages of . . .' has been described by sociolinguists as a division into registers, usually distinguished by their degree of formality, informality, or intimacy. But recent work by sociolinguists and linguistic anthropologists has argued that registers should be understood as constructions, as metalinguistic categories we use to classify, describe, and explain the language we encounter. Asif Agha has described this metalinguistic process as 'enregisterment'. Practices of enregisterment are 'processes whereby distinct forms of speech come to be socially recognized (or enregistered) as indexical of speaker attributes by a population of language users'.[49] This means that (a) we begin to think of co-occurring features of language as constituting a 'distinct form of speech' (which is never one symbol, but a set of connected features); (b) we treat those speech forms as 'indexical of speaker attributes' – we understand those features as pointing to (indicating) a speaker with certain features (defined by class, age, ethnicity, level of formal education, and so on); and (c) those speech forms indicate the speaker attributes only for a limited population of speakers. People sound like English 'southern middle-class' speakers only to a specified group, who habitually make an association between a certain vocabulary and accent with a region of England and a class position (a Martian would not do so, and even a southern middle-class American might not do so). Similarly, someone may sound middle-class to one speaker, 'male' to a second, 'white', to a third, like a 'student' to another, and so on: which speaker attributes are indicated will depend on who is listening. The styles Bakhtin describes are not simply 'there', but that is not because the linguistic features that define them don't exist (people actually drop their aitches, say 'loo' or 'toilet', use the -s suffix for the third person singular of verbs or not, and so on). They are not simple facts because collecting linguistic features into a style and then ascribing a social identity to it, and perhaps an ideological project as well, takes work.

Which might make it sound like the question has been settled: sure, heteroglossia, the buzzing world of socio-ideological languages, has to be made, but the making takes place in everyday life, so that novelists have a buffet of styles to choose from when they sit down to write. Furthermore, sociolinguists have shown that the ironising and stylising of socio-ideological languages are not just the province of novelists; ordinary speakers do it all the time, 'crossing' into forms from groups they don't belong to and using borrowed forms at a distance when it seems appropriate or useful.[50] Heteroglossia, even dialogised heteroglossia, is part of the ordinary social history of language.

But matters are less simple than they seem. A close examination of Agha's argument reveals that the indexing of distinct forms of speech does not take place within the confines of local, everyday speech. What Agha calls 'register competence' requires 'institutionalized practices [that] bring into circulation images of social personhood linked to speech through the circulation of discursive artifacts – [...] oral narratives, printed cartoons, newspapers, magazines, novels, et cetera'[51] Novels! It turns out that the linkage of social types to speech requires the intervention of metalinguistic, mass-produced, reflexive forms like novels. We don't spontaneously do the work of stereotyping and indexing: it's done for us, in the print (and no doubt visual) media that surround us.

It's therefore fair to think Bakhtin has engaged in some sleight-of-hand in his argument. Novels have work to do – they produce images of language, which give a distinct form of speech an identity, an ideology, a context, and a project. But their double-voicedness, their representation of languages also depends on 'a fundamental socio-linguistic heteroglossia and multilanguagedness', drawing on its spontaneous force. The force of heteroglossia, however, is neither fundamental nor spontaneous: it depends on the language-shaping and representing activity of the print and electronic media. Heteroglossia doesn't just exist in the language, as the product of everyday Balzacs, Turgenevs, and Dickenses. It requires a modern, social conception of the world and large narrative forms.

Summary

Dialogism in the novel takes the form of double-voiced discourse, in which language is shaped both by its initial social form – a social dialect, a style, a genre like the personal letter – and the use to which it is put in the novel, the stylistic unity of the work as a whole. The task of the novel is to create the artistic image of such a language, which means to infuse it with historical becoming.

The *Bildungsroman* and the Chronotope (with a Brief Glance at the Future)

There is, among Bakhtin's correspondence, a strange letter from the publisher *Sovetskii pisatel'* to Bakhtin sent in late 1937. In it, the publisher agrees to 'the substitution of an incomplete manuscript by some different one', apparently in response to a letter Bakhtin had sent in September of that year.[52] The incomplete manuscript was the book 'Discourse in the Novel', which Bakhtin had successfully proposed for publication in 1936, but which, for reasons unknown, Bakhtin decided not to continue work on. The new book, 'The *Bildungsroman* and its Significance for the History of Realism', would become the stuff of legend. Rumour had it that one completed manuscript of it was pillaged by Bakhtin for cigarette papers during World War II, while the other was destroyed when the publishing house was bombed. But while the publisher's agreeable response to Bakhtin's request is extant, there is no correspondence about a completed manuscript, nor any particular reason to think one ever existed. What we do have is a long proposal for the book, 37 printed pages in length, and more than 700 pages of handwritten notes for it, which have been transcribed and printed in the *Collected Works* under the title 'On the *Bildungsroman*'.

It's hard not to think that Bakhtin's change of tack was at least partly strategic, for the conspectus and the notes imply a quite conservative book, very much attuned to the literary discussions of the 1930s. Those discussions, as we pointed out in the previous chapter, had focused on what, precisely, a socialist realist novel should look like: what should characterise its hero, whether it was formally a modern version of the classical epic, what it meant for a work to be 'realist' (rather than 'romantic' or 'naturalist'); how it would resemble or depart from the great 'bourgeois realist' works of eighteenth- and nineteenth-century European literature. Soviet critics no longer described their culture as a dramatic break with the past (whether in the spirit of the avant-garde or of a new proletarian culture); they imagined the Soviet Union as the inheritor of the cultural riches of Europe and as the arena in which the great achievements of European humanism would reach a culminating point. Writing about the European literary heritage, as Bakhtin was proposing to do, was therefore fine, even something to be encouraged, so long as it was made clear that the heritage was being squandered in capitalist Europe while it was cultivated in the Soviet Union. Bakhtin was well aware of this: early on in the voluminous notes, he draws attention to '[t]he connection of our theme (the *Bildungsroman*) with the question of the proletariat's use of the literary heritage of the past' (OBild 226).[53]

The *Bildungsroman* proposal seemed to tick all the relevant boxes. Its focus was on the central form of the modern European novel, the *Bildungsroman* or 'novel of cultivation', which narrated the process by which a young man or woman grew, matured, and adjusted to the ways of the modern world. The proposal celebrated the genre's contribution to realism in plot terms and measured the works of the past in terms of how they contributed to the realist project; it examined the European literary heritage as the pre-history of the modern novel; and it placed emphasis on the image of the hero, a central preoccupation of Soviet discussion. Accordingly, the proposal begins with classical antiquity, motors through the Middle Ages, dawdles at more length on the Enlightenment, casts Goethe as the true inventor of the *Bildungsroman*, and concludes with nineteenth- and twentieth-century writing. Although the *Bildungsroman* appears as a peak in this literary landscape, Bakhtin will claim its real importance was preparing the ground for 'the development in the nineteenth century of the synthetic forms of the novel, above all the realistic novel (Stendhal, Balzac, Flaubert, Dickens, Thackeray) and the great Russian novel (Turgenev, Goncharov, Tolstoy, Dostoevsky)' (OBild 194).

Perhaps we shouldn't be surprised that the book itself was never written. The proposal was sent in September 1937, that is, at the height of the purges conducted by the Communist Party, which had forced Bakhtin from his post in Saransk and sent him running for cover, first to his sister's home in Moscow and then to the provincial town of Savelevo. In addition, Bakhtin was not very well, plagued by his osteomyelitis, which would lead to the amputation of his right leg in February 1938. All that would be reason enough not to research and write a long book.

Bakhtin did, however, write rather a lot in the years following the proposal. The *Bildungsroman* project did not produce a book, but it generated those 700 pages of manuscript. To these we can add: another few hundred pages of notes on Rabelais beginning in 1938; an entire book, 'Rabelais in the History of Realism', completed in 1940; 188 pages of notes on the theory of the novel at the end of the 1930s; the lectures 'From the Prehistory of Novelistic Discourse' (1940) and 'The Novel as a Literary Genre' (1941); short manuscript essays on Flaubert, on stylistics in the novel, on the nature of art and the nature of self-consciousness, plus more work on Rabelais including a comparative discussion of Shakespeare, and a short but pointed philosophical text on the nature of the human sciences (early 1940s). It's almost as if the terrible times made Bakhtin work even harder.

It isn't the case, then, that he didn't have time to write – Bakhtin *abandoned* the *Bildungsroman* project. Abandoned it, I suspect, because in the course of working on it he discovered a more fruitful line of enquiry. The moment of discovery is fairly clear in the notes 'On the *Bildungsroman*'. Bakhtin has been discussing how the axis of time intersects with the axis of space in nineteenth-century French realism, and particularly in Balzac and Flaubert. This leads him to the following:

> The examples provided by us of intersections between spatial and temporal series – 'a meeting', 'a parting', 'the road', 'an alien world', 'a castle', 'hosting a salon', 'a small town' – are offered for the time being in an intentionally simplified and abstract form. It is important for us to introduce a single concept, for which these preparatory characterizations have been necessary. In all the analysed cases there is a place where spatial and temporal markers are merged in a meaningful and concrete whole. Time here thickens, it is embodied, it becomes artistically perceptible; space likewise is intensified, it is drawn into the movement

of time, of plot, of history. The marks of time are laid out in space; and space is made meaningful and is measured by time. The term, which we apply to this kind of phenomenon, is *chronotope*, which means in literal translation 'timespace' (or 'spacetime'). (OBild 287–88)

Bakhtin would never look back: the moment is a turning point in his intellectual history, akin to the break between Parts One and Two of the Dostoevsky book. The notes would continue on to a very lengthy discussion of Goethe and his work, in which he would be celebrated not only for producing the mature *Bildungsroman*, but now also for the 'exceptional chronotopicity of Goethe's vision and thought. [...] Everything in this world is *"timespace"*, authentic *chronotope*' (OBild 311). Two different ways of thinking about Goethe's novels: as paradigms of the *Bildungsroman* or as paradigms of 'chronotopicity', a new idea about how time and space are interrelated in narrative. After this break, Bakhtin's notes would go on to trace – following an entirely conventional Soviet literary history – the decline of this 'chronotope' in European modernism, in the works of Proust (where time 'is torn from its real historical fulfillment, it becomes purely subjective duration' (OBild 324)) and Joyce (who represents 'almost some kind of limit point for the retreat from real time and all its real historical indices' (OBild 324)), before briefly singling out Romain Rolland, Jack London, and Thomas Mann for praise. And then, at the halfway point of this long 'laboratory text', the work 'announces the effective opening of a new theme', as the editors have put it, which will become the basis for a 'self-sufficient work', the text we know as 'Forms of Time and of the Chronotope in the Novel'.[54]

The shift is from *Bildungsroman* to chronotope and, in parallel, from Goethe to Rabelais and from literature to popular-festive culture. In the *Bildungsroman* section of the manuscript, Rabelais merits some early brief mentions, and somewhat later in the notes Bakhtin groups Rabelais, Grimmelshausen, and Goethe together as novelists in whose work 'the becoming of the human being has an entirely different character' (OBild 23/331), although Goethe has been discussed at length and Rabelais hardly at all. In the second, 'chronotope' section of the manuscript (assuming the published version is representative), Rabelais is the summit of historical realism, and Goethe finds himself relegated to a few laudatory, but perfunctory mentions. The stakes, however, are not merely terminological or literary-historical: at stake is Bakhtin's entire approach to what he called '*the problem of the assimilation of historical time*' (OBild 279), that is, the question of how novels can represent, through plotting and narrative, the historical becoming that dialogism represented through style.

The Bildungsroman *and the Chronotope*

In the *Bildungsroman* version of literary history, prose writers gradually perfected their narrative technique, moving step by step towards the Goethean plot. The history of narrative before Goethe is a history of progressive approximations to this ideal: from the earliest classical adventure plots to the Enlightenment, static and stolid heroes are gradually made pliable and flexible, to the point in the Enlightenment when plot heroes genuinely 'become', but against the background of a fixed world. In the following century, that fixed world will gradually be dissolved, made pliable in turn by historical becoming, until the Goethean summit is reached. By contrast, literary history under the rubric of the chronotope looks quite different. There is still discussion of classical Greek novels in which heroes wander through exotic locales and of ancient biography and autobiography, but the Enlightenment disappears from view and in its stead is a sudden shift to 'folklore', with its 'popular-mythological fullness of time' (FTC 146/400) and then to Rabelais's wild juxtapositions of sex, eating, death, and defecation.

Historical time is not gradually assimilated over the course of literary history – it is grasped when a writer such as Rabelais discovers and exploits the resources of a popular-festive culture that's always been working beneath the surface. In 'Forms of Time and of the Chronotope in the Novel', Bakhtin briefly mentions the possibilities of an ancient 'folkloric realism' (FTC 151/404) before shifting our attention to the rogue, clown, and fool of medieval popular culture, the parodying, wisecracking, mocking figures we had first encountered in the final chapter of 'Discourse in the Novel'. These figures are brought onstage as the leading examples of 'parodic laughter' (FTC 160/412), tied to the 'chronotope of the people's public square' (FTC 161/413) and embodying a 'right to speak parodically, to not be taken literally, to not be identical with oneself' (FTC 163/415). Now what counts in 'the history of realism' are not incremental improvements in the representation of *Bildung*, but 'all the novelistic forms connected with the transformation of the images of the rogue, clown and fool' (FTC 165/416). Bakhtin, having changed horses from Goethe to Rabelais, is also exchanging an idea of historical realism based on the *Bildungsroman* for one based on carnival and popular-festive culture.

The reader might know how this story ends. Bakhtin will eventually stop writing about the chronotope as well, but will continue writing about Rabelais, who will become the conduit for the energies of carnival and medieval popular-festive culture. The 'Notes on Rabelais', which seem to follow quickly on the notes on the *Bildungsroman*, represents the new project, which will culminate in a book/dissertation in 1940. And yet the novel, as a distinctive issue, does not disappear in Bakhtin's work. For he continues to write about its generic distinctiveness, its style, and its distinctive representation of historical time in a series of talks and short notes from 1940 onwards. His lectures at the Gorky Institute will draw together the idea of carnival laughter, the notion of historical becoming as the object of novelistic writing, a new emphasis on 'contemporaneity', and the idea of dialogising, distancing style. It's this trajectory we want to trace in the following section.

Exposition

In Bakhtin's writing on the *Bildungsroman*, literary history is neatly divided into four historical periods, largely according to whether and how novelistic heroes develop or 'become'. There is a classic period, comprising the 'novel of wandering' (Apulius and Petronius), the novel of ordeal, and ancient biography. Despite significant variations, all the novels in these categories

> exhibit the image of the *finished* hero. All the movement of the novel, all the adventures and events depicted in it transfer the hero through space, move him up the steps on the staircase of the social hierarchy or of life's fortune, distance him from his goals or bring him closer to them (to a bride, to victory, to riches). They change his destiny, they change his position in life, but the hero himself, his character, remains unchanged. The plot of the novel, its composition, its entire inner structure presuppose (postulate) this unchangingness, the hardness of the image of the hero, the static nature of its unity.[55]

It may be that the hero has very few significant attributes (the heroes of the adventure type are basically machines for moving through space), or they have attributes that emerge under ordeal or in the course of their lives; the point is, their attributes do not alter or develop.

The second period is not really a period, but a form, the *Bildungsroman*, the origins of which, Bakhtin argues, stretch back to classical Greece and extend through the Middle Ages and the Renaissance up to the Enlightenment. The defining feature of the *Bildungsroman* is, of course, *Bildung*, the education/cultivation/formation of a central protagonist, so in these cases, the hero does indeed 'become' – there is development, maturation, change. The hero now has a 'dynamic' rather than 'static' unity, and has become a *'variable quantity'* rather than a constant, immobile point (OBild 21/329). 'Changes in the hero acquire *plot significance*' (OBild 21/329), and, in many cases, it is this change that is the unifying arc of the plot itself. But there are *Bildungsroman*s and *Bildungsroman*s. For in all the novels before Goethe (with the apparent exceptions of Rabelais's *Gargantua and Pantagruel* and Grimmelshausen's *Simplicissimus*) the becoming of the hero 'took place against the immobile background of a world that is finished and at its foundation completely solid' (OBild 23/331). In the early *Bildungsroman* the 'world demanded a certain accommodation to it from the human being, it demanded understanding and submission to the existing laws of life' (OBild 23/331). 'The human being became', Bakhtin claims, 'but not the world itself'; in these limited examples of the genre, '[t]he becoming of the hero was, so to speak, his *private affair*' (OBild 23/331).

The third period is occupied by Goethe, because now the dam has broken, and the becoming of the hero

> is not his private affair. He becomes *together with the world*, the historical becoming of the world itself is reflected in him. He is already not within an epoch, but on the border of two epochs, at the point of transition from one to the other. (OBild 23/331)

The problem, however, is that the form has peaked too early. For although Bakhtin will claim that the *Bildungsroman* 'continues to live in the second half of the nineteenth century and in the twentieth century' (OBild 333), he gives no indication of substantial generic change, let alone advance. The novels continue to be written on the basis that Goethe has established, but they don't seem – in Bakhtin's estimation – to be doing anything new.

When Bakhtin rewrites this entire project as a study of the chronotope, the initial, classical material exists in the same three categories, although Bakhtin renames the section on Apulius and Petronius (rather than the 'novel of wandering', it is the 'adventure-everyday novel') and slips it behind the novel of ordeal in his narrative. Why? Because, in this revision of his account of ancient sources, the adventure-everyday novel is more chronotopic than the novel of ordeal. In the latter form, the course of events is, strictly speaking, meaningless. The ancient Greek novels of ordeal Bakhtin discusses typically begin with the sudden eruption of erotic love between a young man and woman, the consummation of which is delayed by a series of obstacles or adventures throughout the novel. But, as Bakhtin puts it, '[t]he hammer of events smashes nothing and forges nothing – it only tests the durability of an already finished product' (FTC 107/363), i.e., the enduring love of the couple. In these novels, chance and accident rule, and events typically have neither a significant cause in the plot nor a significant consequence in the plot – they are simply obstacles to the couple's inevitable reunion. The couple's initial passion and their inevitable union are the only actual events, and everything else takes place in 'an extratemporal hiatus between two moments of biographical time' (FTC 90/346), a hiatus that can be filled by a potentially infinite number of adventures, insofar as every adventure is a meaningless digression.

By contrast, in Apulius's *The Golden Ass*, the logic of chance 'is subordinated to a different, higher logic that encompasses it' (FTC 116/372). 'The *principal initiative*, consequently, belongs to *the hero himself and his character*', even though this initiative is primarily 'negative', consisting of the character's '*guilt, delusion, error*' (FTC 116, 117/372): it is the central character's youthful frivolity and foolishness that set the plot in motion. Furthermore, that plot itself now has direction and consequence built into it: 'the temporal series is now an essential and *irreversible whole*' (FTC 119/375), insofar as it is structured as a series of metamorphoses or changes with a definite sequence. Lucius acts foolishly, is punished (turned into an ass), sees the error of his ways, and is turned back into a (now improved) human being. And while this metamorphosis is, for Bakhtin, a 'mythological shell' (FTC 113/369) for the more fundamental idea of development, it nevertheless endows these novels with a narrative arc: 'guilt – punishment – redemption – blessedness' (FTC 118/374). Apulius thus marks a step forward in the long journey towards the narrativisation of historical becoming.

All of which points to a central ambiguity in the concept of the chronotope – it is at once analytical and normative. Analytical, because it is a description of how narratives intertwine or integrate time and space in their plots or, to be more precise, how movement in time and movement in space is coordinated. There are, accordingly, different sorts of chronotopes in novel writing, each of which is interesting and useful in its own way. But at the same time chronotopicity is a norm or ideal (in Goethe's world, remember, everything was 'authentic chronotope'): there is an ideal form for the assimilation of historical time, a correct way to represent or embody historical becoming. Bakhtin is not merely taking us on a tour of the various types of chronotope; he is charting its perfection in the sphere of narrative.

Although novels of ordeal seem to lack all narrative thrust, they nevertheless contribute an idea of adventure time, focused on departures from the ordinary and everyday course of the world, that will later contribute to the mature novel (including Dostoevsky's works). The adventure-everyday novel in turn contributes the kernel of characterological change, by means of stories that have an irreversible order. Biography and autobiography pitch in as well, contributing the idea that one needs narrative to represent a character fully, that '[h]istorical actuality is an arena for the disclosure and unfolding of human characters' (FTC 141/395), even if the characters themselves are fixed and stable. In our quest for the form that can represent historical becoming, we seem to be headed straight for the *Bildungsroman*, in which all events will contribute to the forward motion of the plot, because they entail medium-term or long-term consequences, and in which every detail – characterological, scenic, geographical, historical – is bound, either directly or indirectly, to this historical movement.

But we never arrive at the *Bildungsroman*; instead, 'Forms of Time and of the Chronotope' takes a strange and surprising turn. Bypassing the *Bildungsroman* completely, it stops to address a phenomenon that concerns both the very distant past and the very distant future, a phenomenon that Bakhtin calls 'historical inversion' and that he dates to an ancient, pre-class stratum of folklore, preceding even the Greek novel. Historical inversion takes place, we're told, when narratives invoke a paradise in the distant past, a Golden Age, an age of heroes, a state of nature (from which we have fallen), and so on. Representations like these are inversions because 'something is depicted as having already existed in the past that actually can be or must be realised only in the future, that, in essence, has the form of a goal, an obligation rather than an actual past' (FTC 147/400–1). Historical inversions project our ideals into a distant, unreachable past, but they also entail a change in the form of these ideals. What is transposed from its place in the future to a place in the past are 'such categories as goal, ideal, justice, perfectedness, the harmonious coexistence of person and society' (FTC 147/400). Located in the past, these categories are embodied in a concrete but idealised world: historical inversions 'attempt to make real that which is considered obligatory or true, to endow it with being, to attach it to a time' (FTC 149/402). Located in the future, these categories have an entirely different significance, being goals or ends that structure our present activity rather than tangible arrangements of things. In the earlier parts of this essay, the chronotope's saturation with time seemed to depend on events 'pushing' the plot forward, demanding continuation; whereas the presence of the future, as an orientating force in the novel, seems to 'pull' events forward, like a magnetic North Pole of time.

We will not meet historical inversion again in Bakhtin's work: its role, it turns out, is to introduce us to two figures, folklore and 'the future', that will be critically important in the rest of Bakhtin's writing. But before examining the unlikely text where those two figures come together, Rabelais's *Gargantua and Pantagruel*, Bakhtin pauses to draw our attention to another force that disguises and deforms the future: medieval Christianity and its eschatological fantasies, which will assume the mantle of cultural reaction previously worn by poetry and myth. 'People are more prepared', Bakhtin notes, 'to extend actuality (the present) upwards, along a vertical of high and low, than to move forward along the horizontal of time.' (FTC 148/401). In the medieval conception, the 'vertical superstructures' of the spiritual and heavenly are something 'extratemporal and eternal' that is nevertheless 'thought of as simultaneous with the given moment, with the present' (FTC 148/401), an ideal sphere counterposed to earthly reality. The implicit contrast is with a concept of the divine as that which makes its presence felt as the need to embody and renew creation by striving for the just, the perfect, and the harmonious along the axis of earthly time.

What follows is a description of the historical struggle between the vertical conception of the just and the good, embodied in chivalric romance, and the horizontal conception of the future, which will be embodied in the work of Rabelais. In the chivalric romance, '[t]he whole world becomes miraculous, and the miraculous itself becomes ordinary (without ceasing to be miraculous). Constant unexpectedness itself ceases to be something unexpected' (FTC 152/405). The presence of the miraculous is the index, of course, of an interpenetration of a higher spiritual world and our ordinary, earthly one. These romances will be followed by the works of Langland and Dante, where '[t]he influence of a medieval, other-worldly vertical is especially strong', lending the works their peculiar organisation (FTC 156/408). Rabelais will appear as the polemical antithesis, the parodic rebuttal to this division of the universe. Drawing on folkloric traditions that express value spatially, he will instantiate what Bakhtin calls 'a direct proportionality of qualitative degrees ("values") to spatiotemporal quantities ("scales")' (FTC 167/418). If something has value, it will be big, and the category of becoming will find spatiotemporal expression in the '*category of growth*' (FTC 168/419) that pervades Rabelais's novel. 'Therefore everything good grows, grows in all relations and on all sides, it cannot but grow, because growth belongs to its very nature' (FTC 168/419). And all this displays 'an extraordinary *faith* [emphasis mine] in earthly space and time, a passion for spatial and temporal distances and expanses that characterises both Rabelais and the other great representatives of the Renaissance (Shakespeare, Camoens, Cervantes)' (FTC 168/419).

Rabelais inherits this direct proportionality from folkloric traditions; but in his hand 'it is counterposed to medieval verticality, it is polemically pointed against it' (FTC 168/420). At the same time, it works in the service of a new conception of history, in which the collective body of humanity becomes the agent, and the earthly world the arena, of action. 'At stake is precisely the possible immortalisation of the earthly on earth, with the preservation of all the earthly values of life – a beautiful physical appearance, blossoming youth, good friends, and the most important thing: the continuation of earthly growth, of development, and of the further perfection of the human being' (FTC 203/452). Bakhtin wants to combine the idea of continual human progress ('growth', 'further perfection') with the immediacy and spontaneity of earthly existence: while there will be no envy of descendants, there will be no asceticism, either, and it is just after this passage that Bakhtin will point us again in the direction of 'the eighteenth century in Germany', in which the '[t]he problem of personal, individual perfection and the becoming of the person, the problem of the perfection (and growth) of the human race, the problem of earthly immortality, the problem of the *Bildung* of the human race, the problem of the rejuvenation of culture through the youth a new generation' (FTC 204/453) are confronted, by Lessing, Herder, and Goethe. Bakhtin believes that these problems will be solved by a narrative chronotope that gives shape and form to this new, future-orientated sense of historical time.

Critique

We could ask what this ideal narrative chronotope would look like (would it be some strange amalgamation of Goethe and Rabelais?), but it's surely more useful to discuss what distinguishes the chronotope from other ideas in narrative theory and analysis, what might make it worth using in preference to the concepts developed by narratologists like Roland Barthes, Gerard Genette, and A. J. Greimas.[56] Two features of the chronotope immediately stand out. First, whereas the focus of classic narratology is on the manipulation of narrative time, Bakhtin – though admitting time has a certain precedence in literature – is interested in the intersection of time and space. The narrative 'function' in Barthes is an event that must have some consequence or else is the consequence of an earlier event: it combines 'logic' (the knock on the door leads to someone answering it) with chronology. But for Bakhtin every narrative event depends on a crossing of space and time. So, for example, 'the event of the meeting lies, as it were, at the point of intersection between a spatial and a temporal series: *one and the same place* defines it just as *one and the same time* does' (OBild 281). Running, journeys, movement of all kinds take time, but they also 'take space', either increasing the space between one event and a following one, or reducing that space. Of course, some events may have a looser connection to space than others. While the ancient Greek novel features all sorts of adventures – abductions, escapes, shipwrecks, and so on – '[t]he adventure events of the Greek novel have no essential connection with the features of the different countries that figure in the novel, with their sociopolitical structure, their culture, their history [...] what happens in Babylon could happen in Egypt or Byzantium and vice versa'

(FTC 100/356). The obvious comparison is with a writer such as Balzac, for whom Paris is not an abstract space, but a historical and social space with its own rules and characteristics, which make certain narrative events possible and others not (it shapes, of course, the kinds of meetings that are plausible, including chance meetings on the Parisian street).

That is to say that the intersection of time and space in a chronotope is simultaneously qualitative – how does the space shape the possible events? – and quantitative – to what degree does the space shape the events? It also makes it possible to focus on certain distinctive chronotopic motifs: the meeting, the missed meeting (same time and different spaces, or same space at different times), the road (where adventures take place), the family home or estate (conceived of as a stable point in space, allowing for generational progression), the 'provincial' town ('a *place of cyclical* everyday time. Here there are no events there is only repetitive "existence"' (OBild 287)), and so on. Bakhtin thinks of such chronotopes as generic features that emerge at some point in history and are then handed down as resources to the next historical period, to be adapted when necessary. The constituent structures of narrative are therefore not, in his view, fundamental plots – like struggle, quest, or communication, as in A. J. Greimas – but chronotopic motifs, to be recycled and combined.

A second distinctive feature: the chronotope does not demand the logical consequentiality of events, as do the narrative theories of Barthes, Todorov, and A.J. Greimas. The Greek novel has an initial erotic meeting, in which the lovers discover one another, and a culminating reunion, but the events in between only retard and obstruct the eventual union of the lovers, and they are otherwise interchangeable. As Bakhtin puts it, it is a plot in which 'chance' plays a decisive role. Discussing the chivalric romance, he'll note how the 'miraculous' event becomes part of the narrative structure. Yes, Bakhtin has a normative concept of the chronotope, a belief that cultures are inching their way towards a realist chronotope in which each event will push things forward, will have some kind of logical weight. But the analyses make space for a variegated narrative world, in which events ruled by chance or miracle can also be accommodated.

We have, however, to guard against one very plausible and dangerous misconception. The slow progress of literary history towards a realist chronotope, in which the hero 'becomes *together with the world*' leads one to imagine that chronotope as a sort of updated version of the nineteenth-century European novel. But a few years after writing about the chronotope, Bakhtin will say this, in the course of an unfinished essay on Flaubert:

> A sharp feeling (a distinct and sharp consciousness) of the possibility of a completely different life and completely different worldview than the life and worldview available in the present is the presupposition of the novelistic image of present life. [...] Not changes within the limits of a given life (progress, decline), but the possibility of a life different in principle with different scales and dimensions.[57]

We know that a realist chronotope would mean that the world changes together with the hero, but Bakhtin is telling us that the novel must present its world as if it could be completely different, drastically and suddenly transformed. In a text on Dostoevsky from the same period, Bakhtin commends '[f]aith in wonder, in the unexpected change in life and one's position in life [...] in the transformation of a slave into a King, the low into the high'.[58]

Did 'faith in wonder' mean Bakhtin's conception of history had parted ways with Marxism? Did it make a reconciliation with the critical discourse about socialist realism impossible? Not at all. In the decade before, his friend Kagan had insisted that Marxism, 'historical materialism', hadn't appreciated its own religious roots. In a letter to his wife in 1924, in which he laid bare his agony over the course of the revolution and his place in it, Kagan claimed that he understood 'the religious essence of the truth of the atheism that comes out of historical materialism'. What was true and valuable in historical materialism was 'a profoundly religious thing, which should be turned against the cult of Lenin by means of all religiosity up to the present day'.[59] For, in fact, the overlap between Bakhtin's evolving idea of historical becoming and the Marxist conception of history was considerable. They were alike, first of all, in claiming that all social arrangements, all culture, were historically changeable and that the essence of the human was to be historical, to alter and transform one's conditions of existence: to 'become *together with the world*' could have easily been a Marxist slogan. Furthermore, both historical becoming and Marx's philosophy conceived of history as an ethically directed process, which moves towards an ethical end: in Bakhtin, a world redeemed by love; in Marx, an emancipated society, in which human labour is no longer alienating. And finally, Bakhtin's emphasis on radical transformation aligned him with Marxism rather than distancing him from it. By putting historical becoming in the foreground of his theory of the novel, Bakhtin was therefore emphasising what his vision of history shared with the ideas of historical change swirling around him. But the sharing was genuine and unforced. Marxist debate might have persuaded Bakhtin it was time to take historical becoming down from the attic, but it didn't force him to put on a costume. It simply reminded him he had an outfit that was suitable for the occasion.

When Bakhtin warns against '[t]he eternal threat of *the present day* to everything that wants to go beyond its limits', he could be talking about people's fear of religious transfiguration, resistance to genuine historical becoming, or bourgeois ideology (which wants to naturalise all present arrangements) from a Marxist perspective. When he invokes the future in the lines that follow, his language teeters on the edge between religion and politics: 'The present day (when it commits violence) always pretends to be a servant of the future. But this future is the future as continuation, the continuity of oppression, not a passage into freedom, not a transfiguration'.[60] These lines, like the writing on Flaubert, were composed around 1943, when the present day could not have been more full of violence and threat. But Bakhtin was also gesturing towards an idea he had developed in a different context, the idea of laughter, which makes its maiden appearance without warning or preparation, in a section of the chronotope essay notionally devoted to the 'idyllic chronotope'. Laughter appears as the aspect of the ancient complex that 'never underwent either religious, mystical or philosophical sublimation' (FTC 236/482), and it is laughter that turns the world upside down, that makes the authoritative look ridiculous, that brings the high down to earth, as Bakhtin will describe at great length in his book on Rabelais.

Summary

A chronotope is a pattern for integrating movement in space with movement in time in a narrative. Although there have been many different chronotopes in the course of literary history, the ideal form would represent all events as part of a ceaseless historical becoming, shaped by a utopian or Messianic future.

The Novel, Contemporaneity, and the Future

Let us pause for a moment to ask the question: where did 'the future' come from in Bakhtin's work? Why did it emerge in tandem with an interest in folklore? I wrote earlier that the effects of Bakhtin's interest in Neo-Kantianism seemed to be deferred until the late 1930s. Why? We don't know. But I have an interesting hypothesis.

Bakhtin had read, we know, Olga Freidenberg's book *The Poetics of Plot and Genre*, which described the narrative techniques of the Greek novel and their roots in myth and folklore.[61] We know this because an indefatigable scholar has actually found the relevant copy of this text in the library of the

Mordovian Pedagogical University in Saransk, which – the library records tell us – Bakhtin looked at in November 1936 (and later again in 1939) and in which he underlined passages emphasising, for example, the role of laughter in an ancient Egyptian papyrus.[62] The sudden appearance of 'folklore' in Bakhtin's work on the chronotope – called 'folklore', not popular-festive culture or carnival – might have something to do with this, as Freidenberg's construction of cultural history separated it into three major periods: myth, folklore, and literature. And, as Nina Perlina has pointed out, Freidenberg, and her fellow semantic paleontologist I. Frank-Kamenetskii, had studied Cassirer intensively in the 1920s and made him a key element of their theoretical framework.[63]

But that is not the central plank of our hypothesis. That rests on a series of letters Kagan wrote to his wife in the summer of 1937, when Bakhtin was in Moscow at his sister's, having escaped from Saransk by the skin of his teeth. On 15 July, Kagan writes: 'Yesterday I was at Boris Vladimirovich's [Zalesski, KH], where Bakhtin was staying. I arrived at 8 and left at 12'. Then on 11 August, 'yesterday from 9 to 12 the Bakhtins were here.' And again on 15 August: 'Yesterday from 11 to 12 I was at the Bakhtins'.[64] In other words, in the summer of 1937 Bakhtin had a lot of long conversations with the man who was his closest philosophical companion and his main conduit for knowledge of Neo-Kantianism. We also know that at some point in 1937 or the year following Bakhtin went back to the works of Ernst Cassirer, making a long conspectus of the second volume of the *Philosophy of Symbolic Forms* (which is entitled *Mythical Thought*), and of Cassirer's *The Individual and the Cosmos in Renaissance Philosophy*.[65] From the conspectus of Cassirer's study of myth we can see that Bakhtin noticed Cassirer's claim (which echoed Cohen) that monotheistic religion had introduced a new *'feeling of the future'*, which made possible the 'time of human *history'*.[66] Cassirer's study of the Renaissance opens with a long discussion of the revolution in worldview initiated by Nicholas of Cusa, who destroyed the medieval vision of a hierarchical order of being, making possible an idea of the world as historical, a discussion that Bakhtin will borrow from liberally when he works on Rabelais.[67] This change – from the vertical order of being in the Renaissance to the horizontal order of being that defines modernity – is first mentioned when Bakhtin begins to discuss the chronotope. There is no smoking pen, but the coincidences point to a conclusion: Bakhtin talks to Kagan and, as a consequence, goes back to some Neo-Kantian sources, which, in turn, lead him in a new direction.

With this shift, Bakhtin's analysis of the novel effectively splits into three streams. There are, first, his continuing attempts to define the distinct style of the novel, now focusing on its roots in ancient and medieval satire and parody, but maintaining, as before, that novels are distinguished by their investment in an indirect, ironising, distanced kind of expression. This stream, fully articulated in 'Discourse in the Novel', will flow into the 1940 lecture/essay 'From the Prehistory of Novelistic Discourse' (which, at the time it was delivered, was also called 'Discourse in the Novel') and into a short fragment dated about 1944 called 'Towards a Stylistics of the Novel'. Second, there is the analysis of chronotope, narrative, and time-consciousness in the novel, sometimes discussed in explicitly narrative terms, sometimes not. Here the major statement is the lecture/essay 'The Novel as a Literary Genre' (1941), to which we should add the drafts 'On the History of the Type (Generic Variety) of Dostoevsky's Novel' (1940–41) and 'On Flaubert' (1944). Finally, there is the analysis of popular laughter and popular-festive forms ('carnival'), treated at great length in the book on Rabelais, the first version of which is completed in 1940, but also discussed in his 1940 entry for the *Soviet Literary Encyclopaedia* on 'Satire', and in the many notes Bakhtin made for revising the Rabelais book – the most important of which are the 'Additions and Amendments to "Rabelais"' of 1944.

There is a good deal of crossover between the works: the book on Rabelais contains many analyses of language and style; the discussions of narrative and time-consciousness point to popular-festive sources; and both sketch out and then slowly fill in a picture of the enemy of the novel, 'official seriousness', in all its varieties.

All this, and during a war that will devastate the Soviet Union and Bakhtin's family as well.

Exposition

'The Novel as a Literary Genre', delivered as a lecture in 1941 and published as an essay subsequently (with the new title 'Epic and Novel'), is organised around a familiar polarity: the ancient epic and the modern novel. Each is the antithesis of the other. In putting things this way, Bakhtin was breaking not only with the prevalent line in Soviet criticism – which held that the Soviet novel should be like a new epic – but also with his own earlier discussions of this relationship.[68] The epic, as Bakhtin defines it, is an elaborate instance of historical inversion, structured by three principles. First, its subject matter is 'a national epic past' (NLG 13/617), that is, stories, legends, or narratives that are already part of 'national' history. It's a 'valorised past of beginnings and peak times' (NLG 19/623), which justifies and grounds the existence of a nation in the present. In the case of Homer – and Bakhtin admitted in the discussion after the lecture that 'I have in mind, above all, Homer in relation to antiquity' – that epic past consists of stories taken from the Trojan cycle of Greek mythology, but we are doubtless all familiar with the kinds of narratives – wars of independence, battles against invaders, long marches and hunger strikes – that ground and explain nations in the present.[69]

Second, this material takes shape as '*national tradition* (and not personal experience and the free inventiveness that grows from it)' (NLG 13/617). By this, Bakhtin means that the narrated stories are authoritative, 'completed, finished and immutable' (NLG 17/621) and, in that respect, distinct from a present that 'is something transitory, it is flow, it is an eternal continuation without beginning or end' (NLG 20/624). The material of this past has a particular form, which dictates that it is not something one knows or represents, but something one remembers and recounts; an epic past is an object of ritual remembrance and reverence, remembrance that seeks to restore and maintain its authority in a fallen present.

Finally, 'the epic world is separated from contemporaneity, i.e., from the time of the bard (author) and his listeners by an *absolute epic distance*' (NLG 13/617). When Homer begins the *Iliad* with 'Sing, goddess, the anger of Peleus' son Achilleus and its devastation', he refers the listener to events that are not just distant in time, but different in form from those of the present. The telling of the events is passed down, but they are in no sense experienced as continuous with the present; the past is not represented as a 'real relative past, connected to the present by uninterrupted temporal transitions' (NLG 19/623). 'From the epic point of view authentic reality belongs only to that *which was*' (OQThN 593), and the present is understood as 'a reality of a lower order in comparison with the epic past' (NLG 19/6240). According to such a philosophy of history, '[t]he future is conceived of either as an essentially indifferent continuation of the present, or as an *end*, the final destruction, a catastrophe' (NLG 20/624). In the present, one can only try to live up to (and fail) the model of the past, or live in dread of the apocalypse to come.

These epic characteristics are systematically contrasted to the 'contemporaneity' of the novel. Even in antiquity, Bakhtin will argue, '[c]ontemporary actuality, flowing and transitory, "common", present, this "life without beginning and end", was an object of representation only in the lower genres' (NLG 20/625). But it is only in modernity – which seems to begin with the Renaissance – that this contemporaneity, as a topic and as a way of thinking about historical time, becomes prevalent through the dominant position of the novel. In the modern novel, the present 'is essentially and in principle unfinished: according to its very essence it demands continuation, it moves into the future, and the more actively and consciously it moves forward into this future, the more tangible and essential is its unfinishedness' (NLG 30/633). Or, as Bakhtin might have put it a few years earlier, it 'becomes'. It would be simple to say that in this conception of history the present takes its bearings from the future rather than the past, but this would ignore the ontological difference between the 'epic' past and the 'novelistic' future. For the future, you'll recall from Bakhtin's earlier comments on historical inversion, consists of a network of linked goals or aspirations – justice, harmony among people, perfectedness – rather than a utopian place, an embodied *picture* of perfection and justice. It is, to borrow Hermann Cohen's terms, a Messianic future, always over the horizon, but with a decisive effect on the present, which thereby becomes profoundly moral or ethical. That's to say that the present, when it takes the form of contemporaneity, demands continuation not because time goes on, but because it has direction: there are tasks to fulfil (echoed in Bakhtin's occasional use of the Neo-Kantian phrase 'not given, but set as a task').

This Messianic strain of the novelistic conception of history will be more in evidence when Bakhtin discusses Rabelais and popular-festive culture. The obvious question for now is how the novel as a form is meant to embody it. In fact, Bakhtin notes several features that distinguish the novel generically from its epic ancestor. First among these is the position or stance of the author in novels, which might be neatly conveyed by the following sentences, with which Balzac opens his novel *Père Goriot*:

> Madame Vauquer, *née* Conflans, is an old woman who for the past forty years has run a family boarding house in the rue Neuve-Sainte-Geneviève, between the Latin Quarter and Fauborg Saint-Marceau. The boarding house, known as the Maison Vauquer, is open alike to men and women, young and old, but no breath of scandal has ever sullied the reputation of this respectable establishment.[70]

'For the past forty years' tells us that the narrator is contemporary with, shares the same temporal space as, the woman and the boarding house he describes, and the narrator assumes the reader shares this space as well, to the extent that they will know where the Latin Quarter and Fauborg Saint-Marceau are and will be familiar with the Paris of 1819, when the novel is set. A novelist, Bakhtin observes, 'can appear in the field of representation itself in any authorial pose, can represent real moments of their own life or make allusions to them, can get mixed up in their heroes' conversations, can openly polemicise with their literary enemies, etc.' (NLG 27/631). In short, the narrator is on the same plane as the represented world. It will turn out this contemporaneity is what makes dialogism, double-voicedness, possible: 'the authorial discourse that represents lies on the same plane as the represented discourse of the hero and can (more precisely: must) enter into dialogical relationships and hybrid combinations with it' (NLG 27-8/631). The same principle accounts for the novel's intimate relationship with and dependence on the extraliterary genres contemporary with it. 'As it is structured in a zone of contact with the unfinished event of contemporaneity, the novel frequently crosses the borders of what is specifically artistic and literary, making use of a moral lesson, a philosophical treatise, a direct political intervention, or degenerating into the raw, unformed spirituality of a confession, a "cry of the soul", etc.' (NLG 33/636).

The distinction between epic and novel is manifest in their plots as well. The epic past is known in advance – whether a particular rendering of it ends here or there is not important. By contrast, novels are afflicted with an '"interest in the ending"' (NLG 32/635): we must want to know – what happens next? The ambiguity of the novelistic ending may be captured by the end of *Père Goriot*, when we are with its hero, Rastignac, who is alone in the cemetery of Père Lachaise:

> Rastignac, now all alone, walked a few paces to the higher part of the cemetery, and saw Paris spread out along the winding banks of the Seine, here the lights were beginning to shine. He eyes fastened almost hungrily on the area between the column in the place Vendôme and the dome of the Invalides, home to that fashionable society to which he had sought to gain admission. He gave this murmuring hive a look which seemed already to savour the sweetness to be sucked from it, and pronounced the epic challenge: "It's between the two of us now!"
> And as the first shot in the war he had thus declared on Society, Rastignac went to dine with Madame de Nucingen.[71]

On the one hand, novels, insofar as they capture a contemporaneity with no predetermined endpoint, must display 'an external and formal, in particular plot, completedness and exhaustiveness' (NLG 31/634). The ending of the novel has to complete an action or movement initiated in the beginning (Rastignac's declaration follows here on the death of the eponymous Goriot); the novel itself must be complete, because the actuality it represents isn't. On the other hand, the novel's ending 'demands continuation, it moves into the future': Rastignac is about to do something else (his further adventures will be represented in other novels from Balzac's series, the *Comedie Humaine*) and the world he inhabits is fundamentally incomplete and open – it has a future.

Finally, Bakhtin returns to the matter of the representation of the hero, which remained a central concern of Soviet criticism. The novelistic hero is not like the epic hero, who is a concatenation of given traits (virtues, failings), all of which are displayed in his or her behaviour. In the 'high-distanced genres', i.e., the epic, the individual is 'absolutely equal to himself', 'completely *externalised*', '[a]ll his potential, all his possibilities up to the end are realised in his external social position, in his whole fate, and even in his external appearance' (NLG 34/637). 'These features of the epic human being', Bakhtin readily acknowledges, '[...] create the exclusive beauty, integrity, crystalline clarity and artistic completeness of this image of the human being, but at the same time', he notes, 'they give rise to its limitations and a certain lifelessness in modern conditions of human existence' (NLG 35/638).

In the novel, 'the transfer of the image of the human being from the distanced plane to the zone of contact with the unfinished event of the present (and consequently, of the future)' (NLG 35/638) changes everything. The individual in the novel is marked by 'an essential dynamism, the dynamism of noncoincidence and inconsistency among the different moments of this image' (NLG 35/638), by 'the inadequacy of the hero to his fate and position' (NLG 37/639), by the hero's possession of 'ideological and linguistic initiative' (NLG 38/640). The novelistic hero is not a harmonious web of traits, but a personality with jagged edges. The inadequacy of the hero to his social position is not just an accidental feature of novels, but is the motor of many novelistic plots: Balzac's Rastignac, the ambitious young man from the provinces, who refuses the role fate assigns him, is just one of many such novelistic heroes. Nor does this inadequacy necessarily issue in stories of fulfilled ambitions: when Bakhtin says the hero 'cannot become once and for all a clerk' (NLG 37/639), he's no doubt thinking of Nikolai Gogol's clerks, whose frustration with their position leads them to madness or death. Initiative can lead heroes to alter their circumstances or to die trying.

All of which might be summed up in Bakhtin's claim that in the novel 'the *subjectivity* of the human being becomes an object of experimentation and representation' (NLG 37/640). Subjectivity, and not 'consciousness': Bakhtin is well aware, by this point, of the work of Proust and Joyce (about which he seems to have had conflicted opinions) and neither represents a hero with initiative. Time in Proust, having been converted into 'a purely subjective duration', amounts to no more than 'a foolish endlessness, which is characteristic also for what would seem to be its antipode, the time of the multi-volume adventure novel' (OBild 324).[72] Joyce, likewise, 'almost some kind of limit point of departure from real time', proves 'that a single empty day is actually the same as an empty eternity' (OBild 324).[73] By subjectivity Bakhtin means not the inner processes of the mind, but the human being as the active agent of speech and action. The noncoincidence of the human being with itself is thus not a matter of sheer human spontaneity or inner freedom, but of its need to achieve something: 'A human being never coincides with itself, insofar as it is always participating in the future' (OQThN 573).

There is, however, one more twist in this tale of literary development. Isn't the novel itself the incarnation of the subjectivity it represents? After all, Bakhtin describes the novel as the 'leading hero in the drama of literary development in modernity' (NLG 7/612), and the opening pages of the lecture/essay make clear that the novel's ambitions are equal to those of its most notorious heroes. 'The Novel as a Literary Genre' opens with the argument that the novel cannot be fitted within the existing theory of genres because its very nature calls into question the way we have thought about genre. Like the heroes it represents within its pages, the novel itself 'becomes *together with the world*', which in this narrative of human history, means that novels participate in the modernisation of the world, in a historical shift from ancient, epic, feudal fixity to the time-consciousness of contemporaneity. The novel can do this because 'it more deeply, essentially, sensitively and rapidly reflects the becoming of actuality itself' (NLG 7/612). It assumes the leading role in modernity (*novoe vremia*, a Russian calque of the German *Neuzeit*) 'because it best expresses the *tendency of becoming* in the modern world; it is, in fact, the only genre born of this modern world and in every respect homogeneous with it' (NLG 7/612). That means that the novel not only narrates and represents 'becoming', the constant development that is the defining feature of contemporaneity, but itself 'becomes'. The novel is therefore, according to Bakhtin, a self-critical genre, constantly evolving, engaged in a constant 'parodying or travestying of the dominant and fashionable varieties of this genre' (NLG 6/611).

In many ways, it's a reprise of the opening of 'Discourse in the Novel'. There Bakhtin had said: you can't understand the style of the novel, and novels appear to have no style at all, if you understand them in terms of poetic style – we therefore need a new 'dialogical' concept of style. Now Bakhtin is saying: the genre of the novel is incomprehensible in terms of the old theories of genre; we need a new 'becoming' or critical concept of genre to understand it (which is why the opening of the essay, deleted from the original Russian publication and the English translation, insists we need a *'philosophy* of poetic kinds and genres' (NLG 608), not just a 'theory').

But just as the former essay made it sound as if you might pluck dialogism and heteroglossia out of 'the social life of discourse [...] in the open spaces of public square and streets', so 'The Novel as Literary Genre' implies that becoming and contemporaneity are ultimately grounded in 'those changes in *actuality itself* that define the novel, that are the cause of its dominance in a given epoch' (NLG 7/612). But the 'changes in actuality' to which Bakhtin refers are not reducible to a series of events, nor can the novel merely reflect them. For in both the novel and its enveloping contemporaneity, what's at stake should not be described as merely a new consciousness of time, a new perception of it, but as a new self-consciousness, because the change in perspective changes the orientation of time itself. Contemporaneity is established when we understand each historical moment *as* a historical moment, as in fact the consequence, intended or not, of human actions. It's the historical consciousness we described earlier with reference to the works of Koselleck, and its emergence, as Koselleck has shown in detail, is a historical event in its own right (one we can only grasp retrospectively). The 'spontaneity of an unfinishable present' (NLG 27/631n), to use a choice phrase of Bakhtin's, derives its force from the fact that we have made the present into something different, something orientated to the future, by acknowledging a human capacity to 'make history', as the old expression goes. The novel therefore has work to do: it's tasked with reworking the present and making it historical.

Critique

Insofar as that task entails novels historicising themselves, engaging in what Bakhtin calls – no doubt with a nod to the political events of the day – 'self-criticism' (NLG 6/611), it might appear that novels are condemned to an endless regress, in which each form falls victim to the parody that will eventually follow it. But not only does that not correspond to the actual history of the novel, it clearly isn't what Bakhtin has in mind. For the present is unfinishable, you might say, for a reason: because it is orientated to a future defined by ideals (justice, perfectedness, harmony), a kind of virtual point to which the present is directed (That it is a virtual point was made clear in a comment Bakhtin made in 1961, when he claimed the key was '[n]ot faith (in the sense of definite faith in Orthodoxy, in progress, in humanity, in revolution, etc.), but *the feeling of faith*, that is, an integral (taking in the whole person) relation to the highest and ultimate value', 61N 294/352). The genre of the novel doesn't engage in 'self-criticism' because each generation sees the previous one as conventional, but because it needs to perfect the becoming that sets a course for that Messianic, but unreachable, future. Or to put the matter sharply: historical becoming doesn't follow from the scientific or anthropological fact that humans make history, but from the moral fact that they are responsible for it. Contemporaneity, the orientation to the future, is the way you experience the present as something morally demanding. The new historical consciousness, Koselleck pointed out, replaced inherited political concepts, such as 'republic' or 'democracy', with concepts of directed historical movement, such as 'republicanism' and 'democratism'; they were, in his words, 'modified by a historical philosophy into concepts of movement which made obligatory intervention into everyday political affairs'.[74]

In the 1920s, in his fragment 'Towards a Philosophy of the Act', Bakhtin insisted on every person's *non-alibi in being* (TPA 40/39), i.e., that they experience responsibility as uniquely addressed to them. In 1941, this non-alibi is guaranteed by the historical experience Bakhtin calls contemporaneity. If this seems like a strange way to think about historical experience, it's because we are used to thinking of historical consciousness and religious consciousness as a zero-sum game. Koselleck had, after all, described historical consciousness as a secular replacement for the Christian belief in apocalypse, the conviction that world was about to end.[75] In Bakhtin, by contrast, religious belief in a Messianic future is precisely what makes historical consciousness possible.

But if this is the case, then historical consciousness is not a matter of progress – something we achieve once and for all after prolonged world-historical effort – but of moral and cultural struggle. Contemporaneity might achieve the upper hand, but it is constantly threatened by the kind of time-consciousness that would erase our responsibility for the future. And indeed, this is borne out by what has been called the Manichean structure of Bakhtin's texts, which continually oppose a cultural form that ought to triumph (dialogism, the novel, the *Bildungsroman*, contemporaneity, carnival) against a form that threatens its success (monologism, poetry, the abstract novel, epic, official seriousness). Bakhtin insisted after his lecture that he adored Homer's epic – 'I am its passionate advocate, I know it by heart, and no novel can inspire in me even a shred of the same pleasure as this epic' – but the epic nevertheless figures as the cultural form that will relieve people of their subjectivity and responsibility, that will turn them into slaves of a glorified national past.[76] Similarly, language may be naturally dialogical, but monological and authoritarian forms are continually produced. In one of the late notes drawn from the 1960s and 1970s, Bakhtin declared with striking confidence that '[t]he speech subjects of the high declamatory genres – priests, prophets, preachers, judges, political leaders, patriarchal fathers, and so on – have passed on. The "writer", simply the writer, the inheritor of their styles, has replaced them all. He either stylises them (poses as a prophet, sermon-giver, etc.) or parodies them (to a greater or lesser degree)' (WN, 132/388-9). In fact, Bakhtin is mimicking, intentionally or not, the structure of some forms of Marxist argument, which, on one hand, expresses confidence in the proletariat's historical mission – it is the universal class that will inevitably

128 Works

bring socialism, in accord with 'iron laws' of historical development – and, on the other hand, portrays the social world as one of unremitting social conflict and struggle, with an uncertain outcome. Likewise, contemporaneity and dialogism ought to be irreversible, but they have to struggle against other forms to succeed.

In the essays on the novel, Bakhtin accentuates the positive, not dwelling on the negative, authoritarian forms. In the discussions of popular-festive culture that follow, however, 'official seriousness' looms large.

Popular-Festive Culture and the Novel

The seed was planted in 'Discourse in the Novel', when Bakhtin, having contrasted the style of poetry and the style of the novel, suddenly and precipitously gave the contrast a political spin. Poetry and its stylistic philosophy, grounded in the 'official socio-ideological heights', was bound to 'the task of the cultural, national and political centralization of the verbal-ideological world', while the novel and its prose kin took its cue from what was happening in 'the social depths, on fairground stages and popular stages, [where] clowning heteroglossia, the mimicry of all "languages" and dialects could be heard, and the literature of fabliaux and Schwänke, street songs, proverbs and anecdotes developed' (DN 273/26).

This world of popular parody, of fairground buffoonery and clowning, disappears from the essay almost as suddenly as it appeared, as Bakhtin spends the next 130 pages on novels and their discourse. But in the final chapter of the book, 'The Two Stylistic Lines of the European Novel', the popular culture of Europe makes a second, extended appearance, as a source for the novels of the Second Stylistic Line, which, as Bakhtin puts it, 'take heteroglossia from below to above: from the depths of heteroglossia they rise to the heights of literary language and overwhelm them' (DN 400/155). It isn't carnival that appears, strictly speaking, but the three figures drawn from medieval popular theatrics that prepare the ground for the novel: the rogue, the fool, and the clown.

Each of these three makes a distinctive contribution to novelistic discourse. The rogue practises a 'jolly deception', the sly telling of falsehoods that everyone knows are falsehoods, but which are meant as a counterpoint to the *'pathos-ridden lies'* told 'in all the high, official, canonized genres' (DN 401/157). The fool offers his 'uncomprehending stupidity' (DN 402/157) as a device for estranging the conventions of social life and 'commonly accepted, canonical and incorrigibly false language with their high-falutin' names for things and events' (DN 403/158). The clown plants the seeds of heteroglossia, engaging in a playful distortion of language: he is 'the one having the right to speak in unacceptable languages and to maliciously distort acceptable languages' (DN 405/160). Together, they provide resources for parodying and satirising 'high pathos and all seriousness and conventionality' (DN 404/160), and it's impossible not to see their descendant in the 'writer' we mentioned a few pages ago, the writer who stylises and parodies the priests, prophets, and preachers.

In fact, when these same three figures make their return engagement in the essay on the chronotope, Bakhtin joins the dots for us. 'The novelist', he tells us, 'stands in need of some kind of formal-generic mask' that will define a position for him, and 'the masks of the clown and the fool, transformed in various ways, come to his aid' (FTC 161/413). They provide a model for the writer who stands askew the world they represent, who does not identify with any character or invest any language with their immediate commitments. But Bakhtin also adds another dimension here: these three figures 'bring with them [...] an essential connection to the theatrical stages of the public square' (FTC 159/411–12).

In a couple of years' time, this connection will occupy nearly all of Bakhtin's attention. The rogue, clown, and fool will turn out to be the reconnaissance party for a much bolder mission: the reconceptualisation of the novel as a form that exploits and shapes the energies of the popular-festive culture of Europe, a culture manifest in not only the carnival practices of medieval and Renaissance Europe, but in folk traditions and legends, in Roman Saturnalia, and in Greek parodic literature. Rabelais will serve as the focal point for this project, but to a great extent he's just a vehicle. In the oral examination of his doctoral dissertation in 1946, Bakhtin said outright that 'the hero of my monograph is not Rabelais, but these popular, festive-grotesque forms, the tradition displayed and brought to light for us in Rabelais's work'.[77] He would provide the entrance point to 'a world of incomplete, unfinishable being'.[78]

A world – not merely a language or a chronotope. As we'll see, one of the most striking features of Bakhtin's writing on Rabelais and popular culture is that he turns what was a way of writing into a way of being. The medieval person, he says in the Rabelais book, lived in two worlds, governed by two different philosophies: an official, usual one, policed by feudal authorities and church institutions and '*a second world and a second life* beyond everything official, in which all medieval people were participants to a greater or lesser degree, in which they *lived* for specific periods of time' (Rab 6/8), the world of popular-festive cults, rituals, and holidays.

What moved Bakhtin to take this bold step? It looks like a happy concatenation of circumstances. Bakhtin had been working intensively on Goethe in 1937, and Goethe's *Italian Journey* impressed him with its sense for the concrete marks of history. 'This feeling of time', he noted, 'permeates the remarkable description of Roman carnival' (OBild 32/299). Rabelais was already beginning to monopolise his attention, no doubt in part because Rabelais had become part of the Soviet canon of 'world literature' (*Gargantua and Pantagruel* appearing in several translations with large print runs), as Katerina Clark has pointed out.[79] It's tempting to think that he came across 'The Historical Psychology of Carnival', by Florens Christian Rang, published in 1928, which suggested that carnival was, indeed, a whole way of life.[80] Tempting, but it's more likely the inspiration for making Rabelais the 'key to this world of grotesque form'[81] was his encounter with the work of Olga Freidenberg, whose *The Poetics of Plot and Genre* he read in 1936 and then again in1939.[82] For Freidenberg argued for the steady persistence and influence of folkloric motifs and plots that had emerged in early agricultural civilisations and would find themselves adapted and transformed in modern literature (Freidenberg had, in addition, worked at ILIaZV since 1922, and clearly knew Voloshinov). And perhaps, if we want to allow ourselves a flight of fancy, Bakhtin was moved by an encounter with the real thing: for the summers of 1935, 1936, and 1937 witnessed mass carnivals in Gorky Park, staged by the Soviet government and attended in huge numbers.[83] Bakhtin's dates in Moscow in 1936 and 1937 make it possible.

Exposition

There are essentially three steps in Bakhtin's argument. The first is that our usual understanding of medieval and Renaissance Europe is fundamentally wrong. We have always understood it as completely dominated by feudal political relationships and the institutions of the Christian Church, when, in fact, these institutions were always complemented by a second culture, the culture organised around popular-festive rituals and forms. The importance of these forms, the degree to which they shaped the consciousness and practice of Europeans, has been woefully underestimated. The second step describes this popular-festive culture, which Bakhtin calls a 'culture of laughter'. The culture of laughter is, on the one hand, polemical: it satirises and calls attention to the conventions of the dominant culture. This involves some reversals, like holidays in which slaves dress up as kings, kings appear as slaves, men as women, and so on. But it also involves putting together what the dominant culture traditionally keeps apart, which results in forms that

Bakhtin calls 'grotesque realism'.[84] But popular-festive culture is not only polemical – it is also a positive vision of humanity. Finally, Bakhtin insists we can only understand Rabelais's writing as an adaptation of imagery and motifs drawn from the culture of laughter. Rabelais takes what are essentially cyclical images of death and rebirth and 'refunctions' them for the Renaissance, turning them into markers of a modern historical consciousness. In describing the literary rendition of becoming, Bakhtin had shifted from Dostoevsky's tortured inner dialogues to the relatively soft stylising of Dickens, Pushkin, and Turgenev. Now he was willing to contemplate something with sharper edges – the fierce satire and wild images of Rabelais.

Indeed, his first task is to demonstrate that the sharp edges, the satires of medieval discourse and the coarse language scattered throughout Rabelais, were in fact marks of a strong ambivalence, that they were not only techniques of negation and critique. His analysis of the prologues to each book of *Gargantua and Pantagruel* notes that often they have a specific satirical target – medieval philosophy, medical authorities, ancient Greek history – but this is secondary to their form and style. The prologue to Book 2, for example, begins as an advertisement for the 'Chronicles of Gargantua' itself, conducted in wildly hyperbolic style, full of superlatives, echoing 'the advertising spirit of a barker on stage or a fairground seller of chapbooks' (Rab 160/173); not only are the Chronicles, according to Rabelais, 'peerless, incomparable', but wrapped in warm linen they are a cure for toothache (Rab 161–62/174–75). But the prologue ends with a torrent of abuse hurled at the unappreciative reader ('may the festers, ulcers and chancres of every purulent pox infect you, mangle you and rend you'), of equal force and absurdity. The excessiveness of each style is a sign of its lack of seriousness: the praise is 'ironic and ambivalent', 'on the border of abuse' (i.e., sarcasm), while the abuse veers towards a cheeky familiarity, to the point where 'the praise abuses and the abuse praises' (Rab 165/179). This ambivalent mixture of praise and abuse is one of the defining features of public square speech.

In the same vein, Bakhtin will point to the vulgarity and indecency of Rabelais's language, where rather than sling mud metaphorically one throws shit and drenches one's opponents in urine. Here the abuse is physical rather than verbal, but it follows a similar logic. On the one hand, shit and urine are the media of 'debasement' (*snizhenie*), a purposeful bringing low and besmirching of people and things. On the other hand, throughout the novel urine and shit fertilise the earth: medicinal springs and the river Rhone turn out to be created by the urinating of Pantagruel and Gargantua. Like the curses they incarnate, 'images of urine and excrement are ambivalent, like all images of the material-bodily depths: they simultaneously debase-kill and regenerate-renew, they are blessing and humiliating, in them death and birth, the sexual act and labour, are completely intertwined' (Rab 151/163). Bakhtin will point to these 'material-bodily depths' – an elaborate name for the bottom half of the human being – as the place where the body expels both one's excrement and one's descendants, the place where life is made and food is digested, the place where the body opens out to the world. As a consequence, it becomes the central zone, an endless source of ambivalent imagery for Rabelais, which reaches something of an apogee in his obsession with tripe. For tripe is, as Bakhtin points out, at once 'the *innards*, the *life* of the human being', 'the swallowing, devouring belly', something eaten, and a form of food associated with excrement (Rab 162/176).

Of course, part of the point of debasement is to turn the apparently spiritual into the grossly material. But the insistent claim of *Rabelais* is that the grossly physiological and the vulgarly material are never just that – they are always, as Bakhtin will put it, 'topographical', part of a wider network of philosophical and cosmic analogies. So, the material-bodily depths will refer not only to human bottoms but to earthly ones as well: Rabelais's world is organised around '[a] mighty move into the depths, into the bowels of the earth and the bowels of the human body' (Rab 370/401). There will be journeys to the underworld, graves dug, people crushed into the dirt, items consumed and consigned to the bowels, all signifying, according to a folkloric logic, simultaneous destruction and renewal.

The historical argument is that the combination of praise and abuse, of death and regeneration, is drawn from practices of ancient and medieval popular culture; Bakhtin will, accordingly, alternate between analyses of Rabelais and catalogues of the cries of Paris and the language of popular rituals. And the implicit source of this ambivalence is the cycles of agricultural life, in which death and new life are inextricably bound up with one another, where excrement is literally an essential element of new growth. Interestingly enough, Bakhtin does not outline the material or economic basis for this cultural imagery in the Rabelais book or dissertation, although he had done so in the chronotope essay that prepared the ground for it (in the chapter on 'The Folkloric Bases of the Rabelaisian Chronotope'). Perhaps it was too obvious to dwell on.

But Bakhtin does not mean by this that the material business of agriculture provided a literal ambivalence, the ambivalence of the soil, if you like, which could then be metaphorically extended to other worlds: he assumes that we are dealing with a series of analogies, spiritual and earthly, with no particular point of origin. In a long and exceptionally interesting series of notes he made while revising the Rabelais thesis – the 'Additions and Amendments to "Rabelais"' of

1944 – he points to Shakespeare as 'cosmic, liminal and topographical: therefore his images – topographical by their very nature – are able to develop such extraordinary power and lifelikeness on the topographical and completely accentuated space of the stage' (AARab 528/688). In Shakespeare, there are no abstract directions or spaces – each point in space or movement, at every level – the stage, the universe, the social structure, the individual – is invested with a topographical meaning by a series of spatial analogies.

That series of analogies includes politics, which means debasement is also a political gesture. 'A push to *the depths*', Bakhtin observes, 'is inherent in fights, beatings, blows: one is subverted, thrown to the ground, trampled in the dirt. Buried' (Rab 370/402). When Bakhtin discusses such a throwdown in the novel itself, the continual thrashing of Catchpole, he argues that 'beating and abuse don't have an everyday and private character, but are symbolic actions directed at *someone higher* – at a "*king*"' (Rab 197/214). Kings are continually brought down to earth in popular festivity, appearing as a clown or slave, in a reversal of roles that calls attention to the transitoriness of all social life. There is accordingly an equation in the series 'uncrowning, travesty, thrashing' (Rab 198/215): bringing the king 'back to earth' can be a matter of taking off his external accoutrements, revealing him as mere flesh and blood, like everyone else. Debasement, on one level a literal grounding of life in the agricultural cycle, can be refunctioned to signify the fundamental equality of all people and the falseness and artificiality of all distinctions of status. Indeed, it's hard not to hear an echo in this material of Bakhtin's older claims about Dostoevsky: that his heroes 'are motivated by the utopian dream of creating some kind of human community that lies beyond existing social forms' (PDA 280/241), which is composed 'of purely human material' (PDA 281/241).

Carnival rituals in which the world is turned upside down – where kings dress as slaves, the poor as kings, priests as minstrels, and so on – are thus interpreted as both critical and utopian. As Bakhtin describes it, '[i]f the clown was originally *disguised* as a king, then now, when his reign is finished, they *dress him up again*, "*travesty*" him, in the attire of a clown' (Rab 197/214). Each gesture – clown to king, king back to clown – is critical and utopian (clowns can be kings, and kings are just clowns in disguise), but the utopianism has two significant dimensions. In an encyclopaedia entry on 'Satire', written at the same time as the dissertation, Bakhtin claimed that satire could be defined as 'the *imagistic negation* of contemporary actuality in its various moments, necessarily including in itself – in one or another form, with different degrees of concreteness and clarity – a positive moment in which a better actuality is asserted' (Sat 373/15). The better actuality would be the one in which there were no kings. And this actuality, Bakhtin is at pains to emphasise, is not so much signified as experienced in carnival. Insofar as a carnival is not a staged performance (it 'does not know footlights, even in rudimentary form' (Rab 7/10)), it creates a public space in which social relationships are transformed:

> The festival was like a temporary suspension of the force of the entire official system with all its prohibitions and hierarchical barriers. For a brief period life came out of its usual legal and ecclesiastical ruts and entered into a sphere of utopian freedom. The very ephemerality of this freedom only strengthened its fantastic nature and utopian radicalism, created in the festive atmosphere of images. (Rab 89/100)

For a brief moment, we are all human material and able to speak to one another as such. That is the first dimension of Bakhtin's utopia.

But in the above scenario the crowd dresses up the clown as a king and then dresses up the clown again *as a clown* (the Russian is *pereodevaiut*, literally, they 're-dress' him). There is a sense in which the clown itself, its particular way of being, is the utopian alternative, insofar as the clown is always in costume, never 'serious', never directly identified with its immediate social role. In preliminary notes for the dissertation Bakhtin claims that '[d]ressing up in its utopian aspect played an enormous role in the history of our consciousness of the world and in particular our consciousness of time, of becoming' (NRab 634).

The clown is never serious, because, of course, clowns are funny, and the laughter they provoke is a feature of the popular-festive culture that Bakhtin dwells on throughout his analysis. Popular-festive culture is a 'culture of laughter': but what could this mean? It clearly refers to the affect itself, insofar as Bakhtin insists that popular-festive culture is affirmative, joyous, a celebration of the abundance and productivity of life. But it also points to the source of laughter, which is a disjunction between the ordinary, the expected (one's given social identity, the usual prohibitions and hierarchic barriers) and some new actuality. Laughter is meant as an expression of distance: a rupture in expectations, the revelation of the ridiculousness of a status or belief, the throwing together of things usually kept artificially apart. This distance from worldly roles, this self-ironising, constitutes a second utopian dimension.

But you can only truly appreciate this dimension of laughter by systematically comparing it with the seriousness it undermines. Fortunately, that is rather easy to do. For while Bakhtin did not spend much time describing the monological novel, the monological poem, or the epic work, seriousness is something he returns to again and again from the late 1930s onwards. As with most of Bakhtin's ideas, this one had a trial run: it's there in Bakhtin's identification of monologism with authoritarian discourse, and with the speech subjects of authoritarian discourse (priests, judges, political leaders, etc.) in 'Discourse in the Novel'. The critical move made in that essay is the identification of monologism not with the impersonal operation of reason, with the faceless operation of language as a neutral system (as it was presented in *Problems of Dostoevsky's Art*), but with the rhetoric of figures having official authority. Serious figures, one might say.

In the Rabelais study itself, this seriousness finds an easy illustration in the structures of medieval life, which already had a reputation for gloom and foreboding. For Bakhtin, these official institutions are held together by the fear they inspire in their subjects, a fear that is based on the intermingling of divine, cosmic power and earthly authority. It is 'fear before everything consecrated and prohibited ("mana" and "taboo") before divine and human power, before authoritarian commandments and prohibitions, before death and punishment after death, before hell and all that is *more terrifying than the earth itself*' (Rab 90–91/102). Elsewhere in the study, Bakhtin will talk of a cosmic fear, 'fear in the face of the immeasurably great and the immeasurably powerful' (Rab 335/363). Medieval political and ecclesiastical institutions were oppressive and brutal. But Bakhtin is asking us to focus on the crucial intertwining of metaphysics and politics here, the way in which these institutions mobilised a vertical conception of the universe, in which earthly forces could embody the sublime power ('immeasurably great') of the divine. The fear Bakhtin singles out is in the end motivated not by a specific danger or threat, but by the absolute gulf that exists between the ordinary individual and royal or ecclesiastical power, a gulf that draws its qualitative depth from the sublimity of the divine.

Bakhtin will happily describe this seriousness as a straightforward affect. In a fragment he titles '*The problem of seriousness*' he opens with: 'Elements of the external expression of seriousness: furrowed brows, terrifying eyes, tensely gathered creases and wrinkles' (TPhFHS 10). But it's important to avoid investing too much in that idea, which has led to some fanciful interpretations of Bakhtin's work, in which playfulness always trumps seriousness. For seriousness in itself is not the problem, but 'official seriousness', that is, the exploitation of seriousness by authoritarian institutions. For that reason, Bakhtin occasionally describes the culture of laughter as just a stage or necessary strategy. Having described the power of popular-festive forms, Bakhtin comments: 'A *new* great seriousness always passes through the crucible of these forms, which burn up the old seriousness' (OQThN 572). Again, while writing the Rabelais text he'll point to '[t]he gloomy character of providentialism and predestination. The joyful character of time and historical process. This is a necessary stage on the path to a new historical (not gloomy) seriousness.'[85]

A new historical seriousness would incorporate the time-consciousness, the sense of historical becoming, characteristic of laughter. For in the end, official seriousness and laughter are distinguished not as affects, but by their conceptions of the historical process, by the ways in which they imagine the future. In his 'Additions and Amendments to "Rabelais"', Bakhtin claims that '[t]o make an image serious means to remove its ambivalence and ambiguousness, its unresolvedness, its readiness to change meaning' (AARab 526/684) and that unreadiness is nowhere better exemplified than in the '[f]orms of monumentalism and heroisation' (AARab 526/685) beloved by kings, queens, and the like. The monument of a leader is meant as an unambiguous vehicle of praise, but, more importantly, it is meant to guarantee the leader a kind of false immortality, an immortality achieved by artificially extending his earthly existence. The hierarchical leader is motivated by '[t]he craving for glory and for the perpetuation of one's *name* (and not nickname) in the memory of descendants, in people's mouths' (AARab 526/685).

An object lesson in the problems caused by this false immortality is available in Shakespeare's tragedies, which Bakhtin analyses immediately following the above comments. The source of tragedy, according to Bakhtin, is located in the protagonist's unwillingness to embrace historical becoming, as exemplified by the generational succession of kings. Thus, Macbeth's fatal acts represent 'the necessary iron logic of self-crowning (and more broadly, the logic of any kind of crowning, of any crown or power, or more broadly still, the logic of any self-asserting life, hostile to replacement and renewal)' (AARab 527/686). Rather than accept the logic of death and rebirth, he asserts himself as an individual, but this royal assertion is just an extreme example of trying to make history, to reach into the future, by simply prolonging one's own existence. This is 'the profound tragedy of *individual* life itself' (AARab 527/687), when it asserts itself against the transformative movement of history. King Lear will have the opposite problem: he tries to die too soon, by giving away his kingdom precipitously.

Bakhtin credited tragedy with a power akin to that of popular-festive culture. It, too, expels fear. 'The *serious* courage of tragedy', however, remains within 'the zone of enclosed individuality' (OQThN 564), pitting the individual against a historical process that will inevitably defeat him or her. 'Tragedy and laughter alike look fearlessly into the eyes of being, they do not erect any illusions, they are sober and exacting' (OQThN 564), Bakhtin says. But in tragedy 'individuality ripens and is completed at the moment of its destruction' (OQThN 564).

Bakhtin will accordingly describe this as a logic of parts and wholes. 'The optimism of the *whole*, defeating every "*partial*" fear' (OQThN 564). Parts – individuals – are guided by interests, local passions that can play a role in history only when they acknowledge their inevitable demise, their transformation by the regenerative logic of death/birth. Immortality is accordingly something only possible at the level of the 'people', each of whom, we can assume, does their bit and then passes on. Monuments, Bakhtin wants to argue, will not do the trick. But neither will faith in the posthumous ascension of one's soul. 'Not the raising of the spirit, but historical progress through children and grandchildren' (NRab 668) is the road to immortality. The individual who believes in their own immortality, whether carved out of spirit or in stone, aims for mere continuity rather than development. In contrast, 'in the carnival sense of the world, the immortality of the people is experienced as unbreakably unified with the immortality of all being that becomes' (Rab 256/278).

The encyclopaedia entry on 'Satire' ends on an interesting note. It remarks that '[a]mbassadors of the future ("ideals") in one or another form and to one or another degree are always present in satire' (Sat 390/34). It's a striking image, pregnant with implications, and it brings to mind another famous invocation of the future, composed a few years earlier by the critic and philosopher Walter Benjamin. In his *Berlin Chronicle* he suggests we consider

> the shock with which we come across a gesture or a word the way we suddenly find in our house a forgotten glove or reticule[.] And just as they cause us to surmise that a stranger has been there, there are words or gestures from which we infer this invisible stranger, the future, who left them in our keeping.[86]

According to Bakhtin, the sharpest satire is full of such words and gestures.

Critique

Objections to Bakhtin's interpretation of Rabelais and to his theory of popular-festive culture were made almost immediately, and none was surprising. After all, Bakhtin had presented a large target. The first set of objections we know about was made at the defence of the dissertation itself, in 1946.[87] It focused on a lack of appreciation for Rabelais's 'humanism' – recall that Bakhtin was using the term 'gothic realism' at this point – and worries that Bakhtin was presenting too medieval a version of an author touted as part of the great tradition of 'world literature'. In the English-speaking world, the Renaissance historian Frances Yates famously responded to *Rabelais and His*

World by claiming that '[a]nyone who knows anything about the Renaissance, and about Rabelais, will know that the Bakhtin method has come up with totally wrong answers'.[88] In Yates's view, Rabelais was a sophisticated humanist, and the popular-festive material did not add anything of substance to his elaborate scholarly and intellectual satires.

But the most probing and influential critiques of this text have been more concerned with the claims made for popular-festive radicalism than with Bakhtin's interpretation of Rabelais. Those critiques focused on the following issues: (1) whether popular-festive culture and carnival were inevitably progressive, as Bakhtin seemed to be arguing; (2) whether carnival was as subversive as Bakhtin presented it; and (3) whether Bakhtin had made a decisive break with his own earlier work, insofar as it seemed to extol the collective, the immortal people, at the expense of the individual.

Is Carnival Progressive?

S. I. Averintsev, an early supporter of Bakhtin in Soviet Russia, noted at once that laughter, and in particular mocking laughter, was by no means always affirmative and progressive. Responding to Bakhtin's claim that 'there is no violence lurking behind laughter' (Rab 95/107), Averinstev points out that 'Christ is mocked' in the Gospels, that uncrowning often led to the murder of the victim, and that there was plenty of laughter in the Soviet Union 'when God was put on trial at Komsomol meetings'.[89] In fact, uncrowning and humiliation, together with the possibility of rebirth, were, Averintsev argues, a standard part of the Stalinist toolkit.

Much the same is true of popular festivity itself, which wasn't, as a matter of historical fact, nearly as universalistic as Bakhtin portrayed it. In their exceptionally shrewd assessment of Bakhtin's analysis of carnival, Peter Stallybrass and Allon White stressed that 'carnival often violently abuses and demonizes *weaker*, not stronger social groups – women, ethnic and religious minorities, those "who don't belong" – in a process of *displaced abjection*'.[90] Among those demonised religious groups were, of course, Jews, who clearly stood outside the entire Christian framework of many carnival events. Carnival in Rome in the fifteenth and sixteenth centuries notoriously included the ritual humiliation of Jews who, along with hunchbacks, young men, donkeys, and bulls, were forced to race naked down the main street while being pelted with stones by 'the people'; for this carnival entertainment the Corso (race-course) was named.[91] As a historical practice – not really a single practice, but a network of somewhat related festive and official events – carnival can hardly be deemed progressive.

Stallybrass and White, having confronted the facts, came up with an interesting strategy. Rather than make carnival as such the focus, one could extract its inversions, debasements, and reversals and make these part of a different series, through which class societies symbolically deal with their conflicts: 'The carnival, the circus, the gypsy, the lumpenproletariat play a symbolic role in bourgeois culture out of all proportion to their actual social importance.'[92] The ruthless suppression of carnival activity in modernising England, which they trace in detail, testifies to this. Their point is that there are marginal groups and activities, in no way central to the politics or economies of their societies, which nevertheless are symbolically charged and thus potentially threatening to an existing or emerging social order. Carnival's mockery and satire aren't necessarily progressive – but they could open the way to ideas and activities that are.

Bakhtin assumed that the universalism he attributes to popular-festive culture can be directly derived from the practice of uncrowning, from grotesque images, from the 'familiar and frank' language of the public square. That satire was not merely negative, but contained 'ambassadors of the future', intimations of a different order or different world, was one of his central claims. The satirising of ranks, however, does not lead inexorably to egalitarianism: Bakhtin has assumed that undermining the complex feudal system of rank and status would simply leave everyone as equals. But universalism entails an alternative principle of social organisation, not the absence of social organisation – it requires procedures and institutions as surely as fiefdoms and papal states. The same holds for the concept of 'the people', which Bakhtin anachronistically applies to the Middle Ages: it's a category that depends on modern political and social structures, not the negation of political structures.

Bakhtin's vision of social and political equality and solidarity – no kings! free and familiar contact! – is not fleshed out with an account of grounding institutions, but the absence is a feature, not a bug. For like Dostoevsky's heroes, Bakhtin 'is motivated by the utopian dream of creating some kind of human community that lies beyond existing social forms', in fact, beyond any imaginable social forms. For investment in any social form, in any human convention, carries the risk of self-asserting life: the difference between clerks and kings is only a matter of degree.[93]

Just Letting Off Steam?

The second objection was well articulated by Terry Eagleton, when he noted that carnival was 'a *licensed* affair in every sense, a permissible rupture of hegemony, a contained popular blow-off as disturbing and relatively ineffectual as a revolutionary work of art'.[94] Was it not, in fact, 'incorporative as well as liberating'?[95] Bakhtin had himself acknowledged and discussed the toleration of carnival in ancient Greece and Rome, as well as in later medieval contexts. Similarly, Bakhtin admits the utopian moment of festivity was always circumscribed and limited: a brief experience of familiarity and equality that would dissipate when it was time to return to the fields and workshops. Did utopian experience motivate its participants, 'the people', to fight for an equality that would last the whole year? As a matter of historical fact, the answer is a clear no. While there were instances of peasant radicalism and movements for social equality in the Renaissance – the English Levellers are an example – there is no evidence I'm aware of that the impetus for them was popular festivity. But, then, this debate is not actually about the fifteenth or sixteenth century.

It's a debate about the present, conducted in twentieth- and twenty-first-century terms. The debate has two dimensions. There is the question of whether cultural practices such as festivals have much political clout at all, whether an 'artificial' experience of liberation and equality fuels a desire for the real thing. But that question depends on our modern conception of cultural practices and our modern worry about their political significance. There is, second, the question of what has been named 'prefigurative' politics, the question of whether it makes sense to establish and practise a form of social life that prefigures a more egalitarian future; this question was raised most sharply by feminists in the latter half of the twentieth century.[96] Does a local and bounded form of a more just mode of life inspire action to change the whole, or does it have a pacifying effect, making life bearable and taking the heat out of social movements?

These are modern questions, requiring modern answers.

Collectivity

In their substantial study, *Mikhail Bakhtin: Creation of a Prosaics*, Gary Saul Morson and Caryl Emerson suggested that the Rabelais book represented a sharp break with Bakhtin's earlier (and later) work. Whereas up to that point Bakhtin had 'tied the individual person to specific events', in the study of Rabelais what inspires Bakhtin is 'not real individual bodies in interaction but the potential for extending, transcending and rendering immortal the collective body'.[97] They were not alone in their suspicions. The Russian critic Mikhail Ryklin thought of the book as something therapeutic, which Bakhtin had written in response to the Stalinist terror and purges of the

1930s.[98] Its 'folkness' was a kind of dialectical reversal of the concepts of 'the people' that were being used to justify the most outrageous official crimes. L. A. Gogotishvili, who had insisted on the primacy of religious consciousness in Bakhtin's work, also interpreted the work on Rabelais as a regression or betrayal. According to Gogotishvili's interpretation, the Rabelais book does not maintain the crucial distinction of author and hero but 'reconciles them in the category of the "generic body"'.[99] In addition, Rabelais's horizontal (discussed earlier in this chapter) is 'hypertrophied to the point where the "present" is denied any significance: everything valuable is located in the future', an 'element of monologism' that Gogotishvili associates with 'the majority of politicized economic doctrines'.[100]

Bakhtin had begun to trade in collectivities before this. Although in the Dostoevsky book dialogism took the form of sharp conversations between individuals, by the time of 'Discourse in the Novel', the voices in play were anonymous, collectively produced styles and socio-ideological languages. If anything, Bakhtin drew a sharp and principled distinction between the 'individual dissonances, misunderstandings or contradictions' (DN 325/79) one found in novels and the deep and profound recesses of social heteroglossia. The emphasis on genres, which unites works on style like 'Discourse in the Novel' with works on plot and narrative like 'Forms of Time and of the Chronotope', was repeatedly justified by the claim that generic form and generic change were where the real action was. When Bakhtin took on the idea of folkloric motifs and plots from Freidenberg and the semantic paleontologists, the collective behind cultural forms became even more anonymous and distant.

As we've established, even the author/hero dyad was not a relation between individuals. Most of 'Author and Hero' described the working of the kinds of cultural forms (biography, confession, etc.) Bakhtin would later call genres. From this perspective, the anonymous forms of popular culture or folklore are not qualitatively different from the forms of authorship Bakhtin discussed ten or fifteen years earlier. The difference is that Bakhtin has realised that the field of cultural forms is a battlefield: the new forms must struggle not with individuality per se, but with forms of 'official seriousness' that make 'self-asserting life' a principle of social organisation.

Summary

Rabelais took popular-festive culture and turned it into a vehicle of historical becoming. The reversals, grotesque forms, and praise/abuse that defined popular-festive culture and its carnivals expressed an ambivalence in the order of the world, a sense of history as depending on death that regenerates, on excrement that fertilises, on the transient nature of all social ranks. Rabelais can use these forms for both debasing, extravagant polemics and as a support for a '[b]road utopian conception (traditional and folkloric, not rationalistically created) that depends, on one hand, on a natural optimism (a faith in material nature) about the continuous victory of rebirth over death [...] and, on the other hand, on the historical progress of knowledge and culture, i.e., on a particular faith in human nature' (NRab 612).

Speech Genres, Utterances, and Metalinguistics

After the furious productivity of the decade from 1936 to 1946, Bakhtin seemed to slow down a bit. He had, for the first time in his life, steady and secure employment, at the Mordovian State Pedagogical Institute in Saransk, where he would teach until retirement in 1961. From 1946 until about 1950, his energies were probably absorbed by the need to revise his dissertation, which would only clear the final hurdle in 1951. All that said, there is something of a lull in Bakhtin's writing from roughly 1945 until 1961, when the arrival of Kozhinov, Bocharov, and Gachev sets off a new round of revision.

Something of a lull quantitatively and something of a lull qualitatively. For the two principal works of the period – the draft for an article 'The Problem of Speech Genres' (1953–54) and the somewhat more rambling 'The Problem of the Text' (1959–60) are restrained in argument, contributions to what might be called 'normal science' rather than clarion calls to rethink the literary enterprise. There is one new concept, 'speech genre', but more significantly, there is a much more conciliatory approach to the problems that had both plagued and stimulated Bakhtin.

The path Bakhtin was taking can be illustrated by looking at a set of notes, named 'Dialogism – II', he made while preparing 'The Problem of Speech Genres'. They open with a series of long quotations from an article by the linguist V. V. Vinogradov called 'Urgent Tasks for Soviet Linguistics (Issues in Literary Scholarship in the Light of J. V. Stalin's Works on Linguistics)': the quotations are on the multiplicity of styles there are within the national language and how best to understand their interrelationships. A few pages later, we find Bakhtin making notes on his own 'Discourse in the Novel'. With his old (and, at that point, still unpublished) text in one hand, and Vinogradov's advice to linguists and literary scholars in the other, Bakhtin created 'The Problem of Speech Genres', a 'Discourse in the Novel' fit for the 1950s.

In the following decade, Bakhtin would return to Dostoevsky, as he prepared the text for a revised *Problems of Dostoevsky's Poetics*. The old Part Two, 'Discourse in Dostoevsky', became chapter 5, and Bakhtin's brief account of adventure plots was replaced by an intricate historical chapter, which attempted to trace Dostoevsky's plots back to Menippean satire. But most of what people read from Bakhtin's final fifteen years are the scribblings, paragraphs, and observations with which he filled four notebooks. Kozhinov, one of Bakhtin's saviours and editors, picked his favourites and published them as 'From Notes Made in 1970–71' and 'Towards a Methodology for the Human Sciences', which we now know had neither Bakhtin's input nor authorisation. Kozhinov chose well: the notes and observations often contain pithy formulations and interesting elaborations of the ideas Bakhtin had cultivated in his earlier years.

Exposition

Like 'Discourse in the Novel', 'The Problem of Speech Genres' is an essay on the stylistics of genre and a warning to all those who indulge in '[t]he isolation of styles from genres' (PSG 65/165). But genre, the central term, has undergone a subtle reworking. It is, in the first instance, a term for the *'relatively stable types'* of utterances (PSG 60/159) we find in language use; in other words, a replacement for the concept of socio-ideological languages. No sooner have we been introduced to the speech genre, however, than the category is divided into primary and secondary forms, with the assertion that '[t]he difference between primary and secondary (ideological) genres is extraordinarily great and principled' (PSG 62/161). For, in fact, Bakhtin has reintroduced the novel, but now in the guise of the secondary genre, defined as the genre that reworks the utterances of the primary genres. Granted, the idea of the secondary genre is more capacious than the idea of the novel – it can take in, for example, scientific research – but the difference in principle between genres that directly embody life practices and those that are reflective, that take the primary genres as their raw material, is something familiar: it's the difference between author and hero, between the aesthetic and the cognitive, between the novel and its subordinate styles. Familiar, but uncannily different, for the new version of the old opposition is neutral, a mere description of genres in a society in which speech genres and novels are facts rather than forms with a project. Heteroglossia finds itself reduced to the simple coexistence of speech types, no longer generating its own social energy. The secondary genres, the very existence of which had once announced 'a radical revolution in the fates of human discourse', now dutifully recombine the primary material for their own purposes.

In general terms, here and in 'The Problem of the Text' Bakhtin appears willing to accept some division of scholarly labour, whereby formal linguistics would focus on grammar and sentences while dialogical study would concentrate its efforts on the utterance:

> Therefore, behind every text stands a system of language. To this language corresponds everything in the text repeated and reproduced, everything repeatable and reproducible, everything that could be given outside the given text (the data). But simultaneously every text (as an utterance) is something individual, unique, and unrepeatable, and in this lies its entire meaning (its project, on account of which it was created).[101]

The study of formal grammar and the study of the style of the utterance are therefore 'two points of view on one and the same concrete linguistic phenomenon', which ideally should be 'organically combined' (PSG 66/167). Thus, the scientific, 'monological' approach to language is divested of all political significance: it's just a different method, with a different object. Treating sentences in the manner of structuralist linguistics is no longer part of a centralising political and cultural project, but just the scientific way of looking at language, legitimate within its limits.

The utterance, now carefully distinguished from the sentence, remains as the new and privileged object of Bakhtin's 'metalinguistics'. But this *'real unit* of speech communication' (PSG 71/172) contains none of the intentionality or force of its 1930s ancestor, 'discourse'. Instead of the seeds of historical becoming, each utterance embodies only a pale 'semantic full-valuedness' (PSG 74/176). Instead of discourse's artistic reworking, all that is left of the novel is the human sciences, which examine language contextually and dialogically (as response, as a contribution to a dialogue), but without the faintest hint of historical becoming.

Critique

It would be wrong, however, to think that Bakhtin had simply given up. Instead, the ethical, political, utopian force that had been condensed in the idea of historical becoming finds itself rerouted into a number of smaller streams. For one thing, Bakhtin finds his own Messiah, whom he labels the superaddressee in his '1961. Notes'. While every speaker, he claims, shapes what they have to say according to a presumed immediate addressee, the very act of speech is shadowed by a Messianic possibility. For 'besides this addressee (the "second" person), the author of an utterance, more or less consciously, presupposes a higher "superaddressee" ("a third"), whose absolutely just responsive understanding is presumed, either at some metaphysical distance or in distant historical time' (61N 126/337). The just responsive understanding is not something one expects, but a utopian, redemptive possibility that animates the utterance from within. For the superaddressee would not just comprehend what one was trying to say, but would retrospectively justify the act of saying it.

In the 'Working Notes from the 1960s and Early 70s', which encompass the two Kozhinov-edited collections, one also finds utopian declarations about the present, declarations in keeping with the belief that we are living in the age of 'contemporaneity' and that the mythic forces have been dealt a near-fatal blow:

> A specific inflection of sobriety, simplicity, democracy, and freedom is inherent in all modern languages. With certain qualifications one can say that they all (especially French) have emerged from the popular and profaning genres, they all, to a certain degree, have been defined by a long and complex process of forcibly removing alien sacred discourse, and sacred and authoritarian discourse in general, with its indisputability, its unconditionality, its absence of qualifications. (WN 132-33/389)

But the extolling of the virtues of the present did not mean Bakhtin was neglecting the future. 'The novel', he remarked in the notes, 'breathes the future' (WN 388). But he now appeared to look to the future in a more strictly temporal sense, as something that, after a sufficiently long wait, might redeem the present (the ambassadors were no longer making voyages from there, it seems). The work's 'significance in great time' (WN 400) depended on one's patience rather than one's ethical orientation: great time depended on an 'endless and unfinished dialogue' (WN 169/433). Bakhtin's ringing declaration that '[n]othing is absolutely dead: every meaning will have its festival of rebirth' (WN 170/435) has often been cited as evidence of his belief in the future. In fact, it reduces 'great time' to a waiting game, in which the future does not structure the present, does not impose demands on it, but can be counted on to redeem all by those with sufficient patience. The Messianic spark had been reduced to the light at the end of the tunnel.

Chapter 5

Reception

As I mentioned at the very beginning of this book, Bakhtin's reception was completely out of joint. Although there were a few reviews of *Problems of Dostoevsky's Art* shortly after it was published, the arrest of its author made public discussion of his work impossible. Contrary to myth, Bakhtin did not disappear from view entirely after that: his lectures at the Gorky Institute in 1940 and 1941 were discussed and his dissertation defence generated a long and serious conversation. But reception was limited to public, oral events – there were no written works to be dissected and evaluated, until the campaign for Bakhtin's rehabilitation began in the early 1960s.

There were, it's true, a few early scattered references to Bakhtin's 1929 book in English, which were probably inspired by Vladimir Seduro's glowing summary of it in a book on Russian Dostoevsky criticism in 1957.[1] But it was the publication of the revised version of his Dostoevsky book in 1963 and of his book on Rabelais in 1965 that gained Bakhtin attention, first in the Soviet Union itself and then in the world beyond.[2] Slavists began to cite Bakhtin as a major 'Formalist' critic of Dostoevsky, and some of them made efforts to extend the notion of the polyphonic novel to other writers, such as Solzhenitsyn.[3] The new interest in Russian Formalism itself, spurred by Victor Erlich's book on the one hand, and the emergence of the Lotman-Uspensky school of semiotics in the Soviet Union on the other, drew attention to Bakhtin as a sort of Formalist fellow-traveller.[4] The approach was appreciative – Bakhtin was considered a significant, important writer – but at the same time muted, in the sense that he was considered just one contributor to an established school of Russian criticism.[5] It's instructive, in that respect, to compare Bakhtin's reception in North America and Britain to the interpretation he received in France, which depended on the offices of the two Bulgarian émigrés I mentioned at the beginning, Tzvetan Todorov and Julia Kristeva. In Kristeva's eyes, it was Bakhtin's break with the project of Formalism that made his work valuable and interesting; for Todorov, who, in fact, composed the first monograph on Bakhtin (*Mikhail Bakhtin: The Dialogical Principle*), Bakhtin was a writer in the line of German Romanticism.[6]

The Dostoevsky book remained the concern of Slavists until 1973, when it was translated for Ardis Press; the Rabelais book followed an entirely different trajectory.[7] A mere three years after its publication in Moscow, it appeared in English translation for MIT Press. Unsurprisingly, its extravagant and unorthodox claims for medieval popular culture provoked sharp reactions: a famously dismissive review by Frances Yates, genuine enthusiasm from scholars beginning to work out the details and method of social history.[8] It became part of the academic literature on Rabelais, cited by Rabelais scholars, and a provocation in the field of social history, where it provided both methodology and inspiration for the new 'history from below'. The preface to the Rabelais book, however, written by Krystyna Pomorska, continued in the earlier vein, describing his Dostoevsky book as belonging 'to the second phase in the development of the Russian Formalist school, the structuralist phase'.[9]

While American and UK Slavists were carefully assimilating Bakhtin into a recognisable, if evolving, tradition of Russian and Slavic criticism, his champions in the Soviet Union were busy establishing as much distance as they could between him and that very same tradition. Bocharov and Kozhinov were fighting valiantly to get more of Bakhtin's work published in book form, which led to the two collections we mentioned at the beginning: *Voprosy literatury i estetiki* [*Questions of Literature and Aesthetics*] in 1975, and *Estetika slovesnogo tvorchestva* [*The Aesthetics of Verbal Art*] in 1979. These two books would, in combination with the existing Dostoevsky and Rabelais texts, eventually constitute the Bakhtin *oeuvre* for the Anglophone world. The editorial decisions that moulded them were therefore crucial. The 1975 collection included two long essays on the novel, destined to be mainstays of Bakhtin's critical influence ('Discourse in the Novel' and the chronotope essay), two transcripts of lectures on the novel, and a fifth piece that seemed wholly out of place, a philosophical critique of Formalism from 1924, which had hardly anything to say about the novel at all.[10] The 1979 collection looks at first glance innocent enough: early philosophy, more material on the novel, and a mix of later work.[11] But that later post-war material, varied as it might be, is unified by a consistent polemic with Soviet structuralism as represented by V. V. Vinogradov in the 1940s and Iurii Lotman later on. At the time, this slant may have looked like a mere by-product of the attempt to get as much Bakhtin out into the world as possible; in retrospect, we can appreciate how much effort went into selecting and shaping the material that appeared. One of the sharpest articulations of Bakhtin's distance from structuralism in the collection was a 1959–61 piece on the philosophy of language titled 'The Problem of the Text in Linguistics, Philology, and the Human Sciences', which systematically distinguished the object of scientific linguistics, language, from the object of the human sciences, the concrete and dialogical utterance. When this work was republished in 1996, we learned that it was, in fact, something of a composite: the editors had attached half the contents of one Bakhtin notebook, dedicated to the reworking of the Dostoevsky book, to the contents of a slightly earlier notebook, in order to create a single work defining Bakhtin's position on language. Similarly, the two powerful collocations of philosophical notes that concluded the 1979 book, 'Towards a Methodology of the Human Sciences' and the 'From Notes Made in 1970–71' turned out – this time when the work was republished in 2002 – to be editorial creations that lifted fragments from a series of notebooks covering a decade and cleverly blended to create two new 'texts' defining the distinctive tasks of the human sciences. Bakhtin had died, and his editors wanted to make sure his position was clear and his originality not in doubt.

Editorial work, however, was only one front in this battle. Bakhtin's defenders in the Soviet Union had begun to create – and create is the right word – a biography for him. They made sure that the rumour that Bakhtin had written texts published under the names of Voloshinov and Medvedev was widely spread and communicated to American scholars.[12] Just as importantly, they began to propagate the interpretation of Bakhtin's life that would underpin the attribution of the disputed texts to Bakhtin. The campaign for Bakhtin 'in a mask' was underway.

When, in the late 1970s, Michael Holquist and Katerina Clark set to work on their biography, they had to depend substantially on the oral testimony of Bakhtin's camp in Russia.[13] When Holquist, working with Caryl Emerson, started to translate the essays on the novel from the 1975 volume (sensibly excluding the odd man out, the critique of Formalism), they had to work with the printed Russian texts rather than manuscript originals, which lay in a private archive. The translations came out as *The Dialogic Imagination* in 1981. In one sense, it's fair to say the Russian slant prevailed, for these two texts ensured that, from that point onwards, Bakhtin would cease to be part of a Formalist-cum-Structuralist tradition and would instead be regarded as an original master thinker. The encounters of the 1960s and 1970s had been earnest and respectful: now theorists read Bakhtin as a brilliant new light in the firmament of literary theory.

Bakhtin was not like structuralism: he saw language as discourse, perpetually 'becoming' and dynamic. But he was not like deconstruction, either, because the slipperiness of discourse seemed to depend on the slipperiness and ambiguity of social context and the social dynamism of heteroglossia. Bakhtin had, it seemed, taken several of the leading melodies of Theory – the fact that we draw on an inherited linguistic system, the semiotic nature of all our ideas, the undecidability of linguistic utterance – and set them in a major key, so that they sounded like ringing humanist declarations rather than a resigned acknowledgement that intentions were futile and history inaccessible. In fact, for a brief moment it looked like the continent Bakhtin had discovered would combine the New World of language-modelled theories with the Old World of historical and ideological criticism. An early review by David Carroll in *Diacritics* – the Talmud, if not the Bible of post-structuralism – claimed that '[w]hat is most clear and forceful in Bakhtin is the way his work opens "the prison-house of language" that most structuralist-formalist approaches have tended to construct without imprisoning us in turn in dialectics, in a history or metahistory'.[14] The neo-Aristotelian Wayne Booth would enthuse about how Bakhtin neatly combined interest in form with interest in textual ideology.[15] Terry Eagleton would join in the enthusiastic chorus with the claim that 'Bakhtin recapitulates *avant la lettre* many of the leading motifs of contemporary deconstruction, and does so, scandalously, in a firmly social context'.[16]

Holquist and Clark's biography, published in 1984, seemed to follow the Russian interpretative line faithfully: they described his early philosophical works – which they called 'The Architectonics of Answerability' – as the core of Bakhtin's program, setting out 'an agenda of topics so basal and complex that not even a lifetime would suffice to think them through'.[17] They explained Bakhtin's shift from philosophy to literary criticism – and his supposed authorship of the disputed texts – as in part a response to his belief that 'he was not going to be able to publish under his own name'.[18] Finally, they described P. N. Medvedev as a 'Soviet careerist' and 'Soviet establishment figure', reinforcing the attacks being made on him by Bakhtin's Russian devotees.[19] The biography was supported by a mass of contextual sources, and the authors confessed to the difficulty of tracking down reliable documentary sources in their preface. Their reliance on unattributed oral testimony (in, for instance, the characterisation of Medvedev) was striking, but, for scholarship on Bakhtin, unexceptional and understandable.[20]

Their apparent indebtedness to the Russian account, however, could not hide their indifference to many of its fundamental interests. Clark and Holquist were Slavists, but they had no deep commitment to the Russian religious tradition, nor did they have any particular attachment to phenomenology or neo-Kantianism (Bakhtin's main philosophical sources). Their interpretative frame for Bakhtin was accordingly secular and, in many respects, recognisably North American. In retrospect, the biography is deceptively structured: the bulk of it is devoted to Bakhtin's life and work until 1929, as *if this were its formative period* (no doubt because this is the period about which the most information was available). But their understanding of Bakhtin's work is largely derived from the work following, not preceding, Bakhtin's linguistic turn (which they believe begins with the disputed texts of Voloshinov, authored by Bakhtin). They acknowledged '[t]he centrality of the self/other distinction in all of Bakhtin's work', but interpreted it as a piece of secular philosophical anthropology.[21] It's characteristic that when introducing the distinction, they grounded it in what they call 'an everyday, garden-variety fact [...]: if, as everyone would admit, no two bodies can occupy the same space at the same time, then my place in existence is unique'.[22] By contrast, for Bakhtin's Russian religious interpreters, the self/other distinction is grounded not in the intuitive truths of space and bodies, but in the relationship between God (the ultimate 'author') and the creatures he has created. As a result, in Clark and Holquist Bakhtin appears as a secular philosopher of language.

That philosophy promised to reconcile the systematic, semiotic aspect of language with the social relationships in which discourse always operated; whether it actually did so was another matter. To a certain degree, Clark and Holquist, as well as Carroll, Booth, and Eagleton, were simply taking Bakhtin at his word. In the preface to the Dostoevsky book, he had insisted that 'a purely formal analysis', such as he was engaged in, 'must grasp every element of artistic structure as a point at which living social forces are refracted', thereby overcoming the limitations of the '[n]arrowly formalist approach' and 'equally narrow ideologism' (PDA 276/4). A few years later he would reiterate this methodological ambition in the opening pages of 'Discourse in the Novel', when he promised to split the difference between 'formalism' and 'ideologism'.

Of course, everything would then depend on what one meant by 'the word when it was understood as a social phenomenon'. At the minimum, it meant that every line of discourse, every utterance, displayed what Bakhtin would call 'addressivity': discourse didn't signify directly, but was always framed and shaped by a situation or respondent. For the Russian religious camp, that respondent was God: the speaker or 'hero' of a discourse can never be understood on its own because it *needs* an author who can make up for its limitedness and mere worldliness.[23] For liberal interpreters of Bakhtin, the *other* addressed was other people: discourse was social or dialogical in the sense that it was always conversational, no matter how mediated and distant one's conversational partner was. As one drifted further Left on the spectrum of Bakhtin criticism, the addressee appeared less and less like a *person*, and more and more like a structure or social situation that framed and re-voiced every instance of speech.

One could therefore believe that Bakhtin had made a decisive break with Formalism and structuralism while holding an understanding of him wholly at odds with other equally un-Formalist interpretations. In the 1980s and 1990s, a hundred flowers of Bakhtin interpretation bloomed, and they were wildly different in colour and shape. The Russian religious interpretation of Bakhtin, in which every interpersonal dialogical encounter echoed the relationship of God to human, found sympathetic exponents in the work of Ann Shukman, Ruth Coates, and Alexandar Mihailovic.[24] In the liberal tradition, exemplified by the critical work of Holquist, Gary Saul Morson, and Caryl Emerson, Bakhtin's dicta on the unrepeatability and uniqueness of the utterance, his insistence on the perpetual possibility of radical transformation, were understood not in religious terms, but as reworkings of a familiar emphasis on the need to attend to the particulars. In their detailed study of Bakhtin, Morson and Emerson claimed Bakhtin provided new reasons for accepting that novels were 'powerful tools for enriching our moral sense of particular situations.'[25]. Dialogue itself was understood as an interaction between individual speakers, though these speakers might represent broader social languages. Its virtues were traditional liberal ones: novels staged 'a complex play of values and tones, as discourses and their speakers orient themselves to each other' – they instantiated the kind of self-reflexiveness that was the hallmark of liberal tolerance.[26] The concreteness of the utterance was assimilated to its everyday, ordinary quality.

The Left thought concreteness meant something quite different. As early as 1974, Fredric Jameson, the dominant presence in American Marxist criticism, had seen in Voloshinov a theoretically sophisticated antidote to the abstractions of structuralism.[27] It was in England and Scotland, however, that Bakhtin found his most dedicated left-wing audience. The Rabelais book had, as I mentioned above, offered a theoretical resource to the growing interest in popular culture, and it was enthusiastically taken up by Tony Bennett, Allon White, and Peter Stallybrass.[28] The burgeoning discipline of social history had forced the world to look carefully at and take seriously a wide range of popular cultural practices from the past. Popular associations, entertainments, and cultural pursuits that had sat under the radar for decades were now interpreted as serious and complex works of culture. In this context, Bakhtin added a new wrinkle. Not only was popular culture complex: it also featured the kind of sophisticated stylistic practice – parody, irony, stylisation – that had heretofore been reserved for novelists. Nor was the territory limited to the past – as cultural studies made the analysis of the present a serious business, Bakhtin's work offered a way to make the unserious elements of popular culture – amusement parks at the beach! – look serious.[29]

It was, however, the essays on the novel, with their talk of official monologism and dialogical-novelistic subversion, that ultimately drew the most attention. Critics like David Shepherd, Craig Brandist, Alastair Renfrew, Graham Pechey, Galin Tihanov, and the author of the present book, to the consternation of their Russian colleagues, took Bakhtin's promise of a sociological stylistics seriously. Where the dominant Russian interpretation wanted to distance Bakhtin as much as possible from his surroundings, to position him above the fray, his socialist and Marxist enthusiasts understood him as a man of his time, deeply entrenched in the ideas and arguments that crisscrossed Russia and Europe in the 1920s and 1930s. As a consequence, if one wanted thick, contextual analysis of Bakhtin's writings in English, the kind of thing traditionally associated with historicism, one turned to Tihanov and Brandist.

That Bakhtin's writings could inspire such fervour, though based on strikingly different construals of what he actually said, naturally raised some eyebrows. Edward Said confessed that he wanted to avoid using the term 'dialogical' on account of 'the cult of Bakhtin'.[30] Paul de Man admired and was intrigued by Bakhtin, but nevertheless wondered 'why the notion of dialogism can be so enthusiastically received by theoreticians of very diverse persuasion'.[31] Robert Young would coolly observe how Bakhtin worked, for liberal and for Marxist critics, as a kind of antidote to post-structuralism:

> Rather than offering an alternative to Derrida in the sense of an oppositional position, Bakhtin seemed to allow the assimilation of some of the more compelling aspects of his thought while placing them within a more acceptable sociohistorical framework. Derrida himself could then be more or less indifferently rejected altogether.[32]

Bakhtin, then, may not have been the critic who drew history and textuality into a perfect braid, but someone who allowed admirers to cut a few corners. Was the enthusiasm of his supporters a matter of projection and wishfulfilment? Did they simply find the solutions they wanted to find? In fairness, Bakhtin's work invited the kind of ambiguities one finds in the wide range of Bakhtin criticism. The new world they glimpsed reflected the ideologies they brought with them, but they were not mere imaginings.

In part, the ambiguities of Bakhtin interpretation stem from the changes that characterised the development of Bakhtin's work itself. Religious interpretations of his work used the philosophical fragments of the 1920s, the Dostoevsky book, and various philosophical titbits from later years as the frame for their discussion. Liberal criticism was most comfortable with the Dostoevsky book, where dialogism is a matter of one voice confronting and provoking another. Marxist and socialist criticism, unsurprisingly, wanted the militant Bakhtin of the 1930s to do the heavy lifting. But in the end, the heterogeneous and even dissonant reception of Bakhtin was made possible, if not inevitable, by the persistent, structural ambiguities in Bakhtin's writing that we have discussed throughout this book.

The question of the ontology of the author was particularly significant. Clark and Holquist had called 'self' and 'other' the primary categories in Bakhtin's thought, but that was not entirely accurate – Bakhtin preferred, even in the early work, to talk of *I* and *other* and, more tellingly, *author* and *hero*. Bakhtin had, indeed, used the model of one person looking at another, seeing the outside of that person (or that person as 'outside', as expression) to describe the author/hero relationship. But in one and the same essay ('Author and Hero') he would describe author and hero as two people, describe them as the relationship of a text to its protagonists, and describe them in terms of the human relationship to an ultimate or supreme outsideness, that is, to God as an author transcending her creaturely heroes. And even when Bakhtin used *author* to mean the author of texts, he oscillated between meaning the physical human being who composed a text and the structure or form of a text.

Problems of Dostoevsky's Art only exacerbated the problem. Dostoevsky is sometimes a conversational partner to his heroes (as if there were two real people chatting), sometimes a 'voice' within the text, and sometimes the text itself ('The author speaks through the construction of their novel not *about* the hero, but *with* the hero', PDA 63/70). 'Discourse in the Novel' made things worse still, when it replaced the dyad of author and hero with that of the 'novel' and the 'languages' represented within it, while at the same time describing the intersection of these two dimensions as 'double-voicing'.

It was not, therefore, outlandish for Morson and Emerson, or Clark and Holquist, to think of dialogue as an interaction between individualised speakers. Nor was it outlandish for the present author and his comrades to think of authorship in broader, sociological terms. In the writing, Bakhtin presented novelistic structures as if they were voices and voices as if they were structures: which is to say that he, in effect, elaborated on a fundamental intuition – that novelistic frames and structures shaped the intentionality or directedness of the speech within them – but never clarified it theoretically.[33] That was the task bequeathed to his interpreters.

The individualist proclivity of American culture inclined its Bakhtin interpreters to reduce structures and languages to voices. In that sense, Bakhtin did, indeed, provide critics hostile to structuralism with a way to discuss novels as complex structures while imagining them as conversations. But the priority of voice was not merely a feature of liberal individualism: it was characteristic of a different kind of Bakhtin criticism as well, which had emerged in parallel with so-called high theory. Feminist criticism and what would eventually be called postcolonial criticism were rapidly gathering momentum through the 1970s and 1980s, and the publication of *The Dialogic Imagination* came at just the right time. In this case, however, the starting point was not individual dialogue but Bakhtin's claim in 'Discourse in the Novel' that in novels 'double-voicedness is deeply rooted in an essential heteroglossia and multilanguagedness'.

In the case of feminist criticism, the timing of Bakhtin's translation could not have been more fortuitous. In the 1980s Dale Spender's *Man-made Language* and the translation of work by Hélène Cixous and other French feminists had sparked a vigorous debate over whether and how the experience of women could be articulated, given the sexism built into the common language.[34] The idea that intentions might be 'refracted' in an inherited language, that a writer at odds with the linguistic resources available could appropriate them and use them against the grain, seemed to offer a middle way between dreams of a pure women's language and resignation before 'man-made language'. From the 1980s onwards, feminist critics used Bakhtin to describe and explain how female authors turned masculinist linguistic form to their own purposes.[35] Typical would be Patricia Yaeger's description of what Eudora Welty did with phrases and figures drawn from Yeats's poetry: 'By "stylizing" an alien text, by assimilating, that is, the other's word into her own heteroglossic style, Welty establishes a distance between the incorporated text and its initial meaning; she opens this text to another point of view.'[36]

The idea that men and women spoke different languages, though powerful, was at least, to some degree, metaphorical. For postcolonial critics there was not the slightest need for metaphor: multilanguagedness, in the perfectly ordinary sense, was normal for nations that had been colonies. When Bakhtin staged a confrontation between a unified, 'centripetal' language and the 'centrifugal' world of popular heteroglossia in the early pages of 'Discourse in the Novel', he had been thinking of how Latin related to the emerging European vernaculars; postcolonial critics had only to put those vernaculars, now the standard languages of powerful European states, in the place of Latin to create a useful model for postcolonial analysis. The question of which language to use, and whether the language of the coloniser could be and should be adapted for postcolonial or revolutionary purposes, had been a pressing issue amongst postcolonial writers: Bakhtin could not have landed on more fertile ground.[37]

Where postcolonial writers wanted to refract their intentions through an imposed colonial language, Bakhtin's claim that novelists express their intentions through indirect double-voicing was a valuable resource. But there was a deeper affinity available between Bakhtin and postcolonial theory. In criticising the very idea of 'race' and racial difference, postcolonial theorists emphasised the ubiquity, the normalcy of ethnic hybridity (as well as the fear and anxiety its possibility awakened in racists). In his *Colonial Desire*, Robert Young saw the analogy with Bakhtin's theory and moved to exploit it.[38] Bakhtin's discussion of hybridisation in 'Discourse in the Novel' suggested that impurity was the rule in language as in biology. Furthermore, the distinction between organic and intentional hybrid utterances suggested that just as ethnic hybridity was a rebuke to purist theories of race, so discursive hybridity undermined the purity required by authoritarian discourse. To close the loop, Young needed only to point out that colonial authority itself required a monological singular language, untainted by the discourse of the colonised. But, of course, just as even the most ostensibly monological utterance is, at some level, a dialogical response to the discourse around it, so, Young observes (citing Homi Bhabha), 'the single voice of colonial authority undermines the operation of colonial power by inscribing and disclosing the trace of the other so that it reveals itself as double-voiced'.[39] Despite its best efforts, colonial discourse ends up producing the very discursive hybridity it needs to repress.

In the United States, the postcolonial appropriation of Bakhtin moved along similar lines. Du Bois's claim that black Americans were afflicted with a 'double consciousness, this sense of always looking at oneself through the eyes of others', uncannily mirrored Bakhtin's notion of a discourse directed 'both at the referent of the speech, as in ordinary discourse, and at *the discourse of an other*, at *someone else's speech*' (PDA 185/105).[40] Henry Louis Gates, Jr., would secure the alignment in his *The Signifying Monkey*, the opening chapters of which were prefaced with quotations from Frederick Douglass and Bakhtin. Gates shrewdly recognised the closeness between the American black vernacular tradition of 'signifyin(g)' – a tradition of rhetorical excess, parody, and irony – and Bakhtin's theory of double-voiced prose.[41]

Bakhtin had argued, from 'Discourse in the Novel' onwards, that the double-voicedness typical of novelistic prose derived its breadth and energy from popular genres and discourse: 'It is precisely here, on a local scale, in the minor "low" genres, on the popular stages, in the fairground squares, in street songs and anecdotes, that techniques were devised for the construction of images of language, for combining discourse with the image of a speaking person, for the objective display of discourse together with a person'

(DN 400–1/156). But Bakhtin did not follow the claim with detailed evidence for it: even the Rabelais study is more about Rabelais than the popular culture of the middle ages. Gates – although this was not his principal aim – makes good on the claim, albeit in an American rather than European context, by showing in detail how black vernacular traditions find themselves translated into African American literary techniques. The association of double-voicing with black double consciousness and postcolonial hybridity set the stage for one of the most productive appropriations of Bakhtin's work.[42]

Was the appropriation appropriate? Was the match between 1930s Bakhtin and postcolonial theory in the 1980s and 1990s as neat as it looked? As before, it would be wrong to say that postcolonial theorists were misinterpreting Bakhtin, but fair to say they took advantage of a significant ambiguity in his work. As I have stressed throughout this book, Bakhtin's project was not to recognise the multiplicity of voices one finds in the social world, to corral and organise an existing heteroglossia, but to describe how voices or socio-ideological languages could and should be made in the first place. To artistically represent language, to create the image of a language entailed infusing language with 'heteroglot becoming' (DN 356/111) by means of plot, narrative, and contextualisation. That infusion was what endowed a social voice with 'its unfinishability, its unclosedness and its indeterminacy', an unfinishability that depended on the power that a Messianic future exercised on the present. When a feminist or postcolonial critic uses the idea of dialogism to explain how one discourse relativises another, how it undercuts its epistemological authority and sure-footedness, this element of Bakhtin's argument is sidelined. But, in fairness, Bakhtin sidelined it, too. The future, apart from some occasional moments, is often a vague and undefined place in Bakhtin's writing. His emphasis on satire and parody, which became stronger and stronger throughout the 1930s, was bound to leave the impression that dialogism was principally an exercise in undercutting authority. And the temptation to frame heteroglossia as the natural condition of discourse, rather than the result of its artistic transformation – or, more radically, as an artistic transformation of discourse in everyday usage – turned attention away from the artistic, redemptive substance of historical becoming.

Critics interested in how the novel undermines colonial or patriarchal authority by double-voicing or dialogised heteroglossia are therefore just playing variations on a theme from Bakhtin. Writers like Young or Bhabha can move with ease from literary to non-literary texts in their discussions of race and hybridity, in part because they don't draw a sharp line between the artistic dialogism of the novel and the dialogism of ordinary language (a line Bakhtin himself smudges quite often). In fact, one could dispense with verbal art altogether, as in James Clifford's influential critique of colonial authority in ethnographic writing, which borrows and develops Bakhtin's idea of polyphony.[43] If critical writing of this type seems to transgress the boundary Bakhtin establishes between artistic and extra-artistic double-voicedness, one is tempted to think: so much the worse for Bakhtin. Nor should we imagine that the application of Bakhtin to social phenomena like colonialism or patriarchy can at best *use* his theory: if one is interested in what the concept of dialogism means for subjectivity, one should look not only to the works of Bakhtin himself, but also to the interpretative work of Young and Bhabha in postcolonial theory, or at Julia Kristeva's discussions of Bakhtin from the 1960s and 1970s.[44]

It would, ironically, be political upheaval in the Soviet Union that finally separated Bakhtin in Russia from Bakhtin abroad. The liberalisation of Soviet cultural life in the 1980s and the eventual implosion of the Soviet Union in 1991 led to the end of censorship, the opening of archives, and a new era in Bakhtin scholarship in the former Soviet Union. The scholarly *Collected Works* which then became possible featured new texts, dramatically new versions of familiar texts, the revelation that some older texts were editorial concoctions, and a strikingly detailed and careful philological commentary (even if much of it was aimed at securing the religious interpretation of Bakhtin's work). The archives were also, however, used by secular-minded critics in Russia such as the late Nikolai Pan′kov and by scholars from the United Kingdom and the United States.

The new sources strengthened the hand of Bakhtin scholars in England, Scotland, and America who had kept a distance from the religious perspective. The general shift in opinion is exemplified by the change in attitudes to the so-called disputed texts of Voloshinov and Medvedev. In the 1980s, the common assumption in American circles was that these works belonged to Bakhtin, and when Harvard University Press re-issued Medvedev's *Formal Method* in 1985, its author was 'M. M. Bakhtin/P. N. Medvedev'. Twenty years later, opinion had drifted steadily to the belief in Voloshinov's and Medvedev's authorship.[45]

These substantial developments in Russian Bakhtin scholarship came too late to have an impact on Anglophone criticism. The Bakhtin surge in England, Scotland, and America had taken place in the 1980s and 1990s, and the established lines of interpretation were more or less set in place before the publication of the Russian *Collected Works*. The result is an odd asymmetry: the Bakhtin corpus in Russia is not the same as the one circulating in the Anglophone countries, because the latter is based on earlier (and faulty) Russian texts. The excellent Bakhtin scholarship of the past twenty years, conducted by philologists in Russia and Slavist Bakhtin scholars abroad, hasn't made much difference to the view of Bakhtin put in place over two decades ago. Bakhtin enthusiasts in the English-speaking world have moved on, having taken what was useful for them from the continent they travelled over. But they haven't just taken – they've made a striking contribution to the meaning and value of Bakhtin's work.

Chapter 6
A Brief Conclusion

In a famous article reflecting on his own position within the sciences, Jürgen Habermas proposed that philosophy should take its existing role of intellectual usher – showing each science to its assigned seat – and 'exchange it for the part of stand-in (*Platzhalter*)'.[1] By this he meant that philosophy could serve as a sort of avant-garde, proposing radical ideas, inspired by scientific problems but not yet supported by evidence, that would eventually be taken up by 'empirical theories with strong universalist claims'.[2] His examples of such ideas were Freud's explanation of symptom formation through repression, Durkheim's idea of the sacred as producer of solidarity, and Chomsky's argument that language acquisition was a kind of hypothesis-testing. Each of these thinkers (along with Weber and Piaget) 'inserted a genuinely philosophical idea like a detonator into a particular context of research', forever changing the field.[3] There have been many arguments about what kind of intellectual Bakhtin was – philosopher, literary critic, cultural theorist? – and whether we should value him for his philosophical contributions or for making more modest, but more solid, contributions to the theory of language or literature. Habermas's shrewd suggestion may provide an answer that makes everyone happy. For Bakhtin was the classic philosopher as stand-in, inserting some genuinely philosophical ideas like detonators into fields of research.

As others have noted, his particular talent was to take the empirical observations of others – on the relationships of author and hero in novels, on the peculiarities of indirect discourse, on the heteroglot nature of languages, on the grotesque features of carnival – and push them to their philosophical limit, using them as levers that would unsettle the way we thought about literature, language, and popular culture. He was never the scholar who first observed the phenomenon that fascinated him: even the apparently foundational split between *I* and *other* had been worked over in philosophy many times before he arrived on the scene. But he was often the scholar willing to draw the most radical consequences from the phenomenon, the writer who could see within indirect discourse the dialogism of language, who could deduce the force of the future from the position of the author in modern novels.

Such insights cannot stand on their own, like philosophical monuments: they demand elaboration, sceptical analysis, testing against empirical material, and so on. The concept of dialogism might compel us to rethink our theories of language and literature, but not as the bare, vague claim that every utterance is dialogical (and it might, in the end, not compel us to rethink our theories as much as we thought, or hoped). The scholars who have complained about the cult of Bakhtin or his philosophical extravagance are for the most part annoyed by those who take the claims in too philosophical a spirit, rather than as invitations to the empirical, scientific task of elaboration and theory-guided research.

Bakhtin's detonators have not, in the end, set off explosions in any disciplines, even if they may have blown a few minds. They can, however, be productively used in the analysis of language and of the sorts of complicated texts we call literary. They have, and they should have, spurred many of us to see things in the details of language and literary style, in the manipulation of time and space, and in construction of literary worlds that we had never seen before.

Notes

Chapter 1

1 Julia Kristeva, 'Une poétique ruinée', in Mikhail Bakhtine, *La poetique du Dostoïevski* (Paris: Seuil, 1970), 5–27.
2 Julia Kristeva, 'The ruin of a poetics', in Stephen Bann and John A. Bowlt (eds.), *Russian Formalism* (Edinburgh: Scottish Academic Press, 1973), 106.

Chapter 2

1 Katerina Clark and Michael Holquist, *Mikhail Bakhtin* (Cambridge, MA: Harvard University Press, 1984).
2 As evidence of Bakhtin's varied sources of support, one could point to the signatories of the petition Vadim Kozhinov put together to persuade the Soviet authorities to publish Bakhtin's Rabelais book in the early 1960s. V. V. Ermilov, an orthodox supporter of socialist realism (and also Kozhinov's father-in-law!), signed, and so did Shklovsky. Although, as Kozhinov entertainingly recounted, when Shklovsky saw that he was being asked to sign a petition with Ermilov's name on it ('with Ermilov, who has abused me?'), he was not pleased. Kozhinov persuaded him by pointing out how impressed people would be when they read his name together with that of his 'worst enemy'. Vadim Kozhinov and Nikolai Pan'kov, 'Kak pishut trudy ili Proiskhozhdenie nesozdannogo avantiurnogo romana' (Vadim Kozhinov rasskazyvaet o sud'be i lichnosti M. M. Bakhtina) ['How they write works, or, the Origin of an unwritten adventure novel (Vadim Kozhinov talks about M. M. Bakhtin's fate and life)'], *Dialog Karnaval Khronotop* 1 (1992), 117–18.
3 V. Kozhinov and S. Konkin, 'Mikhail Mikhailovich Bakhtin: kratkii ocherk zhizni i deiatel'nosti' ['Mikhail Mikhailovich Bakhtin: a brief note on the life and work'], in S. Konkin (ed.), *Problemy poetiki i istorii literatury* (Saransk: Mordovskii gosudarstvennyi universitet, 1973), 5. After this account was debunked, Kozhinov explained that he had got it, second-hand, from a note written by Bakhtin's brother; Kozhinov and Pan'kov, 'Kak pishut trudy', 110–11.

4 It was claimed Bakhtin had smoked the manuscript of a book on the European *Bildungsroman* in the mid-1930s; see S. G. Bocharov, 'Around and about one conversation', *Russian Studies in Literature* 31, 4 (1995), 29–30; Kozhinov and Pan'kov, 'Kak pishut trudy', 113.
5 The claim was repeated in print in V. V. Ivanov, 'Znachenie idei M. M. Bakhtina o znake, vyskazivanii i dialoge dlia sovremmenoi semiotiki', *Trudy po znakovym sistemam* 6 (1973), 44 (translated as V. V. Ivanov, 'The significance of M. M. Bakhtin's ideas on sign, utterance, and dialogue for modern semiotics', in Henryk Baran (ed.), *Semiotics and Structuralism* (White Plains, NY: International Arts and Sciences Press, 1976), 366n101).
6 My principal sources for the following biographical account are: Clark and Holquist, *Mikhail Bakhtin*; S. S. Konkin and L. S. Konkin, *Mikhail Bakhtin: Stranitsi zhizni i tvorchestva* [*Mikhail Bakhtin: Pages from His Life and Work*] (Saransk: Mordovskoe knizhnoe izdatel'stvo, 1993); N. A. Pan'kov, *Voprosy biografii i nauchnogo tvorchestva M. M. Bakhtina* [*Issues in the Biography and Scholarly Work of M. M. Bakhtin*] (Moscow: Izdatel'stvo Moskovskogo universiteta, 2009); 'The Bakhtin Circle: a timeline', in Craig Brandist, David Shepherd, and Galin Tihanov (eds.), *The Bakhtin Circle: In the Master's Absence* (Manchester: Manchester University Press, 2004), 251–75; and N. L. Vasiliev, *Mikhail Mikhailovich Bakhtin i fenomen 'Kruga Bakhtina'* [*Mikhail Mikhailovich Bakhtin and the Phenomenon of the 'Bakhtin Circle'*] (Moscow: Librokom, 2013). Other sources are cited in the notes.
7 See Conv 50–54/57–62.
8 Nikolai Pan'kov has examined M. M. Bakhtin's various résumés and the appropriate university documents; see his N. A. Pan'kov, 'Zagadki rannego perioda (eshche neskol'ko shtrikhov k "biografii M. M. Bakhtina")' ['Mysteries of the early period (a few more lines towards the "Biography of M. M. Bakhtin")'], *Dialog Karnaval Khronotop* 1, 2 (1993), 74–89. The CV in which Bakhtin spends four semesters at Marburg University is described in A. G. Lisov and E. G. Prusova, 'Replika po povodu avtobiograficheskogo mifotvorchestva' ['A rejoinder on the occasion of some autobiographical mythmaking'], *Dialog Karnaval Khronotop* 3 (1996), 161–66.
9 See William Edgerton, 'Iu. G. Oksman, M. I. Lopatto, N. M. Bakhtin i vopros o knigoizdatel'stve "Omphalos"' ['Iu. G. Oksman, M. I. Lopatto, N. M. Bakhtin and the question of the publishing house "Omphalos"'], in M. O. Chudakova (ed.), *Piatye Tynianovskie chteniia* (Riga: 1990), 211–37; O. E. Osovskii, '"Neslyshnyi dialog": biograficheskie i nauchnie sozvuchiia v sud'bakh Nikolaia i Mikhaila Bakhtina' ['"Unheard dialogue": biographical and scholarly echoes in the fates of Nikolai and Mikhail Bakhtin'], in K. G. Isupov (ed.), *M. M. Bakhtin i filosofskaia kul'tura XX veka, chast' 2* (St Petersburg: Obrazovanie, 1991), 43–51.
10 Note that the English translation has mangled this part of the conversation, implying in the lines just before that the party to which Alexander Kerensky belonged, the so-called Trudoviki (the Workers party), was the same as the SRs, the Socialist-Revolutionary Party. It was not.
11 Pan'kov identifies the friend Bakhtin speaks of in this passage as Boris Zalesskii (whose first wife reportedly had an affair with Kerensky); N. A. Pan'kov, 'Tozhe iz

"Kruga Bakhtina": B. V. Zalesskii' ['Another from the Bakhtin Circle: B. V. Zalesskii'], in *Voprosy biografii*, 422–24.

12 On the relationship between the two, see Galin Tihanov, 'Misha and Kolja: thinking the (br)other', *Dialog Karnaval Khronotop* 3 (2001), 135–59. The information on Nikolai's later life is drawn from F. M. Wilson and A. E. Duncan-Jones, 'Biographical introduction', in N. M. Bakhtin, *Lectures and Essays* (Birmingham: University of Birmingham Press, 1963), 1–16.

13 M. V. Iudina, 'Fragment vospominanii (Sem'ia Ugrelidze v Tbilisi. Akademik Tarle. Moi "khozhdenie v mukam")' ['A fragment of reminiscences'], in *Vy spasetes' cherez muzyku* (Moscow: Klassika – XXI, 2005), 142. See also N. I. Nikolaev, 'M. M. Bakhtin v Nevele letom 1919 g.' ['M. M. Bakhtin in Nevel', Summer 1919'], in L. M. Maksimovskaia (ed.), *Nevel'skii sbornik 1: k stoletiiu M. M. Bakhtina* (Sankt Peterburg: Akropol, 1996), 96–97; N. I. Nikolaev, 'Lev Pumpianskii and the Nevel School of Philosophy', in Brandist, Shepherd, and Tihanov, *The Bakhtin Circle*, 125–49.

14 Accounts of the lectures and the founding of the Nevel' Scholarly Association published in a local paper have been reproduced in L. M. Maksimovskaia, 'Gazeta "Molot" (1918–1920)' ['The newspaper "Molot" (1918–1920)'], in Maksimovskaia, *Nevel'skii sbornik 1*, 147–58.

15 *Molot*, 17 May 1919, 1, transcribed in Maksimovskaia, 'Gazeta "Molot" (1918–1920)', 150.

16 On the circle and the school generally, see Brandist, Shepherd, and Tihanov, *The Bakhtin Circle*, in particular David Shepherd, 'Reintroducing the Bakhtin Circle' and Nikolaev, 'Lev Pumpianskii'.

17 M. I. Kagan, 'Avtobiograficheskie zametki' ['Autobiographical notes'], in *O khode istorii* (Moscow: Iazyki slavianskoi kul'tury, 2004), 25; S. I. Kagan and Iu. M. Kagan, 'O pamiatnom, o vazhnom, o bylom: ustnye vospominaniia S. I. Kagan i Iu. M. Kagan' ['About what is remembered, about what is important, about the past: oral reminiscences of S. I. Kagan and Iu. M. Kagan'], *Dialog Karnaval Khronotop* 2 (1995), 178–79.

18 S. I. Kagan and Iu. M. Kagan, 'O pamiatnom', 178.

19 M. I. Kagan, 'Avtobiograficheskie zametki', 27.

20 Nikolaev, 'Lev Pumpianskii', 141.

21 On Vitebsk cultural life in the period and the role of the 'Bakhtin Circle' in it, see Alexandra Shatskikh, *Vitebsk: The Life of Art*, trans. Katherine Foshko Tsan (New Haven: Yale University Press, 2007) and the extremely detailed list of activities in 'The Bakhtin Circle: a timeline', in Brandist, Shepherd, and Tihanov, *The Bakhtin Circle*, 257–62.

22 On Sollertinskii, see L. Mikheeva, *I. I. Sollertinskii: zhizn' i nasledie* [*I. I. Sollertinskii: Life and Legacy*] (Leningrad: Sovetskii pisatel', 1988).

23 On Medvedev's activity in Vitebsk, see Iu. P. Medvedev and Daria Medvedeva, 'The scholarly legacy of Pavel Medvedev in the light of his dialogue with Bakhtin', in Brandist, Shepherd, and Tihanov, *The Bakhtin Circle*, 29–40.

24 B. V. Estifeeva, 'Vospominaniia o Bakhtine: pervoe desiatiletie v Saranske' ['Reminiscences of Bakhtin: the first decade in Saransk'], *Dialog Karnaval Khronotop* 1 (2000), 129.
25 Estifeeva, 'Vospominaniia', 130.
26 'Iz perepiski [From the correspondence]', in M. I. Kagan, *O khode istorii*, 631, 636, 638.
27 N. I. Nikolaev, 'The Nevel School of Philosophy (Bakhtin, Kagan and Pumpianskii) between 1918 and 1925: materials from Pumpianskii's archives', in David Shepherd (ed.), *The Contexts of Bakhtin: Philosophy, Authorship, Aesthetics* (Amsterdam: Harwood Academic, 1998), 35, 37–38.
28 See Conv 157–71/195–211 for Bakhtin's (somewhat digressive) reminiscences about these meetings. The fullest and sharpest account of Bakhtin's activities is from the transcription of his interrogation in 1929; see I. A Savkin, 'Delo o Voskresenii' ['The "Resurrection" Affair'], in Isupov, *M. M. Bakhtin i filosofskaia kul'tura*, 110–11, 113.
29 Notes from the lessons Bakhtin gave to R. M. Mirkina, in the period 1922–27, have been transcribed and published: M. M. Bakhtin, 'Zapisi lektsii M. M. Bakhtina po istorii russkoi literatury. Zapisi R. M. Mirkina [Notes of Bakhtin's lectures on the history of Russian literature, taken by R. M. Mirkina]', in *Sobranie sochinenii, Vol. 2* (Moscow: Russkie slovari, 2000), 213–427. Mirkina herself suggested that the Bakhtins relied heavily on the money Elena Bakhtina made from sewing soft toys; R. M. Mirkina, 'Bakhtin, kakim ia ego znala' ['Bakhtin as I knew him'], *Novoe literaturnoe obozrenie* 2 (1993), 68.
30 See his excellent 'Sociological linguistics in Leningrad: the Institute for the Comparative History of the Literatures and Languages of the West and East (ILJAZV) 1921–1933', *Russian Literature* 63 (2008), 171–200.
31 V. M. Zhirmunskii, *Natsional'nyi iazyk i sotsial'nie dialekty* (Leningrad: Khudozhestvennaia literatura, 1936).
32 The information in this paragraph is drawn from Iu. P. Medvedev, 'Pavel Nikolaevich Medvedev: u istokov sotsiologicheskoi poetiki [PNM: on the sources of sociological poetics]', in P. N. Medvedev, *Sobranie sochinenii, Vol. 1: Istoriia literatury* (Sankt-Peterburg: Rostok, 2018), 3–80.
33 V. N. Voloshinov: 'Po tu storonu sotsial'nogo' ['Beyond the social'], *Zvezda* 5 (1925), 186–214; 'Slovo v zhizni i slovo v poezii: k voprosam sotsiologicheskoi poetiki' ['Discourse in life and discourse in poetry: on questions of sociological poetics'], *Zvezda* 6 (1926), 244–67; *Freidizm: kriticheskii ocherk* [*Freudianism: a critical sketch*] (Moscow: Gosizdat, 1927); 'Noveishie techeniia lingvisticheskoi mysli na zapade' ['The latest trends in linguistic thought in the West'], *Literatura i Marksizm* 5 (1928), 115–49; *Marksizm i filosofiia iazyka: osnovnye problemy sotsiologicheskogo metoda v nauke o iazyke* [*Marxism and the Philosophy of Language: Fundamental Problems of Sociological Method in the Science of Language*] (Leningrad: Priboi, 1929). P. N. Medvedev: 'Uchenyi sal'erizm: o formal'nom (morfologicheskom) metode' ['Scholarly Salierism: on the formal

(morphological) method'], *Zvezda* 3 (1925), 264–76; 'Sotsiologizm bez sotsiologii: o metodologicheskikh rabotakh P. N. Sakulina' ['Sociologism without sociology: on the methodological works of P. N. Sakulin'], *Zvezda* 2 (1926), 267–71; 'Ocherednyi zadachi istoriko-literaturnoi nauki' ['The immediate tasks for literary-historical scholarship'], *Literatura i Marksizm* 3 (1928), 65–87; *Formal'nyi metod v literaturovedenii: kriticheskoe vvedenie v sotsiologicheskuiu poetiku* [*The Formal Method in Literary Scholarship: A Critical Introduction to Sociological Poetics*] (Leningrad: Priboi, 1928). In addition, Medvedev reviewed an enormous number of books and wrote extensively on the poet Aleksandr Blok. Translations of many of the articles cited can be found in Ann Shukman (ed.), *Bakhtin School Papers* (Oxford: RPT Publications, 1983). Medvedev's writings have been collected and edited in P. N. Medvedev, *Sobranie sochinenii*, 2 vols. (Sankt-Peterburg: Rostok, 2018).

34 N. I. Nikolaev, 'Commentary to "K voprosam metodologii estetiki slovesnogo tvorchestva. I. Problema formy, soderzhaniia i materiala v slovesnom khudozhestvennom tvorchestva" ["On Issues in the Methodology of the Aesthetics of the Verbal Artwork 1. The Problem of Form, Content and Material in Verbal Art"]', in M. M. Bakhtin, *Sobranie sochinenii*, Vol. 1 (Moscow: Russkie slovari, 2003), 711–12.

35 See V. Liapunov, V. L. Makhlin, and N. I. Nikolaev, 'Commentary to "Avtor i geroi v esteticheskoi deiatel'nosti" ["Author and Hero in Aesthetic Activity"]', in Bakhtin, *Sobranie sochinenii*, Vol. 1, 496–502.

36 Brian Poole, 'From phenomenology to dialogue: Max Scheler's phenomenological tradition and Mikhail Bakhtin's development from "Toward a Philosophy of the Act" to his study of Dostoevsky', in Ken Hirschkop and David Shepherd (eds.), *Bakhtin and Cultural Theory* (Manchester: Manchester University Press, 2005), 109–35. In brief, Poole argues that in 'Author and Hero' Bakhtin relied on the third edition of Max Scheler's *Essence and Forms of Sympathy*, published in 1926 (and which Bakhtin made a detailed outline of in 1927–28).

37 The two most detailed and thorough statements of the narrative, which I summarise here, are Bocharov, 'One conversation' and Nikolaev, 'Nevel School of Philosophy'.

38 Bocharov, 'One conversation', 21.

39 Bocharov, 'One conversation', 12.

40 See note 35.

41 I take the expression from the editions of books by Voloshinov and Medvedev that came out under the Russian imprint Labirint in the 1990s with the series title 'Bakhtin in a Mask': M. M. Bakhtin, *Bakhtin pod maskoi: v 4 tomakh* [*Bakhtin in a Mask: in 4 volumes*] (Moscow: Labirint, 1993).

42 The conversation is recounted in Bocharov, 'One conversation', 4–9.

43 Letter from Bakhtin to Kozhinov et al., 10 January 1961, reproduced in M. M. Bakhtin and V. V. Kozhinov, 'Iz perepiski M. M. Bakhtina i V. V. Kozhinova (1960–1966)' ['From the correspondence of M. M. Bakhtin and V. V. Kozhinov

166 Notes to pages 19–22

(1960–1966)'], in Pan'kov, *Voprosy biografii*, 496. Kozhinov later claimed that before ever meeting Bakhtin he had been told by three prominent intellectuals – N. A. Berkovskii, V. V. Vinogradov, and V. B. Shklovsky – that Medvedev's book was actually by Bakhtin (see V. V. Kozhinov, 'Kniga, vokrug kotoroi ne umolkaet spory' ['A book over which there are still arguments'], *Dialog Karnaval Khronotop* 4 (1995), 140–41). But he did not mention this in the letter to Bakhtin.

44 S. G. Bocharov, 'Sobytie bytiia' ['The event of being'], *Novyi mir* 11 (1995), 213–14. Meier was a prominent religious intellectual, Vaginov an experimental novelist. Even with the best will in the world, it is hard to see what justifies Bocharov's classification. After all, both Meier and Kagan were supporters of the Soviet regime (as was Pumpianskii after 1927), and Kagan worked for the government.

45 I have already mentioned Medvedev's extraordinary productivity. Below I describe Voloshinov's independent, original work on linguistics and its probable effect on Bakhtin's writing. For a full account of the composition of *Marxism and the Philosophy of Language*, see V. M. Alpatov, *Voloshinov, Bakhtin i lingvistika* (Moscow: Iazyki slavianskikh kul'tur, 2005).

46 Ivanov, 'Znachenie idei M. M. Bakhtina', 44/ 'The significance of M. M. Bakhtin's ideas', 366n101.

47 Nicholas Rzhevsky and V. Kozhinov, 'Kozhinov on Bakhtin', *New Literary History* 25, 2 (1994), 433.

48 Bocharov, 'One conversation', 16.

49 Sergei Averintsev, 'Mikhail Bakhtin: retrospektiva i perspektiva', *Druzhba narodov* 3 (1988), 259.

50 S. G. Bocharov and N. I. Nikolaev, 'Introduction to the Commentaries', in Bakhtin, *Sobranie sochinenii, Vol. 1*, 344–45.

51 Bocharov, 'One conversation', 18.

52 Bocharov, 'Sobytie bytiia', 219.

53 My account of the arrest and interrogation is drawn largely from the accounts in Konkin and Konkin, *Mikhail Bakhtin*, 171–201; and Savkin, 'Delo o Voskresenii'.

54 From the indictment issued by the OGPU in relation to 'Resurrection', quoted in Konkin and Konkin, *Mikhail Bakhtin*, 191.

55 A. V. Lunacharskii, 'O "mnogogolosnosti" Dostoevskogo (Po povodu knigi M. M. Bakhtina "Problemy tvorchestva Dostoevskogo")' ['On the "multivoicedness" of Dostoevsky'], *Novyi mir* 10 (1929), 195–209. The effect of Lunacharskii's review is discussed in S. G. Bocharov, 'Commentary to *Problemy tvorchestva Dostoevskogo*', in M. M. Bakhtin, *Sobranie sochinenii, Vol. 2* (Moscow: Russkie slovari, 2000), 477–79.

56 The article has, in fact, been translated, see Mikhail Bakhtin, 'Experience based on a study of demand among Kolkhoz workers', *Interventions* (2019), 1–17, https://doi.org/10.1080/1369801X.2019.1649184

57 V. N. Turbin, 'Karnaval: religiia, politika, teosofiia [Carnival: religion, politics, theosophy]', in D. Kuiundzhich and V. L. Makhlin (eds.), *Bakhtinskii sbornik 1* (Moscow: Prometei, 1990), 10.

58 The details of Bakhtin's stay and the attack that led to his departure are described in V. I. Laptun, 'Pervyi priezd M. M. Bakhtina v Saransk (1936–1937gg.)' ['M. M. Bakhtin's first stay in Saransk 1936–1937'], in Maksimovskaia, *Nevel'skii sbornik 1*, 61–74.
59 See Conv 189–90/235–36.
60 The correspondence, the CVs, and the charming story are all reproduced in S. G. Bocharov, 'Commentary to "Roman vospitaniia i ego znachenie v istorii realizma" ["The *Bildungsroman* and Its Significance for the History of Realism"]', in M. M. Bakhtin, *Sobranie sochinenii, Vol. 3, Teoriia romana (1930–1961)* (Moscow: Iazyki slavianskikh kul'tur, 2012), 757–65.
61 Bocharov, 'Commentary to "Roman vospitannia"', 762.
62 See the chapter '"World literature"/ "world culture" and the era of the popular front (c. 1935–36)', in Katerina Clark, *Moscow, the Fourth Rome: Stalinism, Cosmopolitanism, and the Evolution of Soviet Culture, 1931–1941* (Cambridge, MA: Harvard University Press, 2011), 169–209.
63 As this episode in Bakhtin's life was 'official', it has been possible to describe it in great detail. See I. L. Popova, 'Istoriia "Rable": 1930–1950-e gody' ['A history of *Rabelais*: 1930–1950'], in M. M. Bakhtin, *Sobranie sochinenii, Vol. 4 (1)* (Moscow: Iazyki slavianskikh kul'tur, 2008), 841–924; N. A. Pan'kov, '"Ot khoda etogo dela zavisit vse dal'neishee..." (Disput o "Rable" kak real'noe sobytie, vysokaia drama i nauchnaia komediia) ['"On the progress of this business the whole future depends..." (The dispute over *Rabelais* as a real event, a high drama, and an academic comedy)'], in *Voprosy biografii*, 91–168.
64 See Pan'kov, '"Ot khoda etogo dela"', 106–8.
65 Letter from Natalia Mikhailovna Perifileva (née Bakhtina) to Boris Vladimirovich Zalesskii, 15 December 1941, reproduced in N. A. Pan'kov, 'M. M. Bakhtin v materialakh lichnogo arkhiva B. V. Zalesskogo' ['M. M. Bakhtin in materials from B. V. Zalesskii's personal archive'], in *Voprosy biografii*, 446–47.
66 M. M. Bakhtin, *Besedy c V. D. Duvakinym* [*Conversations with V. D. Duvakin*] (Soglasie: Moscow, 2002), 320n6.
67 On Bakhtin's short-lived use of the term 'Gothic realism', see N. A. Pan'kov, 'Smysl' i proiskhozhdenie termina "goticheskii realizm"' ['The meaning and origin of the term "gothic realism"'], in *Voprosy biografii*, 382–99.
68 See Kirpotin's letter of 16 December 1974 to Kozhinov, reproduced in N. A. Pan'kov, 'Vokrug "Rable" i Tarle' ['About *Rabelais* and Tarle'], *Dialog Karnaval Khronotop* 4 (1998), 86–87.
69 The point is made forcefully in V. M. Alpatov, 'Zametki na poliakh stenogrammy zashchity dissertatsii M. M. Bakhtina' ['Notes in the margins of the transcript of M. M. Bakhtin's dissertation defence'], *Dialog Karnaval Khronotop* 1 (1997), 70–97.
70 A detailed description of the Commission's action is found in N. A. Pan'kov, '"Rable est' Rable...", ili Kogda VAK na gore svistnet ['"Rabelais is Rabelais.": or when VAK whistles on top of the mountain'], in *Voprosy biografii*, 263–312.

168 *Notes to pages 27–33*

71 It's a classic problem in Bakhtin scholarship. When 'The Problem of Speech Genres' was first published in full, as part of the posthumous 1979 collection, *Estetika slovesnogo tvorchestva* (Moscow: Isskustvo), the editors excised all references to Stalin's article and other references 'of a similar nature'. These excisions have also been made in the version published in the *Collected Works*, with the justification that Bakhtin himself requested that these 'foul adulterations' be removed from the text at publication; L. A. Gogotishvili, 'Commentary to "Problema rechevykh zhenrov" ["The Problem of Speech Genres"]', in M. M. Bakhtin, *Sobranie sochinenii, Vol. 5* (Moscow: Russkie slovari, 1996), 536. This seems fair enough when something is published for general use, but it is unfortunate in a scholarly edition.
72 Estifeeva, 'Vospominaniia', 142.
73 Letter from Kozhinov to Bakhtin, in Bakhtin and Kozhinov, 'Correspondence of Bakhtin and Kozhinov', 486–88.
74 Kozhinov has described his machinations, not always accurately, it seems, in V. V. Kozhinov, '"Tak eto bylo."' ['"That's how it happened."'], *Don* 10 (1988), 156–60.
75 But while Kozhinov's manoeuvring was doubtless impressive, he was not quite the pioneer he had made himself out to be. He had been preceded by Vittorio Strada, an Italian postgraduate student (and member of the Italian Communist Party), who arranged for a revised version of the Dostoevsky book to be published by Einaudi in Turin. The revised version was prepared and delivered to Turin in the summer of 1962, but didn't come out till 1968. Strada has described the process in detail in a public letter (written to counter Kozhinov's very different account of events), in Vittorio Strada, '<Letter, with appended documents>', in V. L. Makhlin (ed.), *Bakhtinskii sbornik III* (Moscow: Labirint, 1997), 373–79. The timing of the two revisions is also discussed in the Russian *Collected Works*: S. G. Bocharov and L. A. Gogotishvili, 'Commentary to "1961 god. Zametki" ["1961 Notes"]', in M. M. Bakhtin, *Sobranie sochinenii, Vol. 5: raboty 1940-х – nachala 1960-х godov* (Moscow: Russkie slovari, 1996), 650–52.
76 A somewhat different account of the Andropov transfer is found in Dmitrii Urnov, 'Vadim i Bakhtin', *Nash sovremennik* (2006), 248 (although Urnov's infatuation with Kozhinov leads one to think he has exaggerated the latter's role).
77 Matt Steinglass, 'International man of mystery: the battle over Mikhail Bakhtin', *Lingua Franca* (1998), http://linguafranca.mirror.theinfo.org/9804/steinglass.html

Chapter 3

1 'Isskustvo i otvetstvennost'', *Den' isskustva*, 13 September 1919, 3–4. It has been reproduced as an appendix in L. M. Maksimovskaia, *Nevel'skii sbornik 1* (Sankt Peterburg: Akropol, 1996) and translated in *Art and Answerability*, 1–3.
2 M. I. Kagan, 'Paul Natorp i krizis kul'tury (1922)' ['Paul Natorp and the crisis of culture'], in *O khode istorii* (Moscow: Iazyki slavianskoi kul'tury, 2004), 93.

3 On Bely, see Alexander L. Dobrokhotov, 'What the Russian symbolists heard in the "music of revolution": philosophical implications', *Studies in East European Thought* 69 (2017), 287–304.
4 Georg Simmel, 'The conflict in modern culture (1918)', in *On Individuality and Social Forms* (Chicago: University of Chicago Press, 1971), 377.
5 Raymond Williams, *Culture and Society, 1790–1950* (London: Chatto and Windus, 1958).
6 The translated version of the interview excludes Rickert's name.
7 Letter from M. I. Lopatto to F[rancesca] Wilson, 5 March 1951, transcribed in William Edgerton, 'Iu. G. Oksman, M. I. Lopatto, N. M. Bakhtin i vopros o knigoizdatel´stve "Omphalos"' ['Iu. G. Oksman, M. I. Lopatto, N. M. Bakhtin and the question of the publishing house "Omphalos"'], in M. O. Chudakova (ed.), *Piatye Tynianovskie chteniia* (Riga: 1990), 235.
8 Hermann Cohen, *Logik der reinen Erkenntnis* [*The Logic of Pure Knowledge*] (Berlin: Bruno Cassirer, 1902); Hermann Cohen, *Ethik der reinen Willens* [*The Ethics of Pure Will*] (Berlin: Bruno Cassirer, 1904); Hermann Cohen, *Ästhetik der reinen Gefühls* [*The Aesthetics of Pure Feeling*] (Berlin: Bruno Cassirer, 1912).
9 On the relationship between Kantianism and Judaism in Cohen's work, see Irene Kajon, 'Critical idealism in Hermann Cohen's writings on Judaism', in Reinier Munk (ed.), *Hermann Cohen's Critical Idealism* (Dordrecht: Springer, 2005), 371–94.
10 See Hermann Cohen, *Religion of Reason Out of the Sources of Judaism*, trans. Simon Kaplan (Atlanta, GA: Scholars Press, 1995), 35–49, 'God's uniqueness'.
11 Cohen, *Religion of Reason*, 64, 67.
12 Cohen, *Religion of Reason*, 92.
13 Cohen, *Religion of Reason*, 93.
14 Robert Gibbs, 'Hermann Cohen's messianism: the history of the future', in Gabriele Motzkin, Helmut Holzhey, and Hartwig Wiedebach (eds.),"*Religion and Reason Out of the Sources of Judaism*": *Tradition and the Concept of Origin in Hermann Cohen's Late Work* (Hildesheim: George Olms Verlag, 2000), 338.
15 M. I. Kagan, 'Kak vozmozhna istoriia?: Iz osnovnikh problem filosofii istorii' ['How is history possible?: one of the fundamental problems in the philosophy of history'], in *O khode istorii*, 199–237.
16 M. I. Kagan, 'Evreistvo i krizis kul'tury (1923)', in *O khode istorii*, 171.
17 Kagan, 'Evreistvo', 174–75.
18 Ruth Coates, 'The first and second Adam in Bakhtin's early thought', in Susan M. Felch and Paul J. Contino (eds.), *Bakhtin and Religion: A Feeling for Faith* (Evanston, IL: Northwestern University Press, 2001), 65.
19 N. K. Bonetskaia, 'M. M. Bakhtin i traditsii russkoi filosofii' ['M. M. Bakhtin and the tradition of Russian philosophy'], *Voprosy filosofii* 1 (1993), 90. According to Bonetskaia, this fundamentally Russian intuition in Bakhtin is challenged in his thoughts by 'alien' Protestant and Jewish ideas (92–93).

20 L. A. Gogotishvili, 'Commentary to "K filosofskim osnovam gumanitarnykh nauk" ["Towards Philosophical Foundations for the Human Sciences"]', in Bakhtin, *Sobranie sochinenii, Vol. 5* (Moscow: Russkie slovari, 1996), 398n8.
21 On Kozhinov's role in the Russian nationalist movement, see Yitzhak M. Brudny, *Reinventing Russia: Russian Nationalism and the Soviet State, 1953–1991* (Cambridge, MA: Harvard University Press, 1998). On his participation in some of the wilder antisemitic conspiracy-mongering, see Marlène Laruelle, 'Conspiracy and alternate history in Russia: a nationalist equation for success?', *Russian Review* 71 (2012), 565–80. In his interviews with Duvakin, Bakhtin, when pressed on the question, insisted Kozhinov was not anti-semitic (Con 201/247). But in another conversation from roughly the same period, Bakhtin is reported as wryly admitting: 'Yes, he is an anti-Semite, but I am a Neo-Kantian. With amendments from Husserl's phenomenology' (both the leading Neo-Kantians and Husserl were Jewish); Maiia Kaganskaia, 'Shutovskoi khorovod' ["A round-dance of fools"], *Sintaksis* 12 (1984), 142.
22 Bocharov, 'Sobytie bytiia' ['The event of being'], *Novyi mir* 11 (1995), 221.
23 Cohen, *Religion of Reason*, 10.
24 M. I. Kagan, 'O religioznom krizise sovremennosti' ['On the religious crisis of contemporaneity'], in *O khode istorii*, 187.
25 M. I. Kagan, Letter to S. I. Kagan, 16 August 1924, transcribed in M. I. Kagan, *O khode istorii*, 642.
26 Aleksandr Blok, 'The twelve', trans. Maria Carlson, http://hdl.handle.net/1808/6598
27 For a discussion of the problem and its history, see Anita Avramides, 'Other minds', in the *Stanford Encyclopedia of Philosophy*, https://plato.stanford.edu/entries/other-minds/
28 A. I. Vvedenskii, *Psikhologiia bez vsiakoi metafiziki [Psychology without Any Metaphysics]* (Petrograd: M. M. Stasiulevich, 1915), 16.
29 Vvedenskii, *Psikhologiia*, 75–76.
30 Edmund Husserl, *Logical Investigations*, trans. J. N. Findlay (London: Routledge and Kegan Paul, 1970), in particular Investigation II.
31 On Red Vienna, see Helmut Gruber, *Red Vienna: Experiment in Working-Class Culture, 1919–1934* (Oxford: Oxford University Press, 1991).
32 Leon Trotsky, *Literature and Revolution* [1923] (Ann Arbor: University of Michigan Press, 1960), 218, 221.
33 Some representative statements can be found in the first three pieces of *LEF*'s initial issue – 'What does Lef fight for?', 'Whom does Lef wrangle with?', 'Whom does Lef warn?, in *LEF* 1 (1923), 1–11, translated in Anna Lawton and Herbert Eagle (eds.), *Russian Futurism through Its Manifestoes, 1912–1928* (Ithaca: Cornell University Press, 1988), 191–201.
34 See the chapter 'Proletarian culture and art', in Trotsky, *Literature and Revolution*, 184–214.
35 Sergei Averintsev, 'Lichnost' i talant uchenogo' ['The personality and talent of a scholar'], *Literaturnoe obozrenie* 10 (1976), 59.

36 'And now, today, when the artist wants to deal with living form, with the living – not the dead – word, he breaks it up and distorts it in his desire to give it a face'; Viktor Shklovsky, 'Resurrecting the word (1914)', in *Viktor Shklovsky: A Reader* (London: Bloomsbury, 2017), 70.
37 The biographical information is taken from N. L. Vasiliev, 'Biograficheskii ocherk' ['Biographical sketch'], in V. N. Voloshinov, *Filosofiia i sotsiologiia gumanitarnykh nauk* (Sankt-Peterburg: Asta Press, 1995), 5–22.
38 The annual reports on Voloshinov's work at ILIaZV have been published as V. N. Voloshinov, 'Lichnoe delo V. N. Voloshinova', *Dialog Karnaval Khronotop* 2 (1995), 70–99. An English translation of them, with useful commentary, is S. V. C. Grillo and E. K. Américo, 'Valentin Nikolaievitch Voloshinov: documented details of his life and work', *Alfa* 61, 2 (2017), doi:10.1590/1981-5794-1709-1.
39 On Bühler and Voloshinov's use of him, see Craig Brandist, 'Voloshinov's dilemma: on the philosophical roots of the dialogic theory of the utterance', in Craig Brandist, David Shepherd, and Galin Tihanov (eds.), *The Bakhtin Circle: In the Master's Absence* (Manchester: Manchester University Press, 2004), 97–124.
40 V. N. Voloshinov, 'Discourse in life and discourse in poetry: questions of sociological poetics', in Ann Shukman (ed.), *Bakhtin School Papers* (Oxford: RPT Publications, 1983), 5–29. / 'Slovo v zhizni i slovo v poezii: k voprosam sotsiologicheskoi poetiki [1926]', in Voloshinov, *Filosofiia i sotsiologiia gumanitarnykh nauk*, 59–86.
41 See Voloshinov, 'Discourse in life', 18–21.
42 As Brian Poole has pointed out, when Voloshinov discusses how social rank is reflected in linguistic style, he lifts his references directly from Cassirer's *Philosophy of Symbolic Forms*; Poole, 'From phenomenology to dialogue: Max Scheler's phenomenological tradition and Mikhail Bakhtin's development from "Toward a Philosophy of the Act" to his study of Dostoevsky', in Ken Hirschkop and David Shepherd (eds.), *Bakhtin and Cultural Theory* (Manchester: Manchester University Press, 2005), 126–27.
43 V. N. Voloshinov, 'Report on work as a postgraduate student, 1927/28: plan and some guiding thoughts for the work *Marxism and the Philosophy of Language*', in Brandist, Shepherd, and Tihanov, *The Bakhtin Circle*, 232 / Voloshinov, 'Lichnoe delo V. N. Voloshinova', 87. The outline, which is very substantial, is one of the strongest pieces of evidence for Voloshinov's claim to be the author of *Marxism and the Philosophy of Language*. The book includes material that is not in the outline, and vice versa.
44 V. N. Voloshinov, 'The problem of the transmission of alien discourse: an essay in sociolinguistic research', in Brandist, Shepherd, and Tihanov, *The Bakhtin Circle*, 223–26 / Voloshinov, 'Lichnoe delo V. N. Voloshinova', 79–80.
45 V. N. Voloshinov, *Marxism and the Philosophy of Language*, trans. Ladislav Matejka and I. R. Titunik (Cambridge, MA: Harvard University Press, 1973), 11n1. Mika Lähteenmäki has made a strong case for how little Voloshinov's philosophy resembled Cassirer's in the end: see his 'Vološinov and Cassirer: a case of plagiarism?', *Historiographia Linguistica* 29, 1/2 (2002), 121–44.

46 Ernst Cassirer, *The Philosophy of Symbolic Forms, Vol. 1: Language*, trans. Ralph Manheim (New Haven, CT: Yale University Press, 1955), 78.
47 Ernst Cassirer, *The Philosophy of Symbolic Forms, Vol. 4: The Metaphysics of Symbolic Forms*, trans. John Michael Krois (New Haven, CT: Yale University Press, 1996), 111.
48 Galin Tihanov, *The Birth and Death of Literary Theory: Regimes of Relevance in Russia and Beyond* (Stanford, CA: Stanford University Press, 2019), 103–8.
49 The story of this brief moment in Soviet literary history is told in Edward J. Brown, *The Proletarian Episode in Russian Literature, 1928–1932* (New York: Columbia University Press, 1953).
50 Galin Tihanov, *The Master and the Slave: Lukács, Bakhtin, and the Ideas of Their Time* (Oxford: Clarendon Press, 2000).
51 Katerina Clark, *Moscow, the Fourth Rome: Stalinism, Cosmopolitanism, and the Evolution of Soviet Culture, 1931–1941* (Cambridge, MA: Harvard University Press, 2011), 18–19.
52 M. M. Bakhtin, 'Fransua Rable v istorii realizma (1940 g)' ['François Rabelais in the History of Realism (1940 version)'], in *Sobranie sochinenii, vol. 4 (1)* (Moscow: Iazyki slavianskikh kul'tur, 2008), 16.
53 That does not mean Bakhtin was a Marxist. When asked about it, he was unambiguous. 'Bear in mind', he told Kozhinov when they met in 1961, 'I am not a Marxist' (Vadim Kozhinov and Nikolai Pan'kov, 'Kak pishut trudy ili Proiskhozhdenie nesozdannogo avantiurnogo romana' (Vadim Kozhinov rasskazyvaet o sud'be i lichnosti M. M. Bakhtina) ['How they write works, or, the Origin of an unwritten adventure novel (Vadim Kozhinov talks about M. M. Bakhtin's fate and life)'], *Dialog Karnaval Khronotop* 1 (1992), 113). When Bocharov asked, in 1974, 'Mikhail Mikhailovich, maybe at one time you were enticed by Marxism?', Bakhtin replied: 'No, never. It interested me, like many other things – Freudianism, even spiritualism. But I was never a Marxist to any degree' (Bocharov, 'Around and about one conversation', *Russian Studies in Literature* 31, 4 (1995), 15, translation altered). Those proclamations relate to Marxism as a political theory and a political commitment. Whether any of Bakhtin's works was consonant with or influenced by Marxism as a philosophy or social theory is a very different question. For even in a text as apparently distant from social affairs as 'Towards a Philosophy of the Act', Bakhtin found time to give Marxism an approving nod. Having dismissed many other ethical philosophies, he noted that historical materialism 'in spite of all its defects and defaults, is attractive to participative consciousness because of its effort to build its world in such a way as to provide a place in it for the performance of determinate, concretely historical, actual deeds' (TPA 20/22). What this wordy sentence meant was that Marxism conceived of the world not as a thing to be contemplated but as constant activity, the constant production of a world, of its social relations, its environment, and so on, and, in that sense, also believed in the priority of ethical reality.

54 See Evgeny Dobrenko, 'Literary criticism and the institution of literature in the era of war and late Stalinism, 1941–1953', in Evgeny Dobrenko and Galin Tihanov (eds.), *A History of Russian Literary Theory and Criticism* (Pittsburgh: University of Pittsburgh Press, 2011), 163–83.
55 Bakhtin, 'Rabelais in the History of Realism', 15.
56 They have been translated in Joseph Stalin, 'Concerning Marxism and linguistics', in *Marxism and Linguistics* (New York: International Publishers, 1951), 9–32.
57 So, for example, in the notes for 'The Problem of Speech Genres', which have been dubbed 'Dialog – II', Bakhtin remarks that the word and the sentence are part of the system of language and 'are its units (the linguistic units) only in its abstract form (according to I. V. Stalin)'; 'Dialog – II', in *Sobranie sochinenii*, Vol. 5, 237. A formal review of Bakhtin's academic department in the Mordovian Pedagogical Institute complimented it on the fact that it had 'not only studied the work of comrade Stalin on linguistics, but also integrated his brilliant utterances into its teaching and scholarly work on questions of linguistics' (V. I. Laptun, 'Arkhivnye materialy o prepodavatel'skoi rabote M. M. Bakhtina v Mordovskom pedinstitute ['Archive materials relating to M. M. Bakhtin's teaching at the Mordovian Pedagogical Institute'], *Dialog Karnaval Khronotop* 1 (1996), 73).
58 Bakhtin's position is complicated by the fact that he was by no means totally hostile to Marr, whose ideas were the object of derision among European, American, and probably many Soviet linguists. Marr and some of the ideas from his Japhetology are directly referred to in the lecture/essay 'Towards a Prehistory of Novelistic Discourse', although these references (TPND 532, 536) were removed from the first published Russian version and so don't appear in the English translation. Alexandar Mihailovic, however, has argued that Bakhtin was deeply opposed to Marr: see his 'Bakhtin's dialogue with Russian Orthodoxy and critique of linguistic universalism', in Felch and Contino, *Bakhtin and Religion*, 121–49.

Chapter 4

1 Bakhtin probably took the term 'architectonic' from the philosophy of Immanuel Kant. Here it is a rough synonym for 'structure'. An architectonic difference is a difference deriving from the structure of the world.
2 Hermann Cohen, *Religion of Reason Out of the Sources of Judaism*, trans. Simon Kaplan (Atlanta, GA: Scholars Press, 1995), 18.
3 Hartwig Wiedebach, 'Aesthetics in religion: remarks on Hermann Cohen's theory of Jewish existence', *Journal of Jewish Thought and Philosophy* 11, 1 (2002), 64.
4 See Liisa Steinby, 'Hermann Cohen and Bakhtin's early aesthetics', *Studies in East European Thought* 63, 3 (2011), 236–38.
5 Bocharov, 'Sobytie bytiia' ['The event of being'], *Novyi mir* 11 (1995), 221.

6 Ruth Coates, 'The first and second Adam in Bakhtin's early thought', in Susan M. Felch and Paul J. Contino (eds.), *Bakhtin and Religion: A Feeling for Faith* (Evanston, IL: Northwestern University Press, 2001), 65, 68–71.
7 L. A. Gogotishvili, 'Varianty i invarianty M. M. Bakhtina' ['The variables and invariables of M. M. Bakhtin'], *Voprosy filosofii* 1 (1992), 117.
8 See Alasdair MacIntyre, *After Virtue* (London: Duckworth, 1982); Marya Schechtman, 'The narrative self', in Shaun Gallagher (ed.), *Oxford Handbook of the Self* (Oxford: Oxford University Press, 2011), 394–416.
9 That is the essential argument of Raymond Williams, *Culture and Society, 1790–1950* (London: Chatto and Windus, 1958).
10 Terry Eagleton, *The Ideology of the Aesthetic* (Oxford: Basil Blackwell, 1990), 3.
11 Note their 'unmergedness' – according to Alexandar Mihailovic, this points to the Chalcedonian formula for the holy Trinity; see his *Corporeal Words: Mikhail Bakhtin's Theology of Discourse* (Evanston, IL: Northwestern University Press, 1997).
12 Bakhtin borrowed this term, 'directedness', from Husserl (the German term is *Gerichtetsein auf*). In Husserl's philosophy consciousness is defined as a combination of intentional states, and consciousness is always intentional because it is 'directed' at something: you think *about* something, feel or see something, respond *to* something. Those different verbs (think, see, respond), however, show us that although consciousness is always directed, it is not always directed in the same way – there are different modes of 'directedness'.
13 Brian Poole, 'Objective narrative theory – the influence of Spielhagen's "Aristotelian theory of 'Narrative Objectivity'" on Bakhtin's study of Dostoevsky', in Jørgen Bruhn and Jan Lundquist (eds.), *The Novelness of Bakhtin* (Copenhagen: Museum Tusculanum Press, 2001), 107–62.
14 Fyodor Dostoevsky, *Crime and Punishment*, trans. Richard Pevear and Larissa Volokhonsky (London: Vintage Classics, 2007), 39.
15 Roland Barthes, 'Introduction to the structural analysis of narratives (1966)', in *Image – Music – Text* (London: Fontana, 1977), 101.
16 M. M. Bakhtin, 'On Questions of Self-Consciousness and Self-Evaluation', *Slavic and East European Journal* 61, 2 (2017), 221/'K voprosam samsoznaniia i samootsenki', in *Sobranie sochinenii, Vol. 5* (Moscow: Russkie slovari, 1996), 74.
17 Bakhtin, 'On Questions of Self-Consciousness', 221/74, 223/74.
18 M. M. Bakhtin, 'Dostoevsky. 1961', in *Sobranie sochinenii, Vol. 5*, 368.
19 See, for example, Boris Eichenbaum, 'How Gogol's "Overcoat" is made', in Robert A. Maguire (ed.), *Gogol from the Twentieth Century* (Princeton, NJ: Princeton University Press, 1974), 269–91.
20 Iurii Tynianov, 'Dostoevskii i Gogol: k teorii parodii (1921)', in *Arkhaisty i novatory* (Leningrad: Priboi, 1929/ reprinted Ann Arbor, MI: Ardis, 1985), 412–55.
21 Anonymous, 'Review of M. Bakhtin, *Problemy tvorchestva Dostoevskogo*', *Oktiabr* 11 (1929), 196.

22 A. V. Lunacharskii, 'O "mnogogolosnosti" Dostoevskogo (Po povodu knigi M. M. Bakhtina "Problemy tvorchestva Dostoevskogo")' ['On the "multivoicedness" of Dostoevsky'], *Novyi mir* 10 (1929), 195.
23 Letter from Bakhtin to Kozhinov, 30 July 1961, 'Iz perepiski M. M. Bakhtina i V. V. Kozhinova', in N. A. Pan'kov, *Voprosy biografii i nauchnogo tvorchestva M. M. Bakhtina* (Moscow: Izdatel'stvo Moskovskogo universiteta, 2009), 517. For Bakhtin's musings about the position of the author in Dostoevsky, see Bakhtin, 'Dostoevsky. 1961', in *Sobranie sochinenii, Vol. 5*, 365–68.
24 S. G. Bocharov, 'Commentary to *Problemy poetiki Dostoevskogo*', M. M. Bakhtin, *Sobranie sochinenii, Vol. 6* (Moscow: Russkie slovari, 2002), 475.
25 Max Weber, *Economy and Society*, trans. Guenther Roth and Claus Wittich (Berkeley: University of California Press, 1921), 4.
26 Isaiah Berlin, 'Two concepts of liberty', in *The Proper Study of Mankind* (London: Chatto and Windus, 1997), 194.
27 M. M. Bakhtin, 'Problemy stilistiki romana' ['Problems in the Stylistics of the Novel'], in *Sobranie sochinenii, Vol. 3* (Moscow: Iazyki slavianskikh kul'tur, 2012), 6.
28 Bakhtin, 'Problemy stilistiki romana', 6.
29 For example: Leo Spitzer, *Stilstudien* (Munich: M. Hueber, 1928); Leo Spitzer, *Italienische Umgangsprache* [*Colloquial Italian Language*] (Bonn and Leipzig: Kurt Schraeder, 1922); L. Iakubinskii, 'O dialogicheskoi rechi' ['On dialogical speech'], *Russkaia rech'* 1 (1923), 96–194; V. M. Zhirmunskii, *Natsional'nyi iazyk i sotsial'nye dialekty* (Leningrad: Khudozhestvennaia literatura, 1936); G. G. Shpet, *Esteticheskie fragmenty* (Petrograd: Kolos, 1922); G. G. Shpet, *Vnutrenniaia forma slova* [*The Inner Form of the Word*] (Moscow: GAKhN, 1927); Ernst Cassirer, *Philosophie der symbolischen Formen, 1* (Berlin: Bruno Cassirer, 1923). It cannot be emphasised too strongly that these are just the tip of the iceberg: the Russian text of 'Discourse in the Novel' refers to critical works by more than sixty authors (of whom a mere sixteen are mentioned in the English translation, and there often with scant bibliographical detail).
30 The excision of more than twenty footnotes (and abridgment of several more) from the original (1975) published version of 'Discourse in the Novel' is an enigma and evidence that the rediscovery of Bakhtin in the 1960s and 1970s has created as many mysteries as the life of the man himself. Indeed, the published 1975 version, which is the basis for the English translation, excluded the text's Introduction, its conclusion, and various lines and paragraphs throughout. There is an unkind and a kind explanation for the absence of so many footnotes. The kind explanation is that the 1975 text was edited from a Bakhtin typescript that had blank spaces for the Roman characters (used for many German language names) that were supposed to be entered later. These blanks were filled in by a different typescript of the text, which was only discovered later by Nikolai Pan'kov, in the archive of Boris Zalesskii (see Pan'kov, 'Tozhe iz "kruga Bakhtina": B. V. Zalesskii' ['Another from the Bakhtin Circle: B. V. Zalesskii'], in *Voprosy biografii*, 426–27). The unkind interpretation can't help noticing that the footnotes excised were to German

(often German-Jewish) and, in a couple of cases, French sources, and that the editor of the text, Vadim Kozhinov, wanted to emphasise Bakhtin's Russianness, perhaps at the expense of foreign influences. One would like to believe the kinder interpretation, but there are good grounds for scepticism: even when footnotes used a Cyrillic transliteration to refer to a German source, they were excised.

31 M. M. Bakhtin, 'Iazyk v khudozhestvennoi literature' ['Language in Artistic Literature'], in *Sobranie sochinenii, Vol. 5*, 287.

32 Craig Brandist and Vladislava Reznik have described the work of these linguists, in particular Boris Larin, Viktor Zhirmunskii, and Lev Iakubinskii, in considerable detail. See Craig Brandist, 'The origins of Soviet sociolinguistics', *Journal of Sociolinguistics* 7, 2 (2003), 213–23; Brandist, 'Sociological linguistics in Leningrad: the Institute for the Comparative History of the Literatures and Languages of the West and East (ILJAZV) 1921–1933', *Russian Literature* 63 (2008), 171–200; and Vladislava Reznik, 'From Saussure to sociolinguistics: the evolution of Soviet sociology of language in the 1920s and 1930s', diss., University of Exeter, 2004, 122–48.

33 See 'The social stratification of (r) in New York City department stores', in William Labov, *Sociolinguistic Patterns* (Philadelphia: University of Pennsylvania Press, 1972).

34 'The logic of nonstandard English', in *Sociolinguistic Patterns*.

35 The *raznochinets* intelligentsia in Russia emerged in the nineteenth century. They were drawn from what might, in England, be called the middling classes – impoverished nobles, merchants, the clergy, and so on – and found work in a rapidly expanding government bureaucracy. They had, however, very little power in the government, which was still dominated as a Tsarist autocracy and, as a result, their ranks became the breeding ground for political and social dissent.

36 Ivan Turgenev, *Fathers and Sons*, trans. Rosemary Edmonds (Harmondsworth, Middlesex: Penguin Books, 1975), 146–47.

37 Marxist because the dynamism, forward movement and change in social relations, derives from the 'contradictory' nature of the social world, which is designed such that its basic functioning entails an inner tension (the tension between an exploited working class and the owners of capital).

38 P. N. Medvedev, *The Formal Method in Literary Scholarship: A Critical Introduction to Sociological Poetics*, trans. Albert J. Wehrle (Cambridge, MA: Harvard University Press, 1985), 24; *Formalnyi metod v literaturnovedenii: kriticheskoe vvedenie v sotsiologicheskuiu poetiku*, in *Sobranie sochinenii, Vol. 2* (Sankt-Peterburg: Rostok, 2019), 62–63.

39 N. A. Pan′kov, 'Stenogramma zasedaniia Uchenogo soveta Instituta mirovoi literatury im. A. M. Gorkogo: Zashchita dissertatsii tov. Bakhtinym na temu "Rable v istorii realizma" 15 noiabria 1946' ['Stenogram of a meeting of the Scholarly Council of the A. M. Gorky Institute of World Literature: the defence of Comrade Bakhtin's dissertation on the theme "Rabelais in the History of Realism", 15 November 1946'], in *Voprosy biografii*, 170.

40 M. M. Bakhtin, 'O Maiakovskom' ['On Mayakovsky'], in *Sobranie sochinenii*, *Vol. 5*, 53.
41 See, for example, Donald Wesling, *Bakhtin and the Social Moorings of Poetry* (Lewisburg, PA: Bucknell University Press, 2003); Michael Eskin, 'Bakhtin on poetry', *Poetics Today* 21, 2 (2000), 379–91.
42 Viacheslav Ivanov, 'The testaments of Symbolism', in *Selected Essays* (Evanston, IL: Northwestern University Press, 2001), 39.
43 L. P. Iakubinskii, 'O zvukakh stikhotvornogo iazyka' ['On the sounds of verse language'], in *Poetika: sborniki po teorii poeticheskogo iazyka* (Petrograd: n.p., 1919), 37, 39.
44 A. Kruchenykh and V. Khlebnikov, 'From *The Word as Such*', in Anna Lawton and Herbert Eagle (eds.), *Russian Futurism through Its Manifestoes, 1912–1928* (Ithaca: Cornell University Press, 1988), 61.
45 Reinhart Koselleck, *Futures Past: On the Semantics of Historical Time* (New York: Columbia University Press, 2004), 236.
46 Koselleck, *Futures Past*, 236.
47 Koselleck, *Futures Past*, 246.
48 Benedict Anderson, *Imagined Communities: Reflections on the Origin and Spread of Nationalism*, rev. ed. (London: Verso, 1991), 22–36.
49 Asif Agha, 'Voice, footing, enregisterment', *Journal of Linguistic Anthropology* 15, 1 (2005), 38.
50 See Ben Rampton, 'From "multi-ethnic adolescent heteroglossia" to "contemporary urban vernaculars"', *Language & Communication* 31 (2011), 276–94, and the issue of the *Journal of Sociolinguistics* 3/4 (1999) dedicated to 'Styling the other'.
51 Agha, 'Voice, footing, enregisterment', 50.
52 Transcribed in Bakhtin, *Sobranie sochinenii*, *Vol. 3*, 758.
53 Some sections of 'On the *Bildungsroman*' have been translated into English (see the list of abbreviations at the beginning of this volume), but most of it has not. Where there is a single number, it indicates the place in the Russian text only.
54 Bocharov, 'Commentary to "Roman vospitaniia i ego znachenie v istorii realizma"', in *Sobranie sochinenii*, *Vol. 3*, 762.
55 M. M. Bakhtin, 'Roman vospitaniia i ego znachenie v istorii realizma' ['The Bildungsroman and Its Significance for the History of Realism'], in *Sobranie sochinenii*, *Vol. 3*, 194–95.
56 See Barthes, 'Introduction to the structural analysis of narratives (1966)'; Gérard Genette, *Narrative Discourse: An Essay in Method*, trans. Jane E. Lewin (Ithaca, NY: Cornell University Press, 1980); A. J. Greimas, 'Narrative grammar: units and levels', *Modern Language Notes* 86, 6 (1971), 793–806.
57 M. M. Bakhtin, 'O Flobere' ['On Flaubert'], in *Sobranie sochinenii*, *Vol. 5*, 132.
58 M. M. Bakhtin, 'K istorii tipa (zhanrovoi raznovidnosti) romana Dostoevskogo' ['On the History of the Dostoevskian Type (Generic Variety) of the Novel'], in *Sobranie sochinenii*, *Vol. 5*, 44.

59 Letter, M. I. Kagan to S. I. Kagan, 16 August 1924, in M. I. Kagan, *O khode istorii* (Moscow: Iazyki slavianskoi kul'tury, 2004), 642. Lenin had died earlier in the year, and the official sanctification of him proceeded in short order.
60 M. M. Bakhtin, 'Rhetoric, to the Extent That It Lies', *Slavic and East European Journal* 61, 2 (2017), 207/ 'Ritorika, v meru svoei lzhivosti', in *Sobranie sochinenii, Vol. 5*, 65, 66.
61 O. M. Freidenberg, *Poetika siuzheta i zhanra* (Moscow: Labirint, 1997).
62 O. E. Osovskii, '"Iz sovetskikh rabot bol'shuiu tsennost' imeet kinga O. Freidenberga": Bakhtinskie marginalii na stranitsakh *Poetiki siuzheta i zhanra*' ['"Among Soviet works O. Freidenberg's book has an enormous value": Bakhtin's marginalia on the pages of *The Poetics of Plot and Genre*'], in V. L. Makhlin (ed.), *Bakhtinskii sbornik IV* (Saransk: MGPI, 2000), 128–34.
63 Nina Perlina, *Olga Freidenberg's Works and Days* (Bloomington, IN: Slavica, 2002), 88–95.
64 'Iz perepiski', in Kagan, *O khode istorii*, 666–68.
65 In an undated letter to Kagan's widow, S. I. Kagan, Iudina asks if Bakhtin can borrow '2 books from Matvei Isaevich's library: Cassirer's 2 volumes on "Language" and "Myth"'. See Letter 311 in Mariia Iudina, *Vysokii stoikii dukh: perepiska 1918-1945 gg* [*A High, Steadfast Spirit: Correspondence 1918-1945*] (Moscow: Rosspen, 2006), 399.
66 M. M. Bakhtin, 'Conspectus of Ernst Cassirer, *Philosophie der Symbolischen Formen,* Zweiter Teil: Das mythische Denken. 1925', in *Sobranie sochinenii, Vol. 4 (1)* (Moscow: Iazyki slavianskikh kul'tur, 2008), 811. Almut Bruckstein has persuasively argued that, although Cassirer is a secular thinker, Cohen's religious Messianism infiltrates itself into his work. See Almut Sh. Bruckstein, 'Practicing "intertextuality": Ernst Cassirer and Hermann Cohen on myth and monotheism', in Jeffrey Andrew Barash (ed.), *The Symbolic Construction of Reality: The Legacy of Ernst Cassirer* (Chicago: University of Chicago Press, 2008), 174–88.
67 See Brian Poole, 'Bakhtin and Cassirer: the philosophical origins of Bakhtin's carnival messianism', *South Atlantic Quarterly* 97, 3–4 (1998), 537–78.
68 The description of the novel as a modern epic, inspired by Hegel, was the centrepiece of George Lukács's famous speech to the Communist Academy in December 1934, which was discussed at length that evening and in two further meetings. The speech and the ensuing discussion were published as Georg Lukács et al., 'Problema teoriia romana' ['Problems in the theory of the novel'], *Literaturnyi kritik* (1935) 2, 214–49, and 3, 231–54.
69 M. M. Bakhtin, 'Zakliuchitel'noe slovo M. M. Bakhtina na obsuzhdenii doklada "Roman, kak literaturnyi zhanr" 24 marta 1941 ['The Concluding Words of M. M. Bakhtin at the Discussion following the Lecture "The Novel as a Literary Genre" 24 March 1941'], in *Sobranie sochinenii, Vol. 3*, 647.
70 Honoré de Balzac, *Père Goriot*, trans. A. J. Krailsheimer (Oxford: Oxford University Press, 1991), 1.
71 Balzac, *Père Goriot*, 263.

72 Later, in the same notes, Proust's *À la recherche du temps perdu* is held up as a great representative of the twentieth-century *Bildungsroman* (OBild 333).

73 We can assume Bakhtin had read the chapters of *Ulysses* that were translated into Russian for the journal *Internatsional'naia literatura* in 1935-36. Joyce is mentioned in the opening line of the long series of notes 'On Questions of the Theory of the Novel' in relation to the problem of 'uninterrupted speech flow', but he garners more significant coverage in a footnote to the 1940 version of the Rabelais study, where Bakhtin credits him with a 'very interesting and significant attempt' at a revival of 'imagistic thinking' (by which he means inner speech); 'Fransua Rable v istorii realizma (1940 g)', *Sobranie sochinenii, Vol. 4 (1)*, 441n208. Some years later, when teaching in Saransk, Bakhtin would describe Joyce as 'a passionate patriot and nationalist, extraordinarily gifted and original', and 'enormously influential' if a bit decadent (quoted in the commentary to 'On Questions of the Theory of the Novel', *Sobranie sochinenii, Vol. 3*, 812). One can only imagine how Joyce would have reacted to such a description.

74 Koselleck, *Futures Past*, 249.

75 Koselleck, *Futures Past*, 232.

76 Bakhtin, 'Zakliuchitel'noe slovo', 647.

77 Pan'kov, 'Stenogramma', 171.

78 Pan'kov, 'Stenogramma', 170.

79 Katerina Clark, *Moscow, the Fourth Rome: Stalinism, Cosmopolitanism, and the Evolution of Soviet Culture, 1931-1941* (Cambridge, MA: Harvard University Press, 2011), 18-19.

80 Florens Christian Rang, 'Historische Psychologie des Karnevals', in Martin Buber (ed.), *Die Kreatur* (Berlin: Verlag Lambert Schneider, 1927), 311-43.

81 Pan'kov, 'Stenogramma', 171.

82 Freidenberg, *Poetika*. On Bakhtin's acquaintance with the book, see Perlina, *Olga Freidenberg* and Osovskii, 'Bakhtinskie marginalii'.

83 See Clark, *Moscow*, 181-82; Claire Shaw, '"A fairground for 'building the new man'": Gorky Park as a site of Soviet acculturation', *Urban History* 38, 2 (2011), 324-44.

84 In fact, in the 1940 dissertation Bakhtin submitted, the popular medieval versions of these forms were called 'gothic realism'. But early criticism of this term – it associated Rabelais with the Dark Ages – persuaded Bakhtin to substitute 'grotesque realism' for 'gothic realism' throughout, in amendments made when Bakhtin revised the dissertation in 1949-50. On the substitution, see N. A. Pan'kov, 'Smysl' i proiskhozhdenie termina "goticheskii realizm" ['The meaning and origin of the term "gothic realism"'], in *Voprosy biografii*, 382-99.

85 Quoted from an archival source in I. L. Popova, 'Commentary to "Dopolneniia i izmeneniia k "Rable" ["Additions and amendments to *Rabelais*"]', in Bakhtin, *Sobranie sochinenii, Vol. 5*, 481.

86 Walter Benjamin, 'Berlin chronicle', in *Selected Writings, Vol. 2: 1927-34* (Cambridge, MA: Harvard University Press, 1999), 634-35.

180 Notes to pages 137–146

87 See Pan′kov, 'Stenogramma'.
88 Frances Yates, 'The last laugh (review of Bakhtin, *Rabelais and His World*)', *New York Review of Books* 13, vi (1969), 21.
89 Sergei Averintsev, 'Bakhtin, laughter, and Christian culture', in Susan M. Felch and Paul J. Contino (eds.), *Bakhtin and Religion: A Feeling for Faith* (Evanston, IL: Northwestern University Press, 2001), 86, 87.
90 Peter Stallybrass and Allon White, *The Politics and Poetics of Transgression* (London: Methuen, 1986), 19.
91 For the gruesome details, see Åsa Boholm, 'Christian construction of the other: the role of Jews in the early modern carnival of Rome', *Journal of Mediterranean Studies* 24, 1 (2015), 37–52.
92 Stallybrass and White, *The Politics and Poetics of Transgression*, 20.
93 Another way to describe the problem is to say that Bakhtin's utopia is a utopia organized around love, but not justice (in this respect he parts ways with Cohen, for whom the Messianic future leads inexorably to politics in the present; see Cohen, *Religion of Reason*, 24–25).
94 Terry Eagleton, *Walter Benjamin or Towards a Revolutionary Criticism* (London: Verso, 1981), 148.
95 Eagleton, *Walter Benjamin*, 149.
96 See Sheila Rowbotham, 'The women's movement and organizing for socialism', in Sheila Rowbotham, Lynne Segal, and Hilary Wainwright, *Beyond the Fragments: Feminism and the Making of Socialism* (London: Merlin Press, 1979), 21–155.
97 Gary Saul Morson and Caryl Emerson, *Mikhail Bakhtin: Creation of a Prosaics* (Stanford, CA: Stanford University Press, 1990), 451, 470.
98 Mikhail K. Ryklin, 'Bodies of terror: theses toward a logic of violence', *New Literary History* 24, 1 (1993), 51–74.
99 Gogotishvili, 'Varianty i invarianty', 125.
100 Gogotishvili, 'Varianty i invarianty', 125–26.
101 M. M. Bakhtin, 'The Problem of the Text in Linguistics, Philology and the Human Sciences', in *Speech Genres and Other Late Essays* (Austin: University of Texas Press, 1986), 105 / 'Problema teksta', in *Sobranie sochinenii, Vol. 5*, 308.

Chapter 5

1 Vladimir Seduro, *Dostoyevski in Russian Literary Criticism, 1846–1956* (New York: Columbia University Press, 1957), 202–32.
2 M. M. Bakhtin, *Problemy poetiki Dostoevskogo* (Moscow: Sovetskii pisatel′, 1963); M. M. Bakhtin, *Tvorchestvo Fransua Rable i narodnaia kul′tura srednevekov′ia i Renessansa* (Moscow: Khudozhestvennaia literatura, 1965).
3 See, for example, Ludmila Koehler, 'Eternal themes in Solzhenitsyn's "The Cancer Ward"', *Russian Review* 28, 1 (1969), 53–65; and Vladislav Krasnov, *Solzhenitsyn*

and Dostoevsky: A Study in the Polyphonic Novel (Athens: University of Georgia Press, 1980).
4 Victor Erlich, Russian Formalism: History – Doctrine (The Hague: Mouton, 1955).
5 Entirely characteristic was Bakhtin's (and Voloshinov's) inclusion in Ladislav Matejka and Krystyna Pomorska (eds.), Readings in Russian Poetics: Formalist and Structuralist Views (Cambridge, MA: MIT Press, 1971), an excellent collection of translations of Russian Formalist articles. Bakhtin was represented by an extract from the stylistics section of Problems of Dostoevsky's Poetics.
6 Julia Kristeva, 'Une poétique ruinée', in Mikhail Bakhtine, La poetique du Dostoïevski (Paris: Le Seuil, 1970); translated as 'The ruin of a poetics'; Tzvetan Todorov, Mikhäil Bakhtine: Le Principe Dialogique (Paris: Le Seuil, 1981).
7 M. M. Bakhtin, Problems of Dostoevsky's Poetics, trans. R. William Rotsel (Ann Arbor, MI: Ardis, 1973).
8 Frances Yates, 'The last laugh (review of Bakhtin, Rabelais and His World)', New York Review of Books 13, vi (1969). Among the historians who took Bakhtin's example to heart were Natalie Zemon Davis, 'The reasons of misrule: youth groups and Charivari in sixteenth-century France', Past and Present 50 (1971), 41–75; and Carlo Ginzburg, The Cheese and the Worms: The Cosmos of a Sixteenth-Century Miller, trans. John and Anne Tedeschi (Baltimore: Johns Hopkins University Press, 1980). Characteristically, Zemon Davis describes Bakhtin as a 'Soviet structuralist' (49).
9 Krystyna Pomorska, 'Foreword', in Mikhail Bakhtin, Rabelais and His World (Cambridge, MA: MIT Press, 1968), viii.
10 M. M. Bakhtin, Voprosy literatury i estetiki (Moscow: Khudozhestvennaia literatura, 1975).
11 M. M. Bakhtin, Estetiki slovesnogo tvorchestva (Moscow: Isskustvo, 1979).
12 For a good example of the claim being spread orally, see Albert J. Wehrle's careful report of information communicated to him by V. N. Turbin (whom he met in 1976 on a research visit to Moscow and whose own evidence was recollections of conversations) in his, 'Introduction: M. M. Bakhtin/ P. N. Medvedev', in Bakhtin/ Medvedev [sic], The Formal Method in Literary Scholarship (Cambridge, MA: Harvard University Press, 1985), xvi. Medvedev's son Iurii caustically described how these claims, which lacked any written backing, gained authority: 'Passed onto the West as rumour, as the opinion of an authoritative person which it would be awkward for a courteous foreigner to dispute, it then returns to us as something having currency in the competent circles of judgement, to which those who launched it can refer and on which they can rely.'; Iu. P. Medvedev, '"Nas bylo mnogo na chelne ..."' ['"There were many of us on the boat ..."'], Dialog Karnaval Khronotop 1 (1992), 98.
13 Katerina Clark and Michael Holquist, Mikhail Bakhtin (Cambridge, MA: Harvard University Press, 1984).
14 David Carroll, 'The alterity of discourse: form, history, and the question of the political in M. M. Bakhtin', Diacritics 13, 2 (1983), 68.

15 Wayne Booth, 'Introduction', in Bakhtin, *Problems of Dostoevsky's Poetics*, trans. Caryl Emerson (Manchester: Manchester University Press, 1984), xiii–xxvii.
16 Terry Eagleton, *Walter Benjamin or Towards a Revolutionary Criticism* (London: Verso, 1981), 150.
17 Clark and Holquist, *Mikhail Bakhtin*, 64.
18 Clark and Holquist, *Mikhail Bakhtin*, 117.
19 Clark and Holquist, *Mikhail Bakhtin*, 114, 111.
20 Noting that Clark and Holquist 'had interviewed many of Bakhtin's friends and disciples', Nina Perlina, in a review of the biography, remarked that nevertheless 'the legends have to be separated from the facts' (Nina Perlina, 'Review of Clark and Holquist', *Russian Review* 45, 4 (1986), 436).
21 Clark and Holquist, *Mikhail Bakhtin*, 94.
22 Clark and Holquist, *Mikhail Bakhtin*, 68.
23 For excellent examples of this interpretative line – excellent because they are representative *and* because they are rigorous and sophisticated – see L. A. Gogotishvili, 'Varianty i invarianty M. M. Bakhtina' [The variables and invariables of M. M. Bakhtin'], *Voprosy filosofii* 1 (1992), 115–33; N. K. Bonetskaia, 'M. M. Bakhtin i traditsii russkoi filosofii', *Voprosy filosofii* 1 (1993), 83–93; N. K. Bonetskaia, 'Bakhtin's aesthetics as a logic of form', in David Shepherd (ed.), *The Contexts of Bakhtin: Philosophy, Authorship, Aesthetics* (Amsterdam: Harwood Academic, 1998), 83–94; and S. G. Bocharov, 'Around and about one conversation', *Russian Studies in Literature* 31, 4 (1995), 4–35.
24 Ruth Coates, *Christianity in Bakhtin: God and the Exiled Author* (Cambridge: Cambridge University Press, 1998); Alexandar Mihailovic, *Corporeal Words: Mikhail Bakhtin's Theology of Discourse* (Evanston, IL: Northwestern University Press, 1997).
25 Gary Saul Morson and Caryl Emerson, *Mikhail Bakhtin: Creation of a Prosaics* (Stanford, CA: Stanford University Press, 1990), 27.
26 Morson and Emerson, *Bakhtin*, 326.
27 Fredric Jameson, 'Review of Voloshinov, *Marxism and the Philosophy of Language*', *Style* 8, 3 (1974), 535–43.
28 Tony Bennett, *Formalism and Marxism* (London: Methuen, 1979); Peter Stallybrass and Allon White, *The Politics and Poetics of Transgression* (London: Methuen, 1986).
29 See, for example, Tony Bennett, 'A thousand and one troubles: Blackpool Pleasure Beach', in Tony Bennett et al., *Formations of Pleasure* (London: Routledge, 1983); Darren Webb, 'Bakhtin at the seaside: utopia, modernity, and the carnivalesque', *Theory, Culture, and Society* 22, 3 (2005), 121–38.
30 Raymond Williams and Edward Said, 'Media, margins and modernity', in Raymond Williams, *The Politics of Modernism* (London: Verso, 1989), 181.
31 Paul de Man, 'Dialogue and dialogism', in *The Resistance to Theory* (Minneapolis: University of Minnesota Press, 1986), 107.

32 Robert J. C. Young, 'Back to Bakhtin', in *Torn Halves: Political Conflict in Literary and Cultural Theory* (Manchester: Manchester University Press, 1996), 38.
33 I've summarised that intuition rather awkwardly, but it is the best I can do. The term 'directedness', though, is awkward for a particular reason: it is a reasonable translation of Bakhtin's term *napravlennost'*, which is, in turn, a Russian translation of a Husserlian term (*Gerichtetsein auf*). On Husserl and Bakhtin, see Chapter 4, n12.
34 A very good summary of the arguments can be found in Deborah Cameron, *Feminism and Linguistic Theory* (London: Palgrave Macmillan, 1992).
35 A brief but very useful account of the feminist use of Bakhtin can be found in Lynn Pearce, *Reading Dialogics* (London: Edward Arnold, 1994), 100–11.
36 Patricia S. Yaeger, '"Because a fire was in my head": Eudora Welty and the dialogic imagination', *PMLA* 99, 5 (1984), 962.
37 See, for example, Tony Crowley's comments on the linguistic situation in Ireland in his 'Bakhtin and the history of the language', in Hirschkop and Shepherd, *Bakhtin and Cultural Theory* (Manchester: Manchester University Press, 1989), 86–88.
38 Robert J. C. Young, *Colonial Desire: Hybridity in Theory, Culture and Race* (London: Routledge, 1995), 18–22.
39 Young, *Colonial Desire*, 21.
40 W. E. B. Du Bois, *The Souls of Black Folk* (London: Longmans, 1965), 2.
41 Henry Louis Gates, Jr., *The Signifying Monkey: A Theory of Afro-American Literary Criticism* (Oxford: Oxford University Press, 1988).
42 On the complexities of this association, see Dorothy J. Hale, 'Bakhtin in African American literary theory', *ELH* 61, 2 (1994), 445–71.
43 James Clifford, 'On ethnographic authority', *Representations* 2 (1983), 118–46.
44 Bhabha discusses what Bakhtin might bring to the idea of agency in his 'The postcolonial and the postmodern: the question of agency', in *The Location of Culture* (London: Routledge, 1994), 245–82. Kristeva's accounts of dialogical subjectivity are found in 'The ruin of a poetics' and 'Word, dialogue and novel', in *Desire in Language: A Semiotic Approach to Literature and Art* (Oxford: Basil Blackwell, 1980), 64–91. For an analysis of Bakhtin's concept of subjectivity, see Daphna Erdinast-Vulcan, *Between Philosophy and Literature: Bakhtin and the Question of the Subject* (Stanford, CA: Stanford University Press, 2013).
45 Evidence for this would be that of the various monographs devoted to Bakhtin published in the past thirty years, not one claimed Bakhtin's authorship for the disputed texts; see (for example) Craig Brandist, *The Bakhtin Circle: Philosophy, Culture, and Politics* (London: Pluto Press, 2002), 4–9; Galin Tihanov, *The Master and the Slave: Lukács, Bakhtin, and the Ideas of Their Time* (Oxford: Clarendon Press, 2000), 7–8; Erdinast-Vulcan, *Between Philosophy and Literature*, 216–17n8.

Chapter 6

1 Jürgen Habermas, 'Philosophy as stand-in and interpreter', in *Moral Consciousness and Communicative Action*, trans. Christian Lenhardt and Shierry Weber Nicholsen (Cambridge, MA: MIT Press, 1990), 15.
2 Habermas, 'Philosophy as stand-in and interpreter', 15.
3 Habermas, 'Philosophy as stand-in and interpreter', 15.

Further Reading

There are, by now, several excellent introductions to Bakhtin's work, as well as many more specialized studies.

General Works

Craig Brandist. *The Bakhtin Circle: Philosophy, Culture, and Politics* London: Pluto Press, 2002. Brandist's study has the virtue of being about the Bakhtin Circle (Bakhtin, Medvedev, Voloshinov) as a whole and it benefits from Brandist's exceptional knowledge of the intellectual history of the period.
Katerina Clark and Michael Holquist. *Mikhail Bakhtin*. Cambridge, MA: Harvard University Press, 1984. This is the only biography extant in English and, while some of it has been superseded by later scholarship, it remains a readable introduction to the work.
Michael Gardiner (ed.), *Mikhail Bakhtin*. 4 vols. London: Sage Publications, 2003. An excellent and extensive collection of Bakhtin criticism and scholarship.
Lynn Pearce. *Reading Dialogics*. London: Edward Arnold, 1994. Pearce's book is more of a how-to guide than a monograph about Bakhtin, but it's extremely useful.
Graham Pechey. *Mikhail Bakhtin: The Word in the World*. London: Routledge, 2007. An excellent exploration of Bakhtin's ideas by a shrewd, perceptive, and theoretically astute critic.
Alastair Renfrew. *Mikhail Bakhtin*. Abingdon: Routledge, 2015. A sharp and intelligent introduction.

More Specialized Studies

Don Bialostosky. *How to Play a Poem*. Pittsburgh: University of Pittsburgh Press, 2017. Not merely a book about Bakhtin and poetry, but a consistently clever and engaging book about how to use Bakhtin to *teach* poetry.

Craig Brandist, David Shepherd, and Galin Tihanov. *The Bakhtin Circle: In the Master's Absence*. Manchester: Manchester University Press, 2004. Fascinating studies on the other members of the Bakhtin Circle.

Caryl Emerson. *The First Hundred Years of Bakhtin*. Princeton: Princeton University Press, 1997. A subtle and very interesting account of the history of Bakhtin's reception and interpretation.

Susan M. Felch and Paul J. Contino. *Bakhtin and Religion: A Feeling for Faith*. Evanston, IL: Northwestern University Press, 2001. Interesting collection of essays on Bakhtin's relation and possible debts to Christian thought.

Ilya Kliger. 'Heroic aesthetics and modernist critique: extrapolations from Bakhtin's author and hero in aesthetic activity'. *Slavic Review* 67, 3 (2008), 551–66. 'Dostoevsky and the novel-tragedy: genre and modernity in Ivanov, Pumpyansky, and Bakhtin'. *PMLA* 126, 1 (2011), 73–87. 'On "genre memory" in Bakhtin'. In Kliger and Boris Maslow (eds.), *Persistent Forms: Explorations in Historical Poetics*, 227–51. New York: Fordham University Press. Shrewd and insightful studies of Bakhtin's theory in its historical context.

Peter Stallybrass and Allon White. *The Politics and Poetics of Transgression*. London: Methuen, 1986. A brilliant historical study of Bakhtin's theory of carnival.

Robert Stam. *Subversive Pleasures: Bakhtin, Cultural Criticism, and Film*. Baltimore: Johns Hopkins University Press, 1992. An inventive and subtle application of Bakhtin's ideas to film, with particular attention to Latin American cinema and carnival.

Galin Tihanov, *The Master and the Slave: Lukács, Bakhtin, and the Ideas of Their Time*. Oxford. Clarendon Press, 2000. A rigorous, insightful comparison of these two figures.

Index

addressee, concept of, 49
aesthetics, in B's thought, 71–74, 81
Agha, Asif, 104–5
Akhmatova, Anna, 44
ambivalence, popular-festive, 131–33, 141
Anderson, Benedict, 102–3
Andropov, Iurii, 29
Andropova, Irina, 29
Apulius, *The Golden Ass*, 112
Aragon, Louis, 25
architectonics, 69
author and hero, distinction of, 42, 49–50, 52, 141, 153
  and literary form, 71–88
  and literary style, 51
authoritarian discourse, 101, 135
avant-gardism, 45
Averbakh, Leopold, 46
Averinstev, S., 20, 46, 138

Bakhtin Circle, 12
Bakhtin, Mikhail Mikhailovich
  arrest and repression of, 2, 20–21, 23
  Bildungsroman project, 105–28
  disputes over biography of, 2–3, 6–8, 148–50
  interpretative disputes over, 16–20, 37–38, 46–48
  obstacles faced, 1–2, 5–6, 21–22, 30–31
  osteomyelitis, 14, 21, 24, 107
  political views, 10, 13
  Rabelais project, 25–27, 28, 55–56, 57, 107, 129–30, 156
  rediscovery of, in 1960s, 2, 5–6, 28–29

Bakhtin, Mikhail Mikhailovich (Works)
  'Additions and Amendments to "Rabelais"', 65, 120, 132–33, 136
  The Aesthetics of Verbal Art, 147
  'Art and Responsibility', 32, 60
  'Author and Hero in Aesthetic Activity', 15, 17–18, 36, 42, 60, 69–73, 81, 141, 153
  'On the *Bildungsroman*', 24, 55, 64, 106–11, 115
  Collected Works, 4, 8, 20, 60, 157
  The Dialogic Imagination, 148, 154
  'Discourse in the Novel', 3, 16, 23, 29, 47–48, 58, 63, 83, 88–105, 109, 120, 125, 128–29, 135, 141, 142, 147, 150, 153–55
  'On Flaubert', 64, 107, 116–17, 120
  'Forms of Time and of the Chronotope in the Novel', 24, 64, 108–18, 129, 132, 141, 147
  'Language in Artistic Literature', 64
  'From Notes Made in 1970-71', 7, 61, 68, 143, 148
  'The Novel as a Literary Genre' ('Epic and Novel'), 25, 29, 64, 68, 102, 107, 120–27
  'From the Prehistory of Novelistic Discourse', 25, 29, 63, 107, 120
  'The Problem of Form, Content, and Material', 17–18, 46–47, 61, 147
  'The Problem of Grounded Peace', 36
  'The Problem of Speech Genres', 27, 58, 66, 142–44, 173n57

187

Bakhtin, Mikhail Mikhailovich (Works) (cont.)
   'The Problem of the Text', 66, 142, 144
   'The Problem of the Text in Linguistics, Philology, and the Human Sciences', 68, 147–48
   Problems of Dostoevsky's Art, 6, 17, 28, 47–48, 52, 62, 75–88, 135, 146, 150, 153
   Problems of Dostoevsky's Poetics, 6, 63, 80, 143, 146–47
   'Problems in the Stylistics of the Novel', 63
   Questions of Literature and Aesthetics, 147
   'On Questions in the Theory of the Novel', 65
   'Rabelais in the History of Realism' (1940), 65, 107, 120
   Rabelais (1965), 6, 20, 66, 130–42, 146–47, 151
   'Satire', 65, 120, 133, 137
   'Towards a Methodology of the Human Sciences', 3, 7, 61, 68, 143, 148
   'Towards Philosophical Foundations for the Human Sciences', 61, 84–86, 135
   'Towards a Philosophy of the Act', 15, 17, 32–39, 42, 60, 69, 72, 127, 172n53
   'Working Notes from the 1960s and Early 1970s', 61, 145
Bakhtin, Mikhail Nikolaevich, 8
Bakhtin, Nikolai Mikhailovich, 9–11, 26, 34
Bakhtina, Ekaterina Mikhailovna, 9, 26
Bakhtina (Bersh-Okolovich), Elena Alexandrovna, 14, 15, 21, 29
Bakhtina, Mariia Mikhailovna, 9, 26
Bakhtina, Natalia Mikhailovna, 9, 23, 26
Bakhtina, Nina, 9, 26
Bakhtina, Varvara Zakharovna, 9, 26

Balzac, Honoré de, 45, 116
   Père Goriot, 122–23
Barthes, Roland, 1, 80, 115, 116
Baudouin de Courtenay, Jan, 16
becoming, historical, 56, 156
   and language, 50–52, 90, 94–98, 105, 144
   and laughter, 136–37, 141
   and Marxism, 117–18
   and narrative, 108–15
   and the novel, 102–3, 122, 125–28, 131
   and unfinishability, 81, 87
Bely, Andrei, 33, 44
Benjamin, Walter, *Berlin Chronicle*, 137
Bennett, Tony, 151
Berkovskii, N. A., 166n43
Berlin, Isaiah, 86
Bhabha, Homi, 155, 156–57
Bildungsroman, 55. See also under Bakhtin, Mikhail Mikhailovich
Blok, Aleksandr, 40, 44
Bocharov, S. G., 2, 142
   and disputed texts, 19
   interpretation of B's works, 17–18, 19, 20, 38, 73, 84
   role of, in rediscovery of B, 28–29, 147
Bonetskaia, N. K., 37
Booth, Wayne, 149, 150
Brandist, Craig, 16, 152, 176n32
Brentano, Franz, 49
Brik, Osip, 45
Briusov, Valerii, 44
Bühler, Karl, 49–50
Bulgakov, Mikhail, 44

carnival, *see* popular-festive culture
Carroll, David, 149, 150
Cassirer, Ernst, 34, 97, 119
   The Individual and the Cosmos, 119
   and Kagan, 11
   Philosophy of Symbolic Forms, 49, 50–52, 90, 119

censorship, 59
Chagall, Marc, 13
Chomsky, Noam, 159
Christianity, 36–38, 73, 113–14
chronotope, 55, 108–18
Chukovskii, K., 17
Cixous, Hélène, 154
Clark, Katerina, 25, 55, 130
Clark, Katerina and Michael Holquist, *Mikhail Bakhtin*, 5, 7–8, 148–50, 153
Clifford, James, 157
Coates, Ruth, 37, 73, 151
Cohen, Hermann, 34–36, 38, 56, 119
  and aesthetic love, 72
  and historical becoming, 98
  and Kagan, 11, 35
  and Messianic future, 103, 122, 180n93
  Religion of Reason, 35, 70
collectivism, 140–41
colonial languages, 154–55
Communist Party, Soviet, 43–44, 53, 57, 107
consciousness, representation of, 84
contemporaneity, 102–3, 110, 121–28, 145. *See also* becoming, future
context, idea of, 30–31
crisis, cultural, 12–13, 32–33, 40
critical realism, 45–46, 54–55
Croce, Benedetto, 49
Crowley, Tony, 183

Dante Alighieri, 114
de Man, Paul, 152
dialogism, 89–105, 127, 159–60
  as author/hero relationship, 75–88
  defined, 76
  origins of term, 17
disputed texts, problem of, 6–7, 18–20, 29, 148–50 *passim*, 157
Dos Passos, John, 55
Dostoevsky, Fyodor, 146
  Brothers Karamazov, 76, 82, 86
  Crime and Punishment, 76, 77–79, 82, 86
  The Double, 82
  Notes from the Underground, 82
  Poor Folk, 82, 86
double consciousness, 155–56
double-voiced discourse, 81–83, 88, 90, 94–98, 105, 123, 153
  and colonialism, 155–57
Douglass, Frederick, 155
DuBois, W.E.B., 155
Durkheim, Émile, 159
Duvakin, V. D., 6

Eagleton, Terry, 139–40, 149, 150
editing of B's work, 59–60. *See also under* V. V. Kozhinov
Eikhenbaum, Boris, 16, 82
Eliot, T. S., 99
Emerson, Caryl, 148, 151. *See also* Morson and Emerson
epic, 120–21, 127
Erlich, Victor, 146
Ermilov, V. V., 28, 161n2
Estifeeva, E. V., 14, 27
ethical reality, 11, 35–36, 40, 73, 172n53
ethical responsibility, 32–39, 40, 69–70, 126–27

fear, 135–36
feminist criticism, 154
Flakserman, G. J., 23
folklore, 114, 119. *See also* popular-festive culture
Frank-Kamenetskii, Izrail', 16, 119
Free Philosophical Association, 44
freedom, B's concept of, 86
Freidenberg, Olga, 16, 141
  Poetics of Plot and Genre, 118–19, 130
Freud, Sigmund, 159
future, idea of, 35, 102–3, 113–15, 118–28, 136–37, 145, 156

Gachev, G., 2, 28, 142
Gates, Henry Louis, Jr, *The Signifying Monkey*, 155–56
Genette, Gerard, 115

genres, 141, 143–44. *See also* novel
Ginzburg, Carlo, 181n8
Goethe, J. W. von, 55, 106, 108, 111, 115
   Italian Journey, 130
Gogol, Nikolai, 124
Gogotishvili, L. A., 37–38, 73, 141
Gorbachev, Mikhail, 8
Gorky, Maksim, 21, 45
Greimas, A. J., 115–16
Grimmelshausen, H. J. C. von, 108
   Simplicissimus, 110
grotesque realism, 131
growth, as analogous to becoming, 114–15
Gumilev, Nikolai, 44
Gurvich, I. N., 12
Gutman, Ia., 12

Habermas, Jürgen, 159
Herder, J. G. von, 115
heroes, and narrative becoming, 110–11, 123–25. *See also* author and hero
heteroglossia, 23, 90, 91–98, 143, 154–57
historical inversion, 113, 120
Holquist, Michael, 151. *See also* Clark and Holquist
Homer, 120–21, 127
Humboldt, Wilhelm von, 50, 97
Husserl, Edmund, 49, 96, 174n12
   Logical Investigations, 41–42
hybridity, 155–57

I and *other*, distinction between, 40–42, 52, 69–74, 159. *See also* author and hero
Iakubinskii, L. P., 16, 48, 92, 100
inner form, 97
intentionality, 96–97
Iudina, M. V., 3, 11–13, 15, 19
   assistance to Bakhtin 21, 25, 26
Ivanov, V. V. (semiotician), 6, 20, 29
Ivanov, Viacheslav (writer), 44, 46, 100

Jameson, Fredric, 151
Joyce, James, 55, 108, 124
Judaism, 34–36

Kagan, M. I., 3, 11–13, 19, 56, 70
   and Cohen, 35–36
   correspondence and meetings with Bakhtin, 14–15, 23, 34, 98, 119
   on cultural crisis, 33, 40
   death of, 24, 26
   and Messianic future, 103
   political views, 13, 117
Kanaev, I. I., 26
Kant, Immanuel, 34, 173n1
Kerensky, Alexander, 10
Khrushchev, Nikita, 5
Kirpotin, V. Ia., 26–27
Koselleck, Reinhart, 102, 126–27
Kozhinov, V. V., 2, 38, 142
   and disputed texts, 19, 20
   as editor, 68, 143, 176n30
   role of, in rediscovery of B, 28–29, 147
Krasnaia nov', 45–46, 53
Kristeva, Julia, 1, 146, 157
Krupskaia, Natalia, 45
Kustanai, exile in, 21–23

'laboratory texts', 24
Labov, William, 92
Lähteenmäki, Mika, 171n45
Langland, William, 114
language
   B's philosophy of, 47–48, 52, 58, 89–105, 142–45, 147–50
   in Rabelais, 131–32
   Voloshinov's study of, 48–52
   see also style
laughter, culture of, 118, 130, 134–36, 138
LEF, 45
Lenin, V. I., 45
Lessing, G. E., 115
Lifshits, Mikhail, 54
Literaturnyi kritik, 54
London, Jack, 108

Lopatto, Mikhail, 9, 10, 34
Lotman, Iurii, 147
love, 70, 72, 85
Lukács, Georg, 45, 54–55, 178n68
  The Historical Novel, 55
Lunacharskii, A. V., 21, 43, 84

Malevich, Kasimir, 13
Mandelstam, Osip, 44
Mann, Thomas, 108
Marr, N. Ia., 16, 57
Marx, Karl, 45, 56
Marxism, 56, 57, 95, 117–18, 127–28, 172n53
Mayakovsky, Vladimir, 45, 99–100
Medvedev, Iu. P., 181n12
Medvedev, P. N., 3, 6, 13, 14, 15–16, 149
  assistance to Bakhtin, 23
  disputed texts of, 18–20, 148, 157
  The Formal Method, 18, 98, 157
  influence of, on Bakhtin, 12, 18, 48
  murder of, 24, 26
Meier, A. A., 19, 21, 37
Messianism, 35, 98, 118, 122, 127, 144–45. *See also* future
metalinguistics, 144
Mihailovic, Alexandar, 151, 173n58, 174n11
modernists, 44–45, 108
modernity, 89–90, 121, 125
Morson, Gary Saul, 151
Morson, Gary Saul, and Caryl Emerson, *Mikhail Bakhtin*, 140, 151, 153
myth, 89–91, 101

Narkompros (Commissariat of Enlightenment), 43
narrative, 79–81, 87, 106–28
  and author and hero, 71, 74
narrator, position of, 122–23
national history and tradition, 120–21
Natorp, Paul, 11, 34
Neo-Kantianism, 47, 49, 118–19, 122
  see also Ernst Cassirer, Hermann Cohen, Paul Natorp

Nevel′, B in, 11–13, 32, 34
Nicholas of Cusa, 119
novel
  force of, 95–98, 101–3
  narrative and form of, 105–28
  and popular-festive culture, 128–42
  as secondary genre, 143
  Soviet debate on, 54–55
  style of, 89–105, 119–20
novelisation, 102

Pan′kov, Nikolai, 157
Pasternak, Boris, 44
Pechat′ i revoliutsiia, 53
Pechey, Graham, 152
people, the, 139
Perlina, Nina, 119, 182n20
personality, theory of, 84–86
Peshkov, Ekaterina Pavlovna, 21
Petrov, G. S., 23
Petrov, Ivan, 20
phenomenology, 41–42, 69
philosophy, role of, 159–60. *See also* aesthetics
Piaget, Jean, 159
plot, functions of, 79, 123. *See also* narrative
poetry, 89, 91, 99–101
politics
  of carnival, 133
  of language, 89–90, 128, 144
  prefigurative, 140
  see also under M. M. Bakhtin, M. I. Kagan
polyphonic novel, 75–88, 157
Pomorska, Krystyna, 147
Poole, Brian, 17, 77, 171n42
popular culture, B applied to, 151
popular-festive culture, 109, 128–42
postcolonial criticism, 154–57
Proletkult, 45, 47, 53
Proust, Marcel, 55, 108, 124
Pumpianskii (Pumpian), L. V., 3, 9, 10, 11–13, 15, 19, 21
  death of, 26
Pushkin, Aleksandr, 44

Pushkin, Aleksandr (cont.)
   'Evgeny Onegin', 99
   'Parting', 72
   'Remembrance', 47

Rabelais, François, 108–9, 114–15, 129–42
   Gargantua and Pantagruel, 110, 130, 131
   see also under M. M. Bakhtin
racial difference, 155
Rang, Florens Christian, 130
RAPP, 53–54
realism, 106, 109, 116–17. See also critical realism, socialist realism
redemption, 72–73
registers and enregisterment, 103–5
religion
   and Marxism, 117–18
   role of, in B's work, 38–39, 72–73, 149–50, 151
   and Russian revolution, 40
   see also Christianity, Judaism
Religious-Philosophical Society, 15, 37
Renfrew, Alastair, 152
responsibility, *see* ethical responsibility
Reznik, Vladislava, 176n32
rogue, clown, and fool, 109, 128–29
Rolland, Romain, 108
Rugevich, A. S., 15
Russian Formalism, 1, 6, 16, 17, 45, 46–48, 52, 146–49
   and style, 82–83, 90, 100–1
Russian nationalism, 38, 57
Russian Orthodoxy, 73
Russian Revolution
   attitudes towards, 10, 13
   cultural aspect of, 40
Russian Symbolism, 100
Russkii sovremennik, 17, 44
Ryklin, Mikhail, 140–41

Said, Edward, 152
Saransk, B in, 23, 27, 142
satire, 131, 133, 139
Saussure, Ferdinand de, 48–49, 58
Scheler, Max, *Essence and Forms of Sympathy*, 52, 165n36
Schiller, Friedrich, 103
Seduro, Vladimir, 146
seriousness, 101, 128, 134–36, 141
Shakespeare, William, 133, 136
Shcherba, Lev, 16
Shepherd, David, 152
Shklovsky, Viktor, 6, 28, 44, 47, 100, 166n43
Shostakovich, Dmitri, 13
Shpet, Gustav, 49, 90
Shukman, Ann, 151
Simmel, Georg, 33
socialist realism, 54–55, 106
socio-ideological languages, 89, 93–98, 143
sociolinguistics, 92
Sollertinskii, I. I., 13, 26
Solzhenitsyn, Aleksandr, 146
   One Day in the Life of Ivan Denisovich 28
Soviet Union
   collapse of, 4, 8, 157
   collectivisation in, 22
   cultural and literary debate in, 15–16, 42–46, 53–57, 100, 106
   see also Russian Revolution
speech genres, 142–44
Spender, Dale, *Man-made Language*, 154
Spengler, Oswald, *The Decline of the West*, 33
Spielhagen, Herbert, 77
Spitzer, Leo, 49
   Italienische Umgangssprache, 52
Stalin, Josef, 13, 27, 44, 53
   on linguistics, 57–58
Stalinism, 53, 90, 138, 140
Stallybrass, Peter, 151

Stallybrass, Peter, and Allon White, *Politics and Poetics of Transgression*, 138–39
Strada, Vittorio, 168n75
Stromin-Stroev, A. R., 20
structuralism, 1, 147–49
style,
  concept of, in B, 81–83, 87–105, 143–44
  novelistic, 89–105, 128–29
  Voloshinov on, 51–52
subjectivity, 124–25, 157
suffering, as origin of ethics, 69–70
Sukhanov, N. N., 23
superaddressee, 144–45

threshold, as crisis, 80–81, 86–88
Tihanov, Galin, 52, 55, 152
Timofeev, L. I., 25
Todorov, Tzvetan, 1, 116, 146
  Mikhail Bakhtin, 146
Tolstoy, Lev, 45
Tomashevskii, Boris, 16
tragedy, 136
Trotsky, Leon, *Literature and Revolution*, 43, 45, 53
Turbin, V. N., 29, 181n12
Turgenev, Ivan, *Fathers and Sons*, 93
Tynianov, Iurii, 82

unfinishability (*nezavershennost'*), 76, 80–81, 86–88, 98, 102, 156
  see also contemporaneity
utopia, 133–34, 139–40, 142
  see also Messianism
utterance, theory of, 58, 143–44

Vaginov, Konstantin, 19
Vinogradov, V. V., 58, 142, 147, 166n43
violence, in carnival, 138
Vitebsk, B in, 13–15
voice, 81–82, 96, 153–54

Voloshinov, V. N., 11, 14, 15–16, 92, 130, 151
  death of, 26
  'Discourse in Life and Discourse in Poetry', 49–50
  disputed texts of, 6, 18–20, 148, 150, 157
  Freudianism, 18
  influence of, on Bakhtin, 3, 12, 18, 48–52, 81
  Marxism and the Philosophy of Language, 18, 50–52
Voronskii, A. K., 43, 45–46, 53
Vossler, Karl, 49, 52
Vvedenskii, A. I., *Psychology without Any Metaphysics*, 41

Weber, Max, 85, 159
Wehrle, Albert J., 181n12
Welty, Eudora, 154
White, Allon, 151. See also Stallybrass and White
Wiedebach, Hartwig, 70
Williams, Raymond, 33, 74
Wittgenstein, Ludwig, 11
world literature, 25, 55–57, 130, 137
World War, First, 32

Yaeger, Patricia, 154
Yates, Frances, 137–38, 147
Yeats, W. B., 154
Young, Robert, 152, 156–57
  Colonial Desire, 155

Zalesskii, B. V., 10, 26, 162–63n11
Zemon Davis, Natalie, 181n8
Zhdanov, Andrei, 57
Zhirmunskii, Viktor, *National Language and Social Dialects*, 16, 92
Zinoviev, Grigorii, 23
Zubakin, B. M., 11–12